CHARMING
SMALL HOTEL
GUIDES

Germany

DUNCAN PETERSEN

HUNTER
PUBLISHING

Germany

DUNCAN PETERSEN

HUNTER
PUBLISHING

Conceived, edited, designed and produced by
Duncan Petersen Publishing Ltd

Consultant editor	Manfred Kohnke
Production editor	Nicola Davies
Art director	Mel Petersen
Editorial director	Andrew Duncan
Designers	Chris Foley and Beverley Stewart

This edition published 2000 by
Duncan Petersen Publishing Ltd,
31 Ceylon Road, London W14 0YP

Sales representation and distribution in the U.K. and Ireland by
Portfolio Books Ltd
Unit 1C West Ealing Business Centre
Alexandria Road
London W13 0NJ
Tel: 0181 579 7748

ISBN 1 872576 98 2

A CIP catalogue record for this book is available from the British Library

AND

Published in the USA by
Hunter Publishing Inc.
130 Campus Drive, Editon, N.J. 08818.
Tel (732) 225 1900 Fax (732) 417 1744

ISBN I-55650-866-2

For details on hundreds of other travel guides and language courses, visit Hunter's Web site at **www.hunterpublishing.com**

Typeset by Duncan Petersen Publishing Ltd
Printed by STIGE SpA, Turin

Contents

Introduction

To this new edition of the *Charming Small Hotel Guide* to
Germany we are pleased to welcome more than a dozen interesting new long entries, dotted throughout the guide, but with
a modest emphasis on the former Eastern Germany. The guide
joins 14 other titles in this now well-established series, covering
destinations in Europe and North America.

These guides are different from other accommodation
guides on the market – designed to satisfy what we believe to
be the real needs of today's traveller.

The most fundamental difference is suggested by the title:
we aim to include only those hotels and guest-houses which are
in some way captivating, and which are small enough to offer
truly personal service, usually from the owner. In Germany,
where success seems to lead inevitably to growth, we have had
a hard time, but most of our recommendations have fewer
than 40 rooms, and only a few have more than 60.

Indeed, this remains the only independently inspected,
selective colour accommodation guide to charming and interesting places to stay in Germany. No hotel pays for an entry.
Beware of imitators who do not admit on the cover that they
accept payments from hotels for inclusion, but only do so in
small print on the inside pages. They say they are selective –
but a quick comparison with this guide will prove that this is a
hollow claim. And if money has changed hands, it is impossible to write the whole truth about a hotel.

The guides are different in other ways, too: their descrip-
tive style is different, and they are compiled differently. Our
entries employ, above all, words: they contain not one sym-
bol. They are written by people with something to say, not a
bureaucracy which has long since lost the ability to distinguish
the praiseworthy from the mediocre. The editorial team is
small and highly experienced at assessing and writing about
hotels, at noticing all-important details. Although we have
made use of reports from members of the public, and would
welcome more of them (see box following this introduction)
we have placed great emphasis on consistency in our selections
and our descriptions.

These are features which will reveal their worth only as you
use your *Charming Small Hotel Guide*. Its other advantages are
more obvious: it contains colour photographs of many of the
entries; and it simplifies the job of finding a hotel to suit your
needs – the entries are presented in clear geographical groups,
and each entry is categorized by the type of accommodation
(for example, country inn or seaside hotel).

Small hotels have always had the special appeal that they can
offer the traveller a personal welcome and personal attention,
whereas larger places are necessarily more institutional. But in
Germany the seeker after small hotels of quality has a particular problem that does not seem to arise to the same extent elsewhere: that the competent and successful hotel-keeper tends
to want to see his business grow. So although there are plenty

of long-established family-run hotels – more than in Britain, in fact – many of the most comfortable and attractive ones are rather large and impersonal. At the same time, our travels in Germany have shown that there are hundreds of small, traditional hotels that are very ordinary indeed – ones which we presume have remained small because their proprietors are unable to attract the customers to justify expansion.

Despite these difficulties, we have been able to identify 360 or so hotels, guest-houses, inns and bed-and-breakfast places that in our view will add to the pleasure of travelling in Germany. The descriptions of these hotels are supplemented by brief notes – contained in area introductions – on dozens of other hotels that are useful to know about, even if in some respects they do not conform to our requirements.

Charming and small

There really are relatively few *genuine* charming small hotels. Despite the compromises we have had to make in Germany, we are particularly fussy about size.

Also, unlike other guides, we often rule out places that have great qualitites, but are nonetheless no more nor less than – hotels. Our hotels are all special in some way.

We think that we have a much clearer idea than other guides of what is special and what is not; and we think we apply these criteria more consistently than other guides because we are a small and personally managed company rather than a bureaucracy. We have a small team of like-minded inspectors, chosen by the editor and thoroughly rehearsed in recognizing what we want. While we very much appreciate readers' reports - see below - they are not our main source of information.

Last but by no means least, we're independent – there's no payment for inclusion.

So what exactly do we look for?
• An attractive, preferably peaceful setting.
• A building that is either handsome or interesting or historic, or at least with a distinct character.
• Ideally, we look for adequate space, but on a human scale: we don't go for places that rely on grandeur, or that have pretensions that could intimidate.
• Decoration must be harmonious and in good taste, and the furnishings and facilities comfortable and well maintained. We like to see interesting antique furniture that is there because it can be used, not simply revered.
• The proprietors and staff need to be dedicated and thoughtful, offering a personal welcome, without being intrusive. The guest needs to feel like an individual.

Whole-page entries
We rarely see all of these qualities together in place; but our

warmest recommendations – whole page, with photograph – usually lack only one or two of these qualities.

Small entries
Lack of space means that some hotel entries have shorter descriptions and no photograph. We consider all these hotels worthy to be in the guide.

How to find an entry
In this guide, the entries are arranged in geographical groups. First, the whole country is divided into 5 regions; we start with Northern Germany and proceed in a southerly direction through Western, Central, Eastern and finally Southern Germany. Each of our regions consists of one or more of the 'Lands' – the states that make up the federation of Germany; and in the guide the entries are grouped into sections usually corresponding to these states. So within Northern Germany, for example, there are sections on Schleswig-Holstein, Hamburg and Niedersachsen.

There are one or two departures from the usual pattern. The Central Germany region consists of only one state: Hessen. The southern state of Bayern, known in the English-speaking world as Bavaria, is split into northern and southern sections because of its physical size and large number of full-page entries.

The region we have called Eastern Germany corresponds to the old East Germany.

Each state section follows a set sequence:

• first comes an Area introduction – an overview of the hotel scene in that state, incorporating brief notes on hotels which have not justified a longer entry – hotels in cities which would otherwise not feature here at all, for example; where the section contains only one or two short entries, these are appended to this introduction;

• then come the main, full-page entries for that state, arranged in alphabetical order by town;

• finally come the shorter, quarter-page entries for that state, similarly arranged alphabetically.

To find a hotel in a particular area, simply browse through the headings at the top of the pages until you find that area – or use the maps following this introduction to locate the appropriate pages. To locate a specific hotel or a hotel in a specific place, use the indexes at the back, which lists the entries alphabetically, first by name and then by place-name.

How to read an entry
At the top of each entry is a coloured bar highlighting the name of the town or village where the establishment is locat-

ed, along with a categorization which gives some clue to its character. These categories are, as far as possible, self-explanatory.

Fact boxes

The fact box given for each hotel follows a standard pattern which requires little explanation; but:

Under **Tel** we give the telephone number starting with the area code used within Germany; when dialling from another country, omit the initial 0 of this code. We also give the **Fax** number, sometimes omitting the code to save space.

Under **Location** we give information on the setting of the hotel and on its car parking arrangements, as well as pointers to help you find it.

Under **Meals** we list the meals available.

The basic **Prices** in this volume – unlike our volume on Britain and Ireland – are per **room**. This year, as a new departure, we are using price bands rather than figures. We normally give the range of prices you can expect to pay, from the cost of the cheapest single room in low season to the cost of the dearest double in high season:

D	under 100 DM
DD	100 DM-200DM
DDD	200 DM-300 DM
DDDD	over 300 DM

If the room price includes breakfast, we say so; otherwise, space permitting, we normally give the price of breakfast separately. We then give the prices of other meals. If room-only or bed-and-breakfast terms are not available, we give either the price for dinner, bed and breakfast (DB&B), or for full board (FB) – that is, all meals included.

Prices include tax and service. Wherever possible we have given prices for 1999, but for many hotels these were not available when the guide was prepared; prices may therefore be higher in 1999 than those quoted, simply because of inflation. But bear in mind also that the proprietors of hotels and guest-houses may change their prices from one year to another by much more than the rate of inflation. Always check before booking.

Under **Rooms** we summarize the number and style of bedrooms available. Our lists of facilities in bedrooms cover only mechanical gadgets, and not ornaments such as flowers or consumables such as toiletries or free drinks.

Under **Facilities** we list public rooms and then outdoor and sporting facilities which are either part of the hotel or immediately on hand; facilities in the vicinity of the hotel but not directly connected with it (for example, a nearby golf course) are not listed here, though they sometimes feature at the end of the main description in the Nearby section, which presents a selection of interesting things to see or do in the locality.

We use the following abbreviations for **Credit cards**:
AE   American Express
DC   Diners Club
MC   MasterCard (Access/Eurocard)
V   Visa (Barclaycard/Bank Americard/Carte Bleue etc)

The final entry in a fact box is normally the name of the proprietor(s); but where the hotel is run by a manager we give his or her name instead.

Glossary of terms
Several German terms which are used in our hotel descriptions (or in hotel names) may be unfamiliar to travellers from other countries. They are explained here:

Autobahn Motorway
Bauern... Farm...
Bier... Beer...
Brau... Brewing...
Burg Castle – though not necessarily a fortress.
*Garni...*Bed & Breakfast only
Garten Garden
Haus House.
Insel Island.
Jagd..., Jäger... Hunting..., hunter....
Kachelofen Ceramic-tiled stove, traditionally wood-burning, often large enough to heat a whole room – a common feature of traditional-style bars and dining-rooms.
Kur Literally 'cure', but not implying illness; the nearest equivalent in Britain is a visit to a health farm.
Landhaus Country-house.
Markt Market.
Mühle Mill.
Rösti Cholesterol-laden Swiss rustic delicacy, based on fried grated potatoes.
Schloss Castle – though not necessarily a fortress.
See Lake.
Stube Literally 'room', but in practice usually a wood-panelled room in which food and drinks are served informally. There are many variations such as *Stuble*, *Stuberl*.
Wasserburg Water-castle – ie, castle with moat.
Wintergarten Conservatory.

Reporting to the guides

Please write and tell us about your experiences of small hotels, guest-houses and inns, whether good or bad, whether listed in this edition or not. As well as hotels in Germany, we are interested in hotels in Britain and Ireland, Italy, France, Spain, Portugal, Austria, Switzerland and other European countries, and those in the eastern and western United States.

The address to write to is:
Duncan Petersen Publishing Ltd
Charming Small Hotel Guides
31 Ceylon Road
London W14 0PY
England.

Checklist
Please use a separate sheet of paper for each report; include your name, address and telephone number on each report.

Your reports will be received with particular pleasure if they are typed, and if they are organized under the following headings:

Name of establishment
Town or village it is in, or nearest
Full address, including post code
Telephone number
Time and duration of visit
The building and setting
The public rooms
The bedrooms and bathrooms
Physical comfort (chairs, beds, heat, light, hot water)
Standards of maintenance and housekeeping
Atmosphere, welcome and service
Food
Value for money

We assume that in writing you have no objections to your views being published unpaid, either verbatim or in an edited version. Names of major outside contributors are acknowledged, at the editor's discretion, in the guide.

If you would be interested in looking at hotels on a professional basis on behalf of the guides, please include on a separate sheet a short CV and a summary of your travel and hotel-going experience.

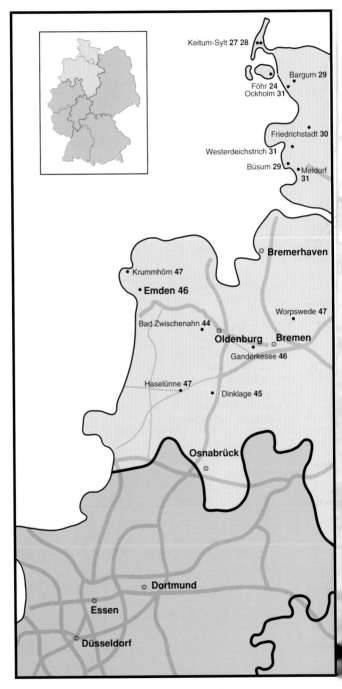

Keitum-Sylt **27 28**

Bargum **29**

Föhr **24**
Ockholm **31**

Friedrichstadt **30**

Westerdeichstrich **31**

Büsum **29** • Meldorf
31

⊚ **Bremerhaven**

• Krummhörn **47**

• **Emden 46**

Worpswede **47**

Bad Zwischenahn **44**
⊚ **Oldenburg** ⊚ **Bremen**

Ganderkesee **46**

Haselünne **47** • Dinklage **45**

Osnabrück
⊚

⊚ **Dortmund**

⊚ **Essen**

⊚ **Düsseldorf**

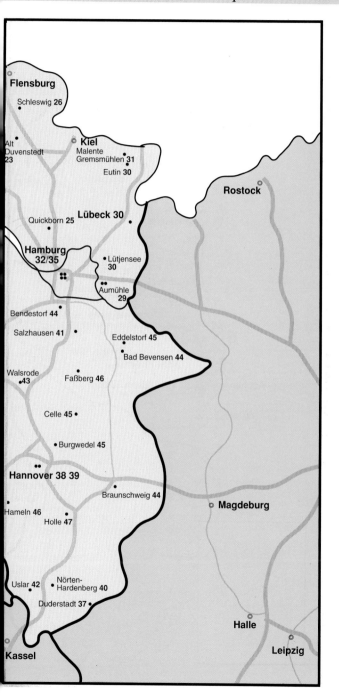

Flensburg

Schleswig 26

Alt
Duvenstedt
23

Kiel

Malente
Gremsmühlen 31

Eutin 30

Rostock

Quickborn 25

Lübeck 30

Hamburg
32/35

Lütjensee
30

Aumühle
29

Bendestorf 44

Salzhausen 41

Eddelstorf 45

Bad Bevensen 44

Walsrode
43

Faßberg 46

Celle 45

Burgwedel 45

Hannover 38 39

Braunschweig 44

Magdeburg

Hameln 46

Holle 47

Uslar 42

Nörten-
Hardenberg 40

Duderstadt 37

Halle

Kassel

Leipzig

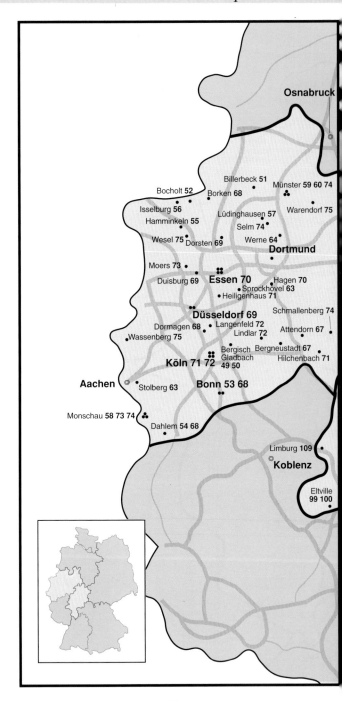

Osnabruck

Billerbeck 51
Bocholt 52   Borken 68   Münster 59 60 74
Isselburg 56   Warendorf 75
Hamminkeln 55   Lüdinghausen 57
Wesel 75 Dorsten 69   Selm 74
Moers 73   Werne 64
                      Dortmund
Duisburg 69   Essen 70   Hagen 70
                  Sprockhövel 63
                  Heiligenhaus 71
              Düsseldorf 69   Schmallenberg 74
Dormagen 68   Langenfeld 72   Attendorn 67
              Lindlar 72
Wassenberg 75
              Bergisch Bergneustadt 67
Köln 71 72   Gladbach Hilchenbach 71
              49 50
Aachen   Stolberg 63   Bonn 53 68
Monschau 58 73 74
          Dahlem 54 68

Limburg 109
Koblenz

Eltville
99 100

14

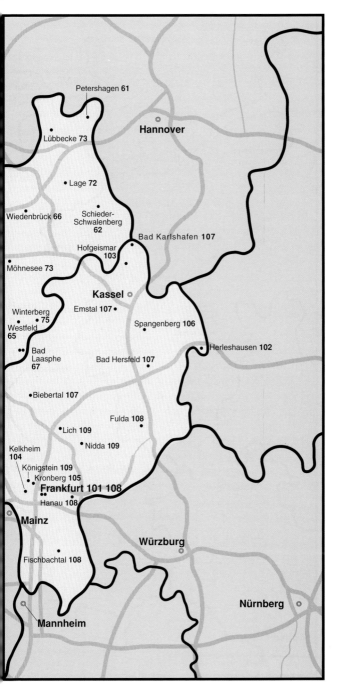

Petershagen **61**

Hannover

Lübbecke **73**

Lage **72**

Wiedenbrück **66**

Schieder-
Schwalenberg
62

Bad Karlshafen **107**

Hofgeismar
103

Möhnesee **73**

Kassel

Emstal **107**

Winterberg
75
Westfeld
65

Spangenberg **106**

Herleshausen **102**

Bad
Laasphe
67

Bad Hersfeld **107**

Biebertal **107**

Fulda **108**

Lich **109**

Nidda **109**

Kelkheim
104
Königstein **109**
Kronberg **105**
Frankfurt 101 108
Hanau **108**

Mainz

Würzburg

Fischbachtal **108**

Nürnberg

Mannheim

Hotel location maps

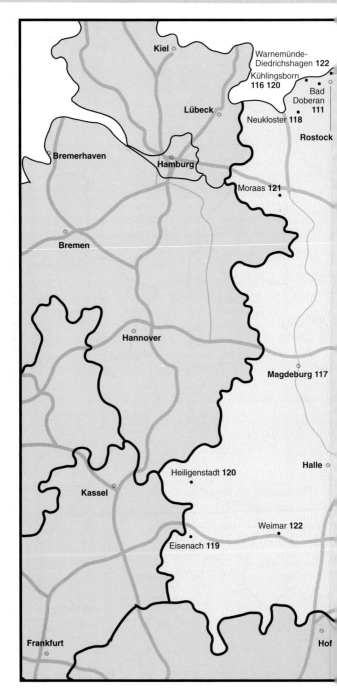

Kiel

Warnemünde-Diedrichshagen **122**
Kühlingsborn **116 120**
Bad Doberan **111**
Lübeck
Neukloster **118**
Rostock

Bremerhaven

Hamburg

Moraas **121**

Bremen

Hannover

Magdeburg **117**

Halle

Heiligenstadt **120**

Kassel

Weimar **122**

Eisenach **119**

Frankfurt

Hof

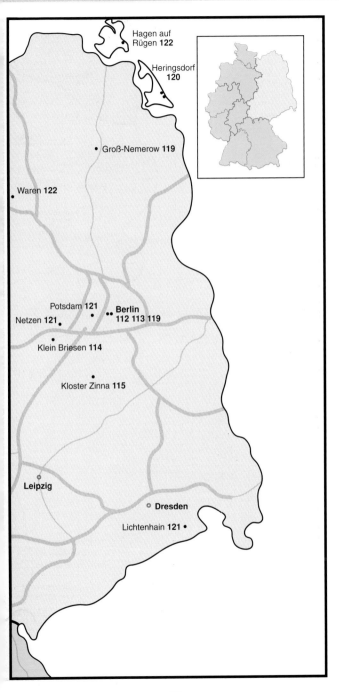

Hagen auf
Rügen **122**

Heringsdorf
120

Groß-Nemerow **119**

Waren **122**

Potsdam **121**

Netzen **121**

Berlin
112 113 119

Klein Briesen **114**

Kloster Zinna **115**

Leipzig

Dresden

Lichtenhain **121**

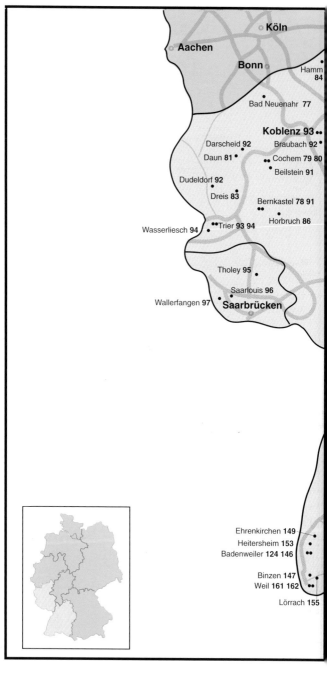

Köln

Aachen

Bonn

Hamm 84

Bad Neuenahr 77

Koblenz 93 ••

Darscheid 92   Braubach 92 •

Daun 81 •   •• Cochem 79 80

                   • Beilstein 91

Dudeldorf 92

Dreis 83

Bernkastel 78 91
••
Horbruch 86

Wasserliesch 94   •• Trier 93 94

Tholey 95 •

Saarlouis 96 •

Wallerfangen 97   Saarbrücken

Ehrenkirchen 149
Heitersheim 153
Badenweiler 124 146

Binzen 147
Weil 161 162

Lörrach 155

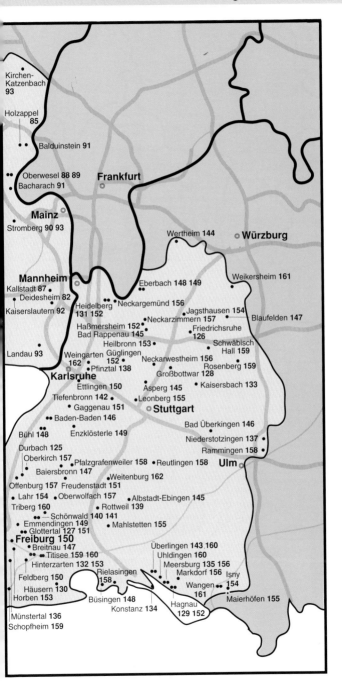

Kirchen-
Katzenbach
93

Holzappel
85

Balduinstein 91

Oberwesel 88 89
Bacharach 91

Frankfurt

Mainz
Stromberg 90 93

Wertheim 144   Würzburg

Mannheim
Kallstadt 87   Eberbach 148 149   Weikersheim 161
Deidesheim 82
Kaiserslautern 92   Heidelberg   Neckargemünd 156
                     131 152   Jagsthausen 154
                Haßmersheim 152   Neckarzimmern 157   Blaufelden 147
                Bad Rappenau 145   Friedrichsruhe
                Heilbronn 153 •   126
Landau 93   Weingarten Güglingen   Schwäbisch
             162   152   Neckarwestheim 156   Hall 159
Karlsruhe   Pfinztal 138   Rosenberg 159
             Großbottwar 128
        Ettlingen 150   Asperg 145   Kaisersbach 133
Tiefenbronn 142   Leonberg 155
        Gaggenau 151   Stuttgart
    Baden-Baden 146
Bühl 148   Enzklösterle 149   Bad Überkingen 146
Durbach 125   Niederstotzingen 137
    Oberkirch 157   Pfalzgrafenweiler 158   Reutlingen 158   Rammingen 158
    Baiersbronn 147   Ulm
                Weitenburg 162
Offenburg 157 Freudenstadt 151
    Lahr 154   Oberwolfach 157   Albstadt-Ebingen 145
Triberg 160   Rottweil 139
        Schönwald 140 141
Emmendingen 149   Mahlstetten 155
    Glottertal 127 151
Freiburg 150
    Breitnau 147   Überlingen 143 160
    Titisee 159 160   Uhldingen 160
    Hinterzarten 132 153   Meersburg 135 156
                Markdorf 156   Isny
Feldberg 150   Rielasingen   Wangen   154
Häusern 130   158   161
Horben 153   Büsingen 148   Maierhöfen 155
                Hagnau
Münstertal 136   Konstanz 134   129 152
Schopfheim 159

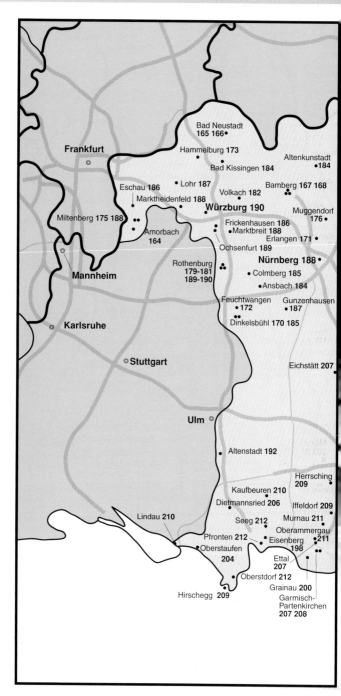

Frankfurt

Bad Neustadt
165 166•

Hammelburg 173
•

Bad Kissingen 184
•

Altenkunstadt
•184

Eschau 186
•

• Lohr 187

Volkach 182
•

Bamberg 167 168
••

Marktheidenfeld 188
•

Würzburg 190

Muggendorf
176 •

Miltenberg 175 188
••

Frickenhausen 186
•
•Marktbreit 188

Erlangen 171 •

Amorbach
164

Ochsenfurt 189
•

Nürnberg 188 •

Mannheim

Rothenburg
179-181
189-190
•••

• Colmberg 185

•Ansbach 184

Karlsruhe

Feuchtwangen
•172

Gunzenhausen
•187

••
Dinkelsbühl 170 185

◦Stuttgart

Eichstätt 207
•

Ulm ◦

Altenstadt 192
•

Herrsching
209
•

Kaufbeuren 210
•

Iffeldorf 209
•

Dietmannsried 206
•

Murnau 211
•

Lindau 210

Seeg 212
•

Oberammergau
•211
••

Pfronten 212
•

•Eisenberg
198

•Oberstaufen
204

Ettal
207
•

◦Oberstdorf 212

Grainau 200

Hirschegg 209
•

Garmisch-
Partenkirchen
207 208

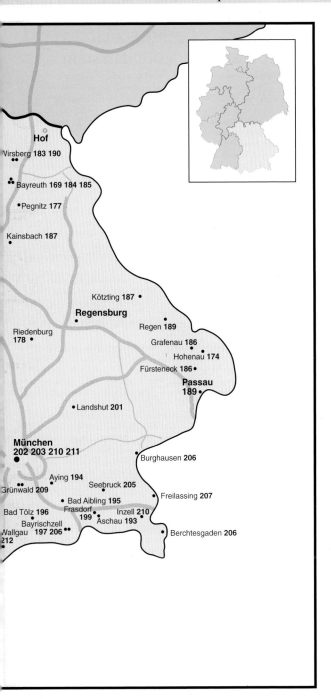

Hof

Virsberg **183 190**

Bayreuth **169 184 185**

Pegnitz **177**

Kainsbach **187**

Kötzting **187**

Regensburg

Regen **189**

Riedenburg **178**

Grafenau **186**

Hohenau **174**

Fürsteneck **186**

Passau 189

Landshut **201**

München 202 203 210 211

Burghausen **206**

Aying **194**

Seebruck **205**

Grünwald **209**

Freilassing **207**

Bad Aibling **195**

Bad Tölz **196**

Frasdorf **199**

Inzell **210**

Aschau **193**

Bayrischzell

Wallgau **197 206**

Berchtesgaden **206**

212

Schleswig-Holstein

Hotels in Schleswig-Holstein

Germany's northernmost 'Land', to the north of the river Elbe, forms an isthmus linking Denmark to the bulk of Continental Europe, with the Baltic Sea to the east and North Sea to the west. For the visitor much of the interest lies, not surprisingly, along the coasts – although in the east there is also an area of lakes and hills, somewhat optimistically known as Holsteinische Schweiz (Holsteinish Switzerland).

Kiel, the capital, is a mainly modern city at the mouth of the busy canal linking the North Sea with the Baltic. Acceptable places to stay in the city include the Kieler Kaufmann (Tel (0431) 88110, fax 8811135, 47 rooms), an elegant, modern hotel adjoining a smart club, and the Wiking (Tel (0431) 673051, fax 673054, 42 rooms), a straightforward modern hotel in the city centre with a restaurant offering gargantuan, if unsubtle, meals. Out of the city centre and more peaceful are the Birke (Tel (0431) 524011, fax 529128, 64 rooms) and Zur Waffenschmiede, a 12-roomed hotel standing in pleasant grounds (Tel (0431) 369690, fax 363994).

The town of Schleswig retains much more of its past, standing at the crossroads of the main roads North/South and East/West. Besides the Waldhotel am Schloss Gottorf, described on page 26, we can recommend a comfortable and welcoming hotel with a nautical flavour, the Strandhalle (Tel (04621) 22021, fax 28933, 28 rooms).

Lübeck, in the Middle Ages the commercial hub of northern Europe, is a still more interesting town, with a splendid old core surrounded by canals. The Kaiserhof, with 70 bedrooms, is rather large for a full entry in this book, but it retains an elegant town-house atmosphere along with a high standard of comfort (Tel (0451) 791011, fax 795083).

We have several entries on the holiday islands off the sandy west coast, of which Sylt is the best-known. Alternatives include the larger (85-room) Stadt Hamburg, a traditional and comfortable hotel in Westerland, a large, elegant resort on Sylt (Tel (04651) 8580, fax 858220), and the Oömrang Wiarthüs, a picturesque 12-roomed hotel with fishermen's bar, at Norddorf on the island of Amrum (Tel (04682) 836, fax 1432). Also in Westerland, the elegant Michelin-starred restaurant of Jörg Müller (Tel (04651) 27788) has three guest-rooms.

Other possibilities in this state include two at Lütjenburg, east of Kiel: Brüchmann am Markt, a simple traditional hotel set, as the name suggests, on the little town's open marketplace (Tel (04381) 7001, fax 6035, 28 rooms); and Ole Liese (Tel (04381) 4374), an elegantly furnished but modest old inn at Panker, a few miles to the north.

This page acts as an introduction to the features and hotels of Schleswig-Holstein, and gives brief recommendations of good hotels that for one reason or another have not made a full entry. The long entries for this 'Land' – covering the hotels we are most enthusiastic about – start on the next page. But do not neglect the shorter entries starting on page 29: these are all hotels that we would happily stay at.

Schleswig-Holstein

Country hotel, Alt Duvenstedt

Töpferhaus

Das Töpferhaus, which lies between Flensburg and Hamburg, is only a 5-minute drive from the motorway. Its peaceful setting in its own grounds on the shore of the Bistensee might well tempt an overnight guest to a longer stay; this is certainly the aim of the manager Jens Diekmann, who took over the controls of the hotel in 1995.

Female chef, Britta Jess, is in charge of the kitchen. Her meals encompass both regional and international specialities. The main restaurant, which has small alcoves, and the other public rooms are decorated in a country house style – simple white-plastered walls complement the exposed beams and solid wooden furniture. The large picture windows, with views across the landscaped terrace and gardens to the lake, contribute to the airy feel. The finishing touches are provided by fresh flower arrangements, in earthenware vases made in the pottery workshop from which the hotel takes its name.

The bedrooms are modern and pleasantly furnished with fitted wall wardrobes and tables, and marble-tiled bathrooms. Some have their own balcony or terrace.

Nearby Rendsburg (5 km) – old town, viaduct; Ostsee (30 km).

24791 Alt Duvenstedt, Am Bistensee
Tel (04338) 333
Fax (04338) 551
Location on edge of Bistensee, 11 km N of Rendsburg; A7 exit Rendsburg/Büdesldorf, 2 km on B 203 towards Eckernförde; car parking
Meals breakfast, lunch, dinner
Prices rooms DD-DDD with breakfast; meals DM40-98

Rooms 27 double, 8 with bath, 2 with shower; 17 single with shower; all rooms have central heating, phone, TV, radio **Facilities** dining-rooms, hall, conference/party room; terrace, tennis court, sauna and solarium, bicycles **Credit cards** AE, DC, MC, V
Children welcome **Disabled** no special facilities **Pets** not accepted **Closed** never
Languages English **Manager** Jens Diekmann

Schleswig-Holstein

Landhaus Altes Pastorat

Since our last edition Landhaus Altes Pastorat has changed owner-ship. The El-Dessoukis, who had been running this delightful place for many years, have retired and a new partnership has taken over consisting of Herrn Freiderichs and Schmidt.

Föhr is one of the larger islands (about 12 km by 9 km) at the north-western extremity of Germany – much quieter than its neigh-bour, Sylt, and a genuine island with no railway-bridge to the main-land. Most of the accommodation is in the arrival port of Wyk; this hotel is not – but it is the one to make for.

The house is a long building of red brick dating from the 17th and 18th centuries, apparently single-storey with the exception of steeply gabled three-storey sections; in fact the roof space accom-modates some of the comfortable bedrooms, their windows poking through the thatch to overlook the lush, flowery back garden. Inside, too, there are flowers, along with art ancient and modern, antiques and books.

The El-Dessoukis placed special emphasis on guests feeling free to 'mellow out' and re-charge their batteries, and assure us that the new owner shares the same philosophy; reports welcome.
Nearby bird sanctuary, cycling, walking.

25938 Insel Föhr, Süderende
Tel (04683) 226
Fax (04681) 5444
Location in middle of old Friesen village on small island; in grounds with ample car parking
Meals breakfast
Prices DB&B DDD per person
Rooms 3 double with shower, 2 single with bath; all rooms have central heating, phone,
hairdrier, TV
Facilities sitting-room, dining-room, library; bicycles
Credit cards not accepted
Children not accepted
Disabled not suitable
Pets not accepted
Closed Oct to Easter
Languages English
Proprietor Knut Friederichs and Sigurt Schmidt

Schleswig-Holstein

Country house hotel, Quickborn

Jagdhaus Waldfrieden

Hamburg is less than half an hour away, but here you are in a different world: this century-old villa, built by a shipping magnate in traditional hunting-lodge style with steeply pitched roofs and mini-turrets, is set in a beautiful little park, its mature trees able to screen out most of the noise of the main B4 road nearby. It is the setting that really makes the place; but Siegmund Baierle is a highly experienced manager of bigger hotels who makes sure that his own small-but-growing enterprise is up to scratch in all respects.

The few bedrooms in the original house are comfortable in an old-fashioned but not particularly atmospheric way. We preferred the more numerous ones added in a brand-new building in 1990: they are not conspicuously modern, and have the attraction of very smart bathrooms. There are several places where you can sit and relax, including a fascinating dining-room with minstrel's gallery, baby grand and hunting trophies. You can also eat in the newly created conservatory (used for breakfast) or at tables under trees in the garden when the weather permits. Cooking is quite ambitious, service impressively helpful.

Nearby walking; Hamburg (23 km).

25451 Quickborn, Kieler Str (B4)
Tel (04106) 3771
Fax (04106) 69196
Location 3 km N of town, just off main road; with large grounds and ample car parking
Meals breakfast, lunch, dinner
Prices rooms DD-DDD with breakfast; Meals DM48-98
Rooms 19 double, 5 single, with bath; all rooms have central heating, phone, hairdrier, TV, minibar, radio
Facilities sitting-room, dining-rooms, breakfast room; terraces
Credit cards AE, DC, MC, V
Children welcome
Disabled access easy
Pets accepted
Closed never
Languages English, French
Proprietor Siegmund Baierle

Schleswig-Holstein

Waldhotel am Schloß Gottorf

No, not another grand old castle, but a fairly modern house set in the grounds of one: Schloß Gottorf is one of the sights of this region, housing Schleswig-Holstein's museum of art and history and museum of prehistory. One way to reach the Waldhotel is to drive across the moat, around the castle and across the moat again, and it is the hotel's peaceful hilly setting in the grounds that are its chief attraction.

The Waldhotel is purpose-built reincarnation of an older building, constructed in 1910, and in any other setting would not merit attention, except perhaps on the grounds of value for money. The rooms vary in style – some rather old-fashioned and dull, others brighter and more modern in style; sadly, the brighter rooms don't necessarily have the best views, down towards the castle. Downstairs, the dining-room is spacious and pleasant, with large windows and flowers on the tables; there is no sitting-room, but a huge sunny terrace compensates.

The Röselers welcome back regular guests as friends and do a good job of offering modest accommodation at a fair price.

Nearby Museum of Art and History, Renaissance Chapel, Nydam Ship, altarpiece in Cathedral.

24837 Schleswig, Stampfmühle 1
Tel (04621) 23288
Fax (04621) 23289
Location on wooded hillside of castle grounds, E of town; with gardens, garages and ample car parking
Meals breakfast, lunch, dinner, snacks
Prices rooms D-DD, with breakfast; child's bed DM16; Meals DM20-50
Rooms 7 double with bath, one single with bath, one family room with bath; all rooms have central heating, phone, minibar, radio; TV on request
Facilities dining-room, café, conference room; terrace
Credit cards AE, MC
Children welcome
Disabled access difficult
Pets accepted (DM5 per night) **Closed** never
Languages English
Proprietor Ute Röseler

Schleswig-Holstein

Benen-Diken-Hof

'Insel auf der insel', goes the motto of this gracious holiday hotel – 'island within the island'. Perhaps that is something of an exaggeration, but this is certainly one of the more exclusive hotels on the island – and looks it, with its Southfork-style drive, ranch-fencing either side. The former owner has retired, and now his son, Claas-Erik Johannsen, runs Benen-Diken-Hof, with his wife, Anja.

The hotel occupies a group of typical thatched, whitewashed houses; the original house was built in 1841, and the 1980s extension is virtually indistinguishable. Inside, it is a confident blend of stylish modern furnishings, well crafted reproductions and genuine antiques. Decorative schemes are restrained, showing off flower arrangements and grandfather clocks to good advantage. There are paintings by local artists on the walls – and in the tiny Captain's Room, used for bridge or chess, seascape murals. Bedrooms are generally bright and uncluttered.

Although only breakfast is advertised, a small selection of dishes is available in the evening for hotel guests. There are some excellent restaurants nearby.

Nearby nudist beaches, birdwatching; Red Cliffs, Westerland (5 km) – resort and casino.

25985 Keitum-Sylt, Süderstr
Tel (04651)93830
Fax (04651)938383
Location in village on E of island of Sylt; in grounds with private car park
Meals breakfast
Prices rooms DD-DDDD; breakfast DM30
Rooms 21 double (5 twin), with bath, 6 single, with shower, 10 family rooms, with bath; all rooms have central heating, telephone, hairdrier, TV, radio; 5 apartments **Facilities** breakfast room, bar, bridge room; indoor pool, sauna, solarium, whirl-pool; sun terrace **Credit cards** AE, DC, V **Children** tolerated **Disabled** access easy **Pets** not accepted **Closed** never **Languages** English, French, Danish **Proprietors** Anja and Claas-Erik Johanssen

Schleswig-Holstein

Country hotel, Sylt island

Seiler Hof

On Sylt even the campsites get booked solid, so it is no surprise that in high season this captivating, cottagey house is booked up by regular visitors a year ahead. One unfortunate side-effect of this is that we were unable to look at the bedrooms; but, to judge by the rest of the house, you need have no worries about them. Some can be used as multi-room apartments.

The Seiler Hof is a typical low-built Friesian house, painted gleaming white, its small-paned windows sheltering under the neat overhanging thatch – very much like the rest of the picturesque village of Keitum. It was built in 1761 for the ancestors of Inken Johannsen – a modest, relaxed lady whose brother owns the grander Benen-Diken-Hof (previous page). The house is tastefully furnished in a mix of rustic and restrained modern styles. The dining-room has a flagstone floor and walls decorated with Dutch tiles – brought back as ballast in sailing ships.

Guest are asked to make their choice of the two dinner menus by midday. If the wholesome home-cooking is not to your taste, there are plenty of alternatives in and around the village.

Nearby nudist beaches, birdwatching; Red Cliffs, Westerland (5 km) – resort and casino.

25980 Keitum-Sylt Ost, Gurstig 7
Tel (04651) 31064
Fax (04651) 35370
Location in middle of village on Sylt island; with garden and car parking
Meals breakfast, dinner
Prices rooms DD-DDD, with breakfast; dinner DM25-45
Rooms 10 double, 5 with bath, 5 with shower; one single with shower; all rooms have central heating, phone, hairdrier, TV, radio
Facilities breakfast room; sauna, steam bath, fitness room, whirlpool
Credit cards none
Children welcome
Disabled not suitable
Pets not accepted
Closed restaurant only, Sun
Languages Danish
Proprietor Inken Johannsen

Schleswig-Holstein

Converted mill, Aumühle

Fürst Bismarck Mühle

Princess von Bismarck turned this mill into a hotel, which is why Jochen Dölger has inherited a collection of Bismarck memorab ilia and furniture. The peaceful setting by woods and water guarantees a steady stream of weekenders from Hamburg.

■ 21521 Aumühle, Mühlenweg 3 **Tel** (04104) 2028 **Fax** (04104) 1200 **Meals** breakfast, lunch, dinner **Prices** rooms D-DD; breakfast DM15, meals from DM22 **Rooms** 7, all with bath or shower, central heating, phone, TV **Credit cards** DC, MC, V **Closed** restaurant only, Wed **Languages** English, French, Spanish

---

Lakeside hotel, Aumühle

Hotel Waldesruh am See

An 18thC hunting lodge in an idyllic position, which largely compensates for the ponderous decoration inside. Dull reds and greens predominate in the public rooms; happily, the spacious bedrooms show a lighter touch.

■ 21521 Aumühle, Am Mühlenteich 2 **Tel** (04104) 3046 **Fax** (04104) 2073 **Meals** breakfast, lunch, dinner, snacks **Prices** rooms D-DD with breakfast; meals from DM14.50 **Rooms** 15, a ll with bath or shower, central heating, phone, TV, minibar **Credit cards** AE, DC, MC, V **Closed** Tue **Languages** English, French

---

Lakeside hotel, Aumühle

Hotel Waldesruh am See

An 18thC hunting lodge in an idyllic position, which largely compensates for the ponderous decoration inside. Dull reds and greens predominate in the public rooms; happily, the spacious bedrooms show a lighter touch.

■ 21521 Aumühle, Am Mühlenteich 2 **Tel** (04104) 3046 **Fax** (04104) 2073 **Meals** breakfast, lunch, dinner, snacks **Prices** rooms D-DD with breakfast; meals from DM14.50 **Rooms** 15, a ll with bath or shower, central heating, phone, TV, minibar **Credit cards** AE, DC, MC, V **Closed** Tue **Languages** English, French

---

Country hotel, Büsum-Deichhausen

Der Rosenhof

New owners, new broom. The Perotkas hail from Switzerland and have set about making this little hotel as stylish as it is comfortable. Leisure facilities include sauna and beauty parlour. Peaceful setting near mud-flats and seaside.

■ 25761 Büsum-Deichhausen, To Wurth 12 **Tel** (04834) 9800 **Fax** (04834) 98080 **Meals** breakfast, lunch, dinner, snacks **Prices** rooms D-DDD with breakfast; Meals from DM15 **Rooms** 23, all with bath or shower, central heating, TV, minibar, radio **Credit cards** not accepted **Closed** restaurant only, Mon **Languages** English

Schleswig-Holstein

Lakeside hotel, Eutin

Voss Haus

Attractive lake and garden views from the terrace of this 300-hundred-year-old building, which has been entirely redecorated recently. New annexe with three apartments next door. Beamed restaurant, extensive menu and wine list. Reports please.

■ 23701 Eutin, Vossplatz 6-10 **Tel** (04521) 70770 **Fax** (04521) 707777 **Meals** breakfast, lunch, dinner **Prices** rooms DD with breakfast; **Rooms** 13, all with bath or shower, central heating, phone, hairdrier, TV, minibar, radio; 3 apartments **Credit cards** AE, MC, V **Closed** never **Languages** English, French, Dutch

Town hotel, Friedrichstadt

Holländische Stube

An attractive group of canalside terraced townhouses, typical of this Dutch-built town. The sitting-rooms and dining-rooms are simple but welcoming, with the occasional antique piece; bedrooms display a little more style.

■ 25840 Friedrichstadt, Am Mittelburgwall 24-26 **Tel** (04881) 93900 **Fax** (04881) 939022 **Meals** breakfast, lunch, dinner **Prices** rooms DD-DDD with breakfast **Rooms** 8, all with shower, central heating, phone, hairdrier, TV, radio **Credit cards** AE, DC, MC, V **Closed** never **Languages** English, Danish

Town hotel, Lübeck

Schwarzwaldstuben

Very few of Lübeck's hotels fall into the charming, small category: the Schwarzwaldstuben is about the best of the bunch. Decoration is somewhat twee, but the hotel is a friendly, central place with very reasonable Prices and pleasant, airy rooms.

■ 23552 Lübeck, Koberg 12-15 **Tel** (0451) 77715 **Fax** (0451) 705414 **Meals** breakfast, lunch, dinner, snacks **Prices** rooms D-DD with breakfast; meals DM14-22 **Rooms** 21, all with shower, central heating, phone, hairdrier; some rooms have minibar, radio **Credit cards** not accepted **Closed** never **Languages** English, Danish

Lakeside hotel, Lütjensee bei Trittau

Fischerklause

This partly thatched hotel has a magnificent setting on the shores of the peaceful Lütjensee. You can enjoy the view through the panoramic windows of the (sadly) bland dining-room, or from the terrace right on the lakeside.

■ 22952 Lütjensee bei Trittau, Am See 1 **Tel** (04154) 7106 **Fax** (04154) 7185 Meals breakfast, lunch, dinner **Prices** rooms D-DD with breakfast; **Meals** from DM28 **Rooms** 15, all with shower, central heating, phone, TV **Credit cards** MC **Closed** Jan, Thu **Languages** English

Schleswig-Holstein

Country hotel, Malente-Gremsmühlen

Weißer Hof

'Garden hotel' is the Heusser-Schmieder family's label, and it is understandable: the low black-and-white hotel is surrounded by pleasant lawns and ponds which are its main attraction. Bedrooms are spacious and comfortable, with a mixture of styles.

■ 23714 Malente-Gremsmühlen, Voßstr 45 **Tel** (04523) 3962 **Fax** (04523) 6899 Meals breakfast, lunch, dinner **Prices** rooms DD-DDD with breakfast; **Meals** DM45-50 **Rooms** 18, all with bath or shower, central heating, phone, TV, minibar, radio **Credit cards** not accepted **Closed** Nov; restaurant only, Tue **Languages** English

Restaurant with rooms, Meldorf

Hotel Dithmarscher Bucht

A neat but ordinary-looking villa, white-walled and tiled, with more to offer than meets the eye – elegant (although largely reproduction) furnishings and a collection of antique toys and puppets.

■ 25704 Meldorf, Helgolandstr 2 **Tel** (04832) 7123 **Meals** breakfast, dinner; lunch Jun to Sep; Sat & Sun **Prices** rooms D-DD with breakfast; meals from DM20 **Rooms** 9, all with bath or shower, central heating, radio **Credit cards** not accepted **Closed** Jan and Feb; Mon **Languages** English

Country hotel, Ockholm-Bongsiel

Gaststätte Bongsiel

A sturdy, red-brick, typically Friesian house on the banks of a slow-flowing river, set in flat open countryside only a few miles from the Danish border. Pleasantly cluttered dining-room and bar; well known for its food, particularly local seafood.

■ 25842 Ockholm-Bongsiel, Bongsiel **Tel** (04674) 1445 **Fax** (04674) 1458 **Meals** breakfast, lunch, dinner **Prices** rooms D with breakfast; meals from DM20 **Rooms** 12, all with shower, central heating **Credit cards** not accepted **Closed** mid-Jan to end Feb; Tue **Languages** German only

Converted farmhouse, Westerdeichstrich

Der Mühlenhof

The area around Büsum is inundated by summer tourists and this solid farmhouse is often fully booked. Despite recent renovations by new owner Rolf Eisenbeisser, rooms and furnishings are simple; the real appeal lies in the windmill restaurant next door, complete with original trappings.

■ 25761 Westerdeichstrich/Büsum, Dorfstr 22 **Tel** (04834) 9980 **Fax** (04834) 99888 **Meals** breakfast, lunch, dinner **Prices** rooms D-DDD with breakfast; meals DM20-50 **Rooms** 17, all with shower, central heating, phone, TV, radio **Credit cards** AE, MC, V **Closed** never **Languages** English, French, Swedish, Italian

Hamburg

Hotels in Hamburg

Set on the river Elbe, Hamburg is Germany's largest port and its second largest city (after Berlin), and one of only two city-states. It attained importance first as a member of the Hanseatic League, an association of ports which monopolized the Baltic and North Sea trade in the Middle Ages, and later as a flourishing and active business and industrial city. Heavily bombed in World War II, the centre is largely modern. Hamburg's thriving nightlife is well known.

Nevertheless there are some peaceful, small and comfortable hotels in Hamburg; the pick of the bunch are described on the following pages. If these are full, we can recommend three other centrally located hotels. The Außen Alster (Tel (040) 241557, fax 2803231, 27 rooms) is a 19thC townhouse with a modern interior; despite its central location, it is relatively peaceful and some rooms have views of the lake, but car parking is a difficulty. Also central and near the Alster lake, but with its own car park and relaxing gardens, is the Prem (Tel (040) 241726), fax 2803851, 52 rooms). An Austrian art collector, Rudolf Prem, converted a pair of townhouses into this elegant hotel and it should therefore be no surprise to find the interior tastefully decorated and scattered with antiques; its restaurant, La Mer, offers interesting food. Our final recommendation is the Wedina (Tel (040) 243011, fax 2803894, 38 rooms), a simple, quiet and friendly hotel on the edge of the Alster lake with its own garden and swimming-pool; it has no restaurant but that is no problem in central Hamburg.

Outside the centre there are more possibilities. The Haus Lindtner at Harburg, for example, has 17 rooms and a pleasant garden (Tel (040) 790090, fax 790 9952) and the Mellingburger Schleuse at Sasel is a peaceful 250-year-old farmhouse (Tel (040) 602 4001, fax 602 27912, 40 bedrooms).

City hotel, Hamburg-Pöseldorf

Garden Hotel

Part of a matching set of three little hotels, with over 60 rooms in total, which are popular with media people. The designer has had a field day, giving each room an individual modern treatment. Breakfast in a conservatory. Beautiful garden, of course.

■ 201448 Hamburg 13, Magdalenenstr 60 **Tel** (040) 414040 **Fax** (040) 4140420 **Meals** breakfast, snacks **Prices** rooms DDD-DDDD; breakfast DM20 **Rooms** 17, all with bath or shower, central heating, air-conditioning, phone, hairdrier, TV, minibar, radio **Credit cards** AE, DC, MC, V **Closed** Christmas **Languages** English, French, Spanish

This page acts as an introduction to the features and hotels of Hamburg, and gives brief recommendations of good hotels that for one reason or another have not made a full entry – as well as containing our one short entry for the city. The long entries for this 'Land' – covering the hotels we are most enthusiastic about – start on the next page.

Hamburg

Town house hotel, Hamburg

Hotel Abtei

The Abtei is that rare bloom, a city hotel that is conveniently central but also offers peace and personality. It starts with the advantage of being set in a quiet, upmarket residential area: ancient chestnut trees line the street outside (once the drive to an old abbey). The position has other advantages, too: the smart Hamburg shops are just a walk away, boats can be hired on the Aussenalster just around the corner and the airport is only 15 minutes away by car.

Built in 1887, this elegant building was converted into a hotel in 1978 by the present owners, Petra and Fritz Lay, but it still retains the atmosphere of a private home. Its high-ceilinged rooms are beautifully furnished with elegant English antiques and lovely fabrics; built-in stereo in the impressive marble bathrooms may sound over the top, but there is nothing florid in the decoration.

Both breakfast and afternoon tea can be enjoyed in the lush garden, and the Lays have recently opened a dining-room for the service of dinner, with the emphasis on regional French and Italian food. Note that smoking is discouraged.

Nearby Kunsthalle, Botanical Gardens, port, view from TV tower.

20149 Hamburg,
Abteistrasse 14
Tel (040) 442905
Fax (040) 449820
Location in quiet one-way street just W of Aussenalster, N of city centre; garden, 2 garages, limited car parking
Meals breakfast, dinner, snacks
Prices rooms DDD-DDDD with breakfast; meals DM60-120

Rooms 11 double, all with bath; all rooms have central heating, phone, hairdrier, TV, minibar, radio
Facilities sitting-room, dining-room, bar
Credit cards AE, DC, MC, V
Children tolerated
Disabled no special facilities
Pets not allowed
Closed never **Languages** English, French, Italian
Proprietor Fritz Lay

Hamburg

Riverside hotel, Hamburg-Blankenese

Strandhotel Blankenese

Blankenese, once a fishing village, is now a smart residential suburb of Hamburg, its large residences set on a steep slope with narrow streets winding down to the estuary of the Elbe – over a mile
wide at this point. This glorious little art nouveau house, painted
gleaming white, faces directly on to the river. It was built as a
hotel in the early years of this century, and retains abundant original features – cornices, moulded ceilings, stained-glass windows,
glazed doors – although the enthusiastic new owners have
embellished the beach terrace, making a restful spot for a drink.

The setting is very much part of the hotel's appeal, and the
river-view rooms are clearly to be preferred – the best being
admirably spacious and beautifully proportioned, with an effective blend of antique furniture (meant to be used, not just
admired) and modern art. The latter is a particular enthusiasm of
Christian Peters, and pervades the house; the airy breakfast room
overlooking the Elbe is used as a gallery by local artists.

Satisfying food is served in the intimate dining-room, but there
is also a wide choice of restaurants along the Elbe.

Nearby sailing, golf, horse-riding; Wedel (5 km) – ship-saluting
ceremony (Willkomm-Höft).

22587 Hamburg 55,
Strandweg 13
Tel (040) 861344
Fax (040) 864936
Location on shore of Elbe in
smart district 15 km E of
middle of city; with garden
and car parking
Meals breakfast, lunch,dinner
Prices rooms DD-DDDD;
breakfast DM18, meals
DM25-55
Rooms 11 double, 4 with
bath, 7 with shower; 4 single,
all with bath; one suite; all
rooms have central heating,
phone, hairdrier, TV,
minibar, radio **Facilities**
dining-room, breakfast room,
art gallery; terrace, private
beach, sauna **Credit cards**
AE, DC, MC, V **Children**
welcome **Disabled** no special
facilities **Pets** accepted
Closed never **Languages**
English, French **Proprietors**
Christian Peters, Franz Kroll

Hamburg

Town villa, Hamburg

Hotel Hanseatic

The two years Wolfgang Schüler spent in London hotels must have made a strong impression, judging by the elegant hotel that he opened in 1979. A decanter of sherry is placed all the rooms, many of which are furnished with English antiques. For breakfast there is a choice of 15 teas served in silver teapots with toast and home-made jams. Above all, the dapper Herr Schüler himself, with his excellent clipped English and impeccable manners, is almost a caricature of the English themselves.

The white-fronted Patrician townhouse lies near Alster lake in a smart residential area of Hamburg. It has the atmosphere of an exclusive club: there is no hotel sign, and most of the guests hear of the Hanseatic by word of mouth. You are encouraged to linger over breakfast with a newspaper, or to sit and talk in the elegant drawing room, where you can serve yourself from the drinks cabinet. The bedrooms are immaculate, combining the atmosphere of a private house with all the comforts of a large hotel.

It is only a ten minute drive into town – alternatively in the summer, guests can visit the sights by Alster ferry from the quay a few minutes' walk away.

Nearby boat-trips round harbour, fine arts museum.

22299 Hamburg 60, Sierichstr 150
Tel (040) 485772
Fax (040) 485773
Location on main road in residential aread 10 mins from middle of city, NE of Außenalster; with garages
Meals breakfast
Prices rooms DD-DDDD; breakfast DM27.50
Rooms 13 double with bath; all rooms have central heating, phone, hairdrier, TV, minibar, radio
Facilities drawing-room, breakfast room
Credit cards none
Children welcome
Disabled not suitable
Pets not accepted
Closed never
Languages English, French
Proprietor Wolfgang Schüler

Niedersachsen

Hotels in Niedersachsen

The 'Great Northern Plain' of Niedersachsen (Lower Saxony) as a whole is hardly a popular tourist spot, but it is more varied than you might expect. For instance, there are the rich and fertile foothills of the Harz and Weber mountains in the south.

The region's main seaport is Bremen, but it is not part of Niedersachsen; like Hamburg, it is an independent city-state. We have no particular recommendations for central Bremen, although it does of course have the usual smart big hotels. But on the northern outskirts is the Landhaus Louisenthal, a classical-style mansion with home-like furnishings (Tel (0421) 232076, fax 236716, 60 rooms). There are other recommendable hotels not far away: the Hof Hoyerswege (Tel (04222) 2071, fax 5306) is a comfortable 20-roomed hotel with peaceful gardens only 15 miles south-west of Bremen at Ganderkesee. Further west, in the resort of Bad Zwischenahn, is the Seehotel Fährhaus, which has 54 bedrooms and offers magnificent views across the lake (Tel (04403) 6000, fax 4717). The East Friesian Islands, just off the coast, have fine windswept beaches and are excellent for bird-watching; we recommend the Strandeck on the car-free island of Langeoog – a very comfortable hotel offering sumptuous food (Tel (04972) 755, fax 6277, 42 rooms).

The biggest city in the state itself is Hannover; in addition to our main entries, bear in mind the Alpha-Tirol (Tel (0511) 131066, fax 341535, 15 rooms) in the centre, or the Landhaus Köhne am See (Tel (05131) 91085, fax 8367, 26 rooms) on the outskirts. Further east, in Wolfsburg, is the Ludwig am Park, a 38-roomed hotel near the town park and with an excellent restaurant (Tel (05362) 51051, fax 65214).

The Lüneburger Heath was once a vast moorland but this is gradually diminishing as its infertile soil is improved. In the town of Lüneburg, stay at the Hotel Zum Heidkrug, a restaurant-with-rooms housed in a delightful Gothic-style building (Tel (04131) 31249, fax 37688, 7 rooms), or the Stumpf, a simple little hotel on the outskirts (Tel (04134) 215). Further south, the beautiful old town of Celle is distinguished not only by its architecture but also by the exceptionally elegant Fürstenhof, a Relais & Châteaux hotel partly located in a splendid palace (Tel (05141) 2010, fax 201120, 75 rooms).

We have no full entries for Osnabrück, the major city of the south of Lower Saxony. If you need a place to stay there, try the elegant Residenz, (Tel (0541) 586358, fax 571847, 22 rooms), the historic Walhalla (Tel (0541) 27206, fax 23751, 27 rooms) or the Waldhotel Felsenkeller, a 30-roomed hotel at Bad Iburg 10 miles south (Tel (05403) 825, fax 804).

This page acts as an introduction to the features and hotels of Niedersachsen, and gives brief recommendations of good hotels that for one reason or another have not made a full entry. The long entries for this 'Land' – covering the hotels we are most enthusiastic about – start on the next page. But do not neglect the shorter entries starting on page 44: these are all hotels that we would happily stay at.

Niedersachsen

Town hotel, Duderstadt

Zum Löwen

Whatever antique character this old house had previously hung on to was knocked out of it during its thorough renovation in 1988, and as a result the smart new-look Zum Löwen is certainly open to the criticism that it lacks character. The bedrooms, in particular, are rescued from complete anonymity only by restrained use of Laura Ashley-style floral prints; the furniture is production-line stuff.

But the production line in question is a respectable one, its products durable, comfortable and easy on the eye. And the overriding impression the hotel makes on the visitor is of thorough attention to detail. You may not be captivated by what the interior designer was trying to do, but you have to admire the execution. This is particularly true of the various public areas – the swish, panelled 'gourmet' dining-room, the pine-and-pinks bar and the glass-roofed café, leading to the neatly tiled terrace.

Not least of the hotel's attractions is the excellent cooking – creative, competent, satisfying. Lighter snack meals are available in the bar.

Nearby ancient town hall, half-timbered houses, St Cyriakus Church.

37115 Duderstadt, Marktstr 30
Tel (05527) 3072
Fax (05527) 72630
Location on main pedestrian street of town 32 km E of Göttingen; with garages
Meals breakfast, lunch, dinner
Prices rooms DD-DDDD, with breakfast; meals DM40-110
Rooms 28 double, 24 with bath, 4 with shower; 8 single with shower; all rooms have central heating, phone, TV, hairdrier, minibar, radio, safe
Facilities dining-room, breakfast room/café, conference room, children's playroom; terrace, indoor swimming-pool, sauna **Credit cards** AE, DC, MC, V **Children** very welcome **Disabled** access easy; lift/elevator; wheelchair available **Pets** accepted
Closed 1-9 Jan
Languages English, French
Manager Andreas Pastuszka

Niedersachsen

Country house hotel, Hannover

Landhaus Ammann

The Landhaus is (despite its name and our corresponding categorization) well placed both for the city centre and for Hannover's exhibition halls. Not surprisingly, it attracts business custom – and a generous expense account would certainly be useful here.

But even those travelling at their own expense may find Helmut Ammann's prices justified by his smooth combination of elegant country-house atmosphere with city convenience and service, and – not least – first-class food. The kitchens come under Herr Ammann's personal aegis, and the food lives up to its Michelin star. It is modern in its presentation, with an emphasis on distinctive flavours and much use of herbs from the garden, and is complemented by a cellar of over 500 wines. The dining-room is elegantly designed in soft colours, the tables are widely spaced and beautifully set with good linen and porcelain – but you can also eat outside on the sheltered terrace with a view of the garden and woods. The bedrooms, too, are elegant, in cool shades with dark-wood furniture and well equipped bathrooms; the best are very spacious.

Nearby Herrenhausen Gardens, Museum of Lower Saxony.

30173 Hannover,
Hildesheimer Str 185
Tel (0511) 830818
Fax (0511) 843 7749
Location on edge of woods,
on S side of city, near
Südschnellweg; with garden
and ample car parking
Meals breakfast, lunch,
dinner
Prices rooms DDD-DDDD
with breakfast; menus DM80-
150

Rooms 12 double, 2 suites,
all with bath; all rooms have
central heating, phone,
hairdrier, TV, minibar, radio,
trouser press
Facilities dining-room, bar
Credit cards AE, DC, MC, V
Children very welcome
Disabled level access to
ground floor **Pets** accepted
Closed never **Languages**
English, French, Swedish
Proprietor Helmut Ammann

Niedersachsen

Suburban restaurant with rooms, Hannover

Georgenhof

Like Landhaus Amman, on the diametrically opposite side of town, the Georgenhof is one of Hannover's most highly regarded restaurants – or rather it contains one of them, known as Stern's. Heinrich Stern is head of the kitchen, while his wife Renate looks after the front of house. The food is expensive, modern in presentation but essentially simple.

The setting is as much of an attraction to diners as is the food. As you would expect, the dining-rooms are immaculate: glittering table settings (with artistically arranged vegetation) and stylish modern wood chairs against a simple, almost austere background of plain walls and dark beams, with only the minimum of ornamentation. Immediately outside is an attractive terrace where tables are set, and beyond that a reedy, weedy pond with an illuminated fountain. The creeper-covered walls of the hotel and the lush trees form a secluded haven.

The bedrooms are as uncluttered as the dining-rooms, with the emphasis on comfort but with enough attention to detail – such as harmoniously framed prints on the walls – to lift them out of the ordinary. The staff are helpful.

Nearby Herrenhausen Gardens, Berg Garden.

30167 Hannover 1,
Herrenhäuser Kirchweg 20
Tel (0511) 702244
Fax (0511) 708559
Location in NE edge of city, close to Herrenhausen Gardens; in grounds with ample car parking
Meals breakfast, lunch, dinner, snacks
Prices rooms DD-DDDD, with breakfast; DM40 for children under 6 in parents' room; Meals DM36-166

Rooms 5 double, 8 single, 1 family room, all with bath; all rooms have central heating, phone, hairdrier, TV, minibar; m ost have radio
Facilities restaurant, conference room; terrace
Credit cards AE, DC, MC, V
Children very welcome
Disabled not suitable
Pets tolerated
Closed never
Languages English
Proprietors Stern family

Niedersachsen

Country hotel, Nörten-Hardenberg

Burghotel Hardenberg

Given that the name means 'castle-hotel' and that this is a member of the Gast im Schloss group, you might expect this establishment somewhat to resemble a castle. But no: the romantic crenellated ruin on the hilltop is the hotel's picturesque backdrop, not the hotel itself.

But little else about Burghotel Hardenberg disappoints the visitor. The building – a long, three-storey, timbered affair forming three sides of a courtyard and crisply painted in black-and-white – has been an inn since around 1700, and now presents a very satisfactory combination of modern comfort and traditional atmosphere. Several of the bedrooms have been refurbished and have pretty contrasting fabrics.

The hotel's main restaurant, newly revamped and christened Novalis, serves ambitious, creative food in the modern manner that is highly regarded by the locals; the separate modern Burgmühlen restaurant, with its glossy conservatory, tends towards regional traditions. There is a new owner at Burghotel Hardenberg; we welcome further reports.

Nearby ruined castle; Northeim (10 km) and Einbeck (20 km) – wooden houses.

37176 Nörten-Hardenberg, Im Hinterhaus 11a
Tel (05503) 9810
Fax (05503)981666
Location in woodland on fringe of village, 11 km N of Göttingen; with garden, garages, ample car parking
Meals breakfast, lunch, dinner, snacks
Prices rooms DD-DDD, with breakfast; meals DM16-128
Rooms 38 double, 14 with bath, 14 with shower; 7 single, 4 with bath, 3 with shower; all rooms have central heating, phone, TV, minibar, safe, fax **Facilities** 2 dining-rooms, bar, conservatory, conference room; riding, golf, sauna, solarium, **Credit cards** AE, DC, MC, V **Children** welcome **Disabled** access easy **Pets** accepted in bedrooms only **Closed** 24 Dec **Languages** English, French, Spanish **Proprietor** Ralf O. Leidner

Niedersachsen

Farmhouse hotel, Salzhausen

Josthof

Here is a rarity. There is no shortage in Germany of hotels occupying ancient houses, or of hotels that have been in business for 350 years, or of places that have been in the family for 35 years. But there are very few that are as entirely unmodernized as this farmhouse – typical of the Lüneberg Heath region, with its timbered red-brick walls, and low thatched roof.

The name relates to the building's former use as a tax-collection point. But that does not mean it is boring or functional. Not only is the house itself warmly inviting, with its massive beams, red-tiled floors and huge, solid antiques; but also the young, friendly staff strike just the right note of informality.

The bedrooms, split between the main building and an equally antique-looking annexe, come as a slight disappointment; in making sure that they are comfortable, the proprietors have neglected the charm factor. But the best are notably spacious.

This is a region for bracing walks and the rustic dining-room – the heart of the hotel, with an enormous tiled stove – serves appropriately robust food in fortifying portions. The wine list is surprisingly extensive, and there is a cupboard full of spirits.

Nearby Lüneburg Heath – nature reserve; Lüneburg (20 km).

21376 Salzhausen, Am Lindenberg 1
Tel (04172) 292
Fax (04172) 6225
Location behind church on edge of small town on Lüneburg Heath, 45 km SE of Hamburg; with garden and ample parking for cars
Meals breakfast, lunch, dinner, snacks
Prices rooms D-DDD, with breakfast; Meals DM25-75

Rooms 14 double, 2 single, with bath; all rooms have central heating, phone, hairdrier, TV, minibar, radio
Facilities dining-room, *Stube;* terrace
Credit cards AE, DC, MC, V
Children welcome **Disabled** access easy; some ground-floor rooms **Pets** accepted
Closed Christmas Day
Languages English
Proprietor Jörg Hansen

Niedersachsen

Menzhausen

Uslar is an old town surrounded on three sides by the Solling-Vogler nature reserve, and the Menzhausen is its main hotel and restaurant. The original building dates from the 16th century and looks the part, with a colourfully ornamented half-timbered façade. In the 30 years that it has been in the hands of the Körber family it has been considerably altered and extended – most recently by the addition of a whole new building separated from the old core by a street and linked by a covered footbridge.

The new part, largely designed by Herr Körber himself and opened only in 1990, is a striking reinterpretation of the traditional Weserrenaissance style. It contains smart leisure facilities as well as comfortable, spacious bedrooms with carefully designed stained-wood furniture and swish bathrooms. The rooms in the old part are not particularly captivating. The dining-room, on the other hand, has plenty of beams and cosy niches.

Herr Körber is something of a wine buff, and his cellar is of vinous as well as architectural note; tastings are organized. Food is regionally based, with plenty of game in evidence. Snacks are available in the bar.

Nearby walking; boat-trips on Weser (10 km).

37170 Uslar, Lange Str 12
Tel (05571) 2051
Fax (05571) 5820
Location in pedestrian precinct in old town 35 km NW of Göttingen; with garden, car parking
Meals breakfast, lunch, dinner
Prices rooms DD-DDDD, with breakfast; meals DM20-70
Rooms 28 double, 24 with bath, 4 with shower (6 twin); 9 single with shower; 3 family rooms with bath; all have central heating, phone, TV; some have hairdrier, minibar
Facilities dining-room, *Bierstube*, wine cellar, conference room; terrace, indoor pool, sauna **Credit cards** AE, DC, MC, V
Children welcome **Disabled** some ground-floor rooms; lift/elevator **Pets** well-behaved dogs **Closed** never **Languages** English, French
Proprietor Fritz Körber

Niedersachsen

Country guest-house, Walsrode

Landhaus Walsrode

Walsrode lies only a few kilometres from the major motorways through northern Germany, and is an excellent stopping-off point. At the end of a long day in the car, the tree-lined drive leads the weary traveller to a peaceful setting and a personal welcome from the owner, Lieselotte Wolff.

The 400-year-old red-tiled former farmhouse stands in its own extensive parkland gardens at the edge of the wood. While retaining a homely feel, Frau Wolff has transformed the interior into an elegant guest-house, marked by her good taste. The bedrooms are spacious and uncluttered; the furniture is mainly modern, but each room contains one selected antique piece and a few old paintings and prints on the walls.

In principle, only breakfast is served, but a simple cold evening meal can also be arranged. In the evening Frau Wolff encourages guests to mingle around the fireplace in the large drawing room, where drinks are served from a wardrobe-sized cabinet, or in smaller groups in the conversation room or card room. There is also a reading-room for the less sociable, with shelves full of books, periodicals and newspapers.

Nearby Tropical bird park (3 km), leisure park, golf course.

29664 Walsrode, Oskar-Wolff-Str 1
Tel (05161) 8053
Fax (05161) 2352
Location near centre of small town 60 km N of Hannover, 3 km E from exit 27 of E234; garages and car parking
Meals breakfast, snacks
Prices rooms D-DDD, with breakfast
Rooms 11 double, 6 with bath, 5 with shower (2 twin); 6 single, 2 with bath, 3 with shower; 2 apartments with bath; all rooms have central heating, phone, TV
Facilities breakfast room, hall, sitting-room, conference room, library; heated outdoor swimming-pool
Credit cards AE, MC
Children very welcome
Disabled ground-floor room
Pets large dogs not allowed in breakfast room **Closed** 15 Dec to 15 Jan **Languages** English
Proprietor Frau L Wolff

Niedersachsen

Country hotel, Bad Bevensen

Grünings Landhaus

A tranquil spot despite the popularity of the eponymous Lothar Grüning's ambitious cooking. After a comprehensive revamp, the bedrooms have shed their matronly style for a more opulent look.

■ 29549 Bad Bevensen, Haberkamp 2 **Tel** (05821) 98400 **Fax** (05821) 984041 **Meals** breakfast, lunch, dinner **Prices** rooms DD-DDD with breakfast; meals from DM60 **Rooms** 25, all with bath, central heating, hairdrier, phone, minibar, radio **Credit cards** not accepted **Closed** 1 Dec to 17 D ec; 6 Jan to 31 Jan **Languages** English

---

Sub el, Bad Zwischenahn

Hotel Am Kurgarten

A plush, elegantly furnished and richly decorated modern hoTel with every comfort. Public rooms are an unrestrained mish-mash of styles and patterns; bedrooms, happily, are plainer and more tasteful, with opulent marble bathrooms.

■ 26160 Bad Zwischenahn, Unter den Eichen 30 **Tel** (04403) 59011 **Fax** (04403) 59620 **Meals** breakfast **Prices** rooms D-DDD with breakfast **Rooms** 19, all with bath or shower, central heating, phone, hairdrier, TV, radio **Credit cards** AE, MC, V **Closed** never **Languages** English

---

Country hotel, Bendestorf

Landhaus Meinsbur

The long thatched roofs of this immaculate red-brick and timber house give many of the comfortable, flowery bedrooms an attic- like feel. Beams, leather furniture and Persian carpets predom~inate. Popular, rustic restaurant.

■ 21227 Bendestorf, Gartenstr 2 **Tel** (04183) 6088 **Fax** (04183) 6087 **Meals** breakfast, lunch, dinner **Prices** rooms DD-DDD with breakfast; meals DM30-40 **Rooms** 16, all with bath or shower, central heating, phone, hairdrier, TV, minibar, radio **Credit cards** DC, MC, V **Closed** never **Languages** English

---

City hotel, Braunschweig

Ritter St Georg

The city's oldest timbered building – with prettily painted ceilings in the restaurant and bar – is also one of its most comfortable hotels. Stylishly simple bedrooms, the best notably spacious.

■ 38100 Braunschweig, Alte Knochenhauerstr 12-13 **Tel** (0531) 13039 **Fax** (0531) 13038 **Meals** breakfast, lunch, dinner, snacks **Prices** rooms DD-DDDD; breakfast DM15; meals DM70 **Rooms** 22, all with bath or shower, central heating, phone, hairdrier, TV, minibar, radio **Credit cards** AE, DC, MC, V **Closed** restaurant only, Feb; Sun **Languages** English, some French

Niedersachsen

Village inn, Burgwedel

Marktkieker

A deceptively olde-worlde timber-and-brick building from the outside, bristling with mod cons inside (including a 'green' energy system). But much charm remains: old beams criss-cross the rooms, furnished in a comfortable mixture of styles. Free local sports facilities.

■ 30938 Burgwedel 1, Am Markt 7, Grossburgwedel **Tel** (05139) 7093 **Fax** (05139) 894065 **Meals** breakfast **Prices** rooms DD-DDD with breakfast **Rooms** 16, all with bath or shower, central heating, air-conditioning, phone, TV **Credit cards** AE, DC, MC, V, **Closed** 22 Dec to 5 Jan **Languages** English

---

Town inn, Celle

Utspann

A real gem, this former tannery, in the old part of town, just inside the north wall. Comfortable bedrooms have been decorated in a busy, countrified style, but with unusual flair. A cobbled courtyard and new restaurant add to the charm.

■ 29221 Celle, Im Kreise 13 **Tel** (05141) 92720 **Fax** (05141) 927252 **Meals** breakfast, lunch, snacks, dinner **Prices** rooms DD-DDD (supplement during exhibitions), breakfast DM 16; **Meals** from DM40 **Rooms** 23, all with bath, central heating, phone, hairdrier, TV **Credit cards** AE, DC, MC, V **Closed** Christmas **Languages** English, Spanish

---

Country hotel, Dinklage

Burghotel Dinklage

'Country' is somewhat generous – Dinklage is a small town. But the Burghotel is set in woods, and smartly rustic in style, with warm wooden furnishings in the very comfortable bedrooms. Suave, cool dining-rooms.

■ 49413 Dinklage, Burgallee 1 **Tel** (04443) 8970 **Fax** (04443) 897444 **Meals** breakfast, lunch, dinner **Prices** rooms DD-DDD with breakfast; meals from DM30 **Rooms** 53, all with b ath or shower, central heating, phone, TV, minibar, radio; some have hairdrier **Credit cards** AE, DC, MC, V **Closed** never **Languages** English, French, some Spanish

---

Country house hotel, Eddelstorf

Hansens Hof

An old estate, tastefully converted with a mix of stylish modern and more traditional furnishings. There is a strong equestrian influence – guests can bring or borrow horses, but riding is not mandatory.

■ 29575 Eddelstorf, Alte Dorfstr 2 **Tel** (05807) 1255 **Fax** (05807) 1304 **Meals** breakfast, lunch, dinner, snacks **Prices** rooms D-DD with breakfast; meals DM18-45 **Rooms** 23, al l with bath or shower, central heating, phone, TV, radio; some rooms have minibar **Credit cards** AE, DC, MC **Closed** never **Languages** English

Niedersachsen

Town hotel, Emden

Heerens Hotel

Not a particularly pretty town, but a pretty enough hotel on the fringe of the canal-ringed centre – a white-and-yellow villa with smooth modern furnishings in its panelled dining-room, and smart, spacious bedrooms.

■ 26725 Emden, Friedrich-Ebert-Str 67 **Tel** (04921) 23740 **Fax** (04921) 23158 Me als breakfast, lunch, dinner **Prices** rooms DD-DDD with breakfast; meals DM45 **Rooms** 21, all wit h bath or shower, central heating, phone, hairdrier, TV, radio **Credit cards** AE, DC, MC, V **Closed** restaurant only, Sat; Sun evening **Languages** English, Swedish

---

Village inn, Faßberg-Müden

Niemeyer's Posthotel

Much altered over the years, this family-run coaching inn now plays host to conferences and attracts guests looking for well-ordered, comfortable accommodation. Set in manicured gardens, with the Südheide nature reserve beyond.

■ 29326 Faßberg-Müden, Hauptstr 7 **Tel** (05053) 98900 **Fax** (05053) 989064 **Meals** breakfast, lunch, dinner, snacks **Prices** rooms DD-DDD with breakfast; meals from DM25 **Rooms** 39, all with central heating, phone, hairdrier, TV, minibar, radio **Credit cards** MC, V **Closed** never Languages English

---

Country hotel, Ganderkesee-Bookholzberg

Landhaus Hasbruch

The renovated bedrooms of this traditionally painted forest-girt hotel may be depressingly uniform, but there is abundant compensation in the rustic character of the panelled bars and dining-rooms. Unpretentious, satisfying food.

■ 27777 Ganderkesee 2-Bookholzberg, Hedenkampstr 20 **Tel** (04223) 92190 **Fax** (04223) 9 21930 **Meals** breakfast, lunch, dinner, snacks **Prices** rooms DD with breakfast; **Meals** from DM30 **Rooms** 12, all with shower, central heating, phone, TV, radio **Credit cards** MC **Closed** never **Languages** English, French, Dutch

---

Town house hotel, Hameln

Krone

In the old part of this timbered house in central Hameln, you will enjoy a happy mix of comfort and character (low ceilings, beams, modern wood-and-brass furniture). Annexe and public rooms are less stylish. Piped music and dim lighting throughout.

■ 31785 Hameln, Osterstr 30 **Tel** (05151) 9070 **Fax** (05151) 907217 **Meals** breakfast, lunch, dinner, snacks **Prices** rooms DD-DDDD **Rooms** 34, all with bath or shower, central heating, phone, TV, minibar; some have hairdrier, radio **Credit cards** AE, DC, MC, V **Closed** never **Languages** English, French

Niedersachsen

Town hotel, Haselünne

Burghotel

A historic brick-built mansion, including a 160-year-old bed among its treasures; not all the bedroom furniture is so special. Breakfast is served in the wooden-walled *Bauernstube* – for other meals, there is a restaurant under the same ownership next door.

■ 49740 Haselünne, Steintorstr 7 **Tel** (05961) 1544 **Meals** breakfast **Prices** rooms D-DD with breakfast **Rooms** 17, all with bath or shower, central heating, phone, TV, minibar, radio **Credit cards** AE, DC, MC, V **Closed** never **Languages** English

---

Village inn, Holle-Astenbeck

Gutsschenke des Fürsten zu Münster

Appealing timber-framed inn, reassuringly popular with locals who come for filling meals. Overnight guests must try to ignore the sound of the traffic on the busy road outside; those who do will be rewarded by the Gerhardt's friendly informality inside.

■ 3118 Holle-Astenbeck **Tel** (05062) 1866 **Meals** breakfast, lunch, dinner **Prices** rooms D-DD with breakfast **Rooms** 28, all with shower, central heating, phone **Credit cards** AE, DC, V **Closed** Mon; lunch Mon to Wed **Languages** English

---

Country hotel, Krummhörn-Greetsiel

Witthus

With canals and windmills all around, you might be in the Netherlands at this tasteful hotel, tea-room, garden-café and art gallery in one, and indeed you almost are. Great care has been taken over everything, including the harmonious bedrooms.

■ 26736 Krummhörn 3, Kattrepel 7-9 **Tel** (04926) 540 **Fax** (04926) 1471 **Meals** breakfast, lunch, dinner, snacks **Prices** rooms DD-DDD with breakfast; meals from DM20 **Rooms** 14, all with shower, central heating, phone, hairdrier, TV, radio **Credit cards** MC, V **Closed** 25 Nov to 25 Dec **Languages** English, Dutch

---

Town hotel, Worpswede

Eichenhof

It is hard to believe this long, low, whitewashed building is in the middle of town. Mature trees, meadow and ponds form a shield against urban life, and Marita Monsees looks after guests with easy charm - reports have been good. Simple, light bedrooms and breakfast room are spotless.

■ 27726 Worpswede, Ostendorfer Str 13 **Tel** (04792) 2676 **Meals** breakfast **Prices** rooms DD-DDD with breakfast **Rooms** 18, all with bath or shower, central heating, phone, hairdrier, TV, minibar, radio **Credit cards** AE, DC, MC, V **Closed** 3 Nov to 12 Dec **Languages** English

Nordrhein-Westfalen

Hotels in Nordrhein-Westfalen

Here is the industrial heartland of modern Germany, centred on the intensely developed Ruhr basin between Duisberg and Dortmund. But here also are historic cities and castles – and no shortage of desirable small hotels.

Köln (Cologne) is the most attractive of the cluster of large industrial cities in the centre of this region. As well as the three hotels we describe in detail, you might like to bear in mind the Altstadt (Tel 01221) 2577851, fax 2577853, 30 rooms); Landhaus Gut Keuchhof (Tel (02234) 76033, fax 78687, 50 rooms); the St Maternus, a pleasant restaurant-with-rooms (Tel (0221) 393633, fax 393245, 10 rooms); and the Spiegel (Tel (02203) 61046, fax 695653), a 27-bedroomed hotel near the airport.

Far less interesting, but the capital of the whole region, is the fashion-conscious, commercial and administrative city of Düsseldorf, on the fringe of the industrial Ruhr. If our two main recommendations are booked up, you could try the Rhein-terrasse (Tel (0211) 996990, fax 996 9999, 42 rooms), the Haus am Zoo (Tel (0221) 626333), fax 626536, 22 rooms) or, close to the exhibition halls, Villa Viktoria (Tel (0211) 469 000, fax 469 00601, 40 suites); none is central but all are relatively small and have some character. Bonn is the small and unremarkable capital city of what was West Germany. Nevertheless it is worth a visit and we can add the Jacobs (Tel (0228) 232822, fax 232850, 43 rooms) as an alternative to our two detailed recommendations.

Away to the north of the Rhine – and the big cities – is the Westphalian plain, flat and green and scattered with castles, manors and farms. The Schmelting at Reken (Tel (02864) 311, fax 1395, 23 rooms) or the Ratshotel Rudolph at Ahaus (Tel (02561) 2051, fax 2055) would make good stopping-off places; further north still, we can recommend the Schlosshotel Surenburg at Hörstel, not a castle as its name suggests, but a welcoming and modern 23-roomed hotel in the grounds of an old castle (Tel 05454) 7092, fax 7251). At Harsewinkel, more or less midway between our recommendations at Warendorf and Wiedenbrück, is the Poppenborg, a smart and ambitious restaurant with 18 very modestly priced rooms (Tel (05247) 2241).

Further possibilities in the more mountainous Sauerland (E of the Ruhr) are the Landhotel Gasthof Schütte in Schmallenberg (Tel (02975) 82501, fax 82522, 58 rooms), an ancient and beautiful country inn; the Hubertus (Tel (02972) 5077, fax 1731, 24 rooms), also in Schmallenberg; and the Haus Hilmeke (Tel (02723) 8171, fax 80016), a 27-roomed hotel in Lennestadt. Near Siegen, to the south, is the Alten Flecken in Freudenberg, a modernized timbered house (Tel (02734) 8041, fax 1277, 25 rooms).

This page acts as an introduction to the features and hotels of Nordrhein-Westfalen, and gives brief recommendations of good hotels that for one reason or another have not made a full entry. The long entries for this 'Land' – covering the hotels we are most enthusiastic about – start on the next page. But do not neglect the shorter entries starting on page 67: these are all hotels that we would happily stay at.

Nordrhein-Westfalen

Manor house hotel, Bergisch Gladbach

Schlosshotel Lerbach

Nothing but praise from recent visitors to this new entry in our guide: "English guests are certain to appreciate the traditional country house comfort of the bedrooms, each one individually decorated with antique pieces, four posters, half-testers and brass bedsteads. The place exudes refinement and relaxation".

Built on the site of a medieval castle, the place in question is an ivy-covered late-19thC manor house complete with sturdy stone tower and rambling outbuildings, set in its own extensive grounds, with woods, a lake on which you can fish, and a tennis court. The stables are now a beauty centre, with pool.

The hotel is approached along a curving driveway, and austere lobby, with its great stone fireplace, its stone pillars and its hunting trophies belies the softness and luxury of the bedrooms, the friendliness of the staff, and the excellence of the cooking, for which chef Dieter Müller has won two Michelin stars. Less formal and business-oriented is the hotel's second restaurant, Schlosschänke, which serves "classical cuisine in the country house style", and there is a delightful terrace where meals and drinks can be taken in warm weather.

Nearby forest walks, golf.

51465 Bergisch Gladbach, Lerbacher Weg
Tel (02202) 2040
Fax (02202) 204940
E-mail lerbach@relaischateaux.fr
Location on E side of Bergisch, 17 km E of Cologne in own grounds; ample car parking
Meals breakfast, lunch, dinner
Prices rooms DDDD, with breakfast; meals from DM70,
Rooms 44 double, 3 single, 7 suites, all with bath; all rooms have central heating, phone, fax, TV, radio, CD player, minibar, hairdrier
Facilities sitting-room, dining-rooms, bar, conference rooms, terrace; beauty centre, tennis court
Credit cards AE, DC, MC, V
Children accepted **Disabled** no special facilities **Pets** accepted **Closed** never
Languages English, French
Proprietor Kurt Wagner

Nordrhein-Westfalen

Country hotel, Bergisch Gladbach

Waldhotel Mangold

Waldhotel Mangold is most definitely a family concern. It was the present owner's father who in 1927 founded a small hostelry on the site, at the edge of the forest in the peaceful Milchborntal. Hans Mangold was born there – he took over the hotel in 1966 on his father's death, has tirelessly expanded and improved it, and intends to hand it on to his children.

 The building is not particularly attractive from the outside, although the setting remains peaceful. The reception and sitting areas in the oldest part of the house are all old beams and solid oak antiques, with a fireplace and beautiful carved wooden staircase. The much-expanded restaurant area contains many striking features: a carved wooden gateway, specially commissioned stained glass windows and an highly unusual hand-beaten brass ceiling. The seven bedrooms in the main building were recently refurbished – orthopaedic beds and state-of-the-art bathrooms providing a touch of luxury. The other bedrooms in a separate annexe are comfortable and immaculately kept. An attractive alternative to the city-centre hotels of Cologne, 17 kilometres away.

Nearby forest walks, golf.

51429 Bergisch Gladbach - Bensberg, Am Milchborntal 39-43
Tel (02204) 95550
Fax (02204) 955560
Location in wooded suburb, 17 km E of Cologne; in grounds with ample car parking
Meals breakfast, dinner, snacks
Prices rooms DD-DDD with breakfast; meals from DM60
Rooms 18 double (6 twin), 3 single, with bath; all rooms have central heating, phone, TV; most rooms have hairdrier, minibar
Facilities dining-rooms, conference room, bar, *Stube*
Credit cards AE, MC, V
Children welcome **Disabled** some ground-floor rooms
Pets not accepted **Closed** restaurant only, Sun eve, Mon
Languages English, French
Proprietor Hans Mangold

Nordrhein-Westfalen

Town inn, Billerbeck

Domschenke

Billerbeck is one of the many small towns that does not rate a mention in the tourist guides but has a quiet old part (now pedestrianized) at its centre. The Domschenke is well named: you can step out of its front door and into the cathedral whose twin spires dominate the skyline for miles around.

It was a 17thC house originally, but has been much renovated and extended in recent years, to the extent that it now seems something of a reproduction, both inside and out. The clear exception to this is the bar, part of which has conspicuously ancient beams. But replica or not, the beamed dining-room is cheerfully rustic. The bedrooms are comfortable rather than full of character – uncluttered and restrained in decoration, with new but traditional-style furniture; unusual shapes (such as an alcove accommodating a double bed) lend extra interest to some rooms.

The hotel has been in the eagerly helpful Groll family for over 130 years, and the youthful kitchen brigade is now competently led by the son of the household, Frank. He has added modern dishes to the repertoire of Westphalian specialities.

Nearby Schloss Darfeld (10 km); Merfelder Bruch (10 km).

48727 Billerbeck, Markt 6
Tel (02543) 4424
Fax (02543) 4128
Location opposite cathedral in pedestrianized middle of little town 32 km E of Münster; with garages and private parking
Meals breakfast, lunch, dinner
Prices rooms D-DD, with breakfast; Meals DM15-48
Rooms 18 double (5 twin), 5 single, 2 suites, all with bath; all rooms have central heating, phone, TV; most rooms have radio
Facilities dining-room, restaurant, stube, TV room
Credit cards AE, DC, MC, V
Children welcome
Disabled no special Facilities
Pets tolerated
Closed never
Languages English, French
Proprietor Josef Groll

Nordrhein-Westfalen

Country hotel, Bocholt-Barlo

Schloß Diepenbrock

The first glimpse of the hotel Schloß Diepenbrock as you approach it along a tree-lined country road is of the classical yellow façade and twin turrets of the castle itself – so it comes as something of a disappointment to discover that the restaurant and most bedrooms are housed in a modern building overlooking the lake. There are four beautiful guest rooms on the first floor of the moated castle, but since it is still very much the Baron's home they are generally let only by special arrangement.

If you are determined to sleep within the moat there is always the tower room, a perfectly round double room with thick walls and small windows at the base of one of the turrets. The modern annexe rooms are comfortable and have pleasant views of the lake and castle grounds, but lack any real character. The restaurant enjoys a solid reputation and is furnished in a rustic style with wood panelling and tiled floor.

You can expect a friendly welcome from the young staff, and indeed from the Baron and his wife, who are actively involved in the management of the hotel.

Nearby Town hall; Xanten (20 km) – archaeological park, St Victor's Cathedral.

46397 Bocholt-Barlo,
Schloßallee 5
Tel (02871) 3545
Fax (02871) 39607
Location 15 km NE of A3 Essen/Arnhem motorway, 5 km N of Bocholt; parking
Meals breakfast, lunch, dinner, snacks
Prices rooms DD-DDD; breakfast DM17.50; meals DM47-89
Rooms 18 double (8 twin), 3 single, 2 suites, all with bath; all rooms have radio, central heating, phone, TV, minibar
Facilities dining-room, breakfast room, sitting-room, conference room; terraces, fishing, golf, riding
Credit cards AE, DC, MC, V
Children very welcome
Disabled ground-floor rooms
Pets not accepted **Closed** never **Languages** English, French, Spanish, Greek
Proprietor Freiherr Wilhelm von Graes

Nordrhein-Westfalen

Schloßhotel Kommende Ramersdorf

The Kommende Ramersdorf is a fairy-tale château, complete with countless turrets and spires. But the hotel itself is to be found in converted stable buildings around a small inner courtyard. No need for disappointment: this makes for a small hotel of friendly proportions with a low-key, personal touch.

The castle stands in lovely grounds at the top of a steep drive, though not entirely isolated from traffic noise. The main building is now a museum and also houses Herr Bartel's impressive collection of restored antiques. Some of these have found their way into the hotel, unobtrusively but helpfully run by his wife Barbara; in principle, they are for sale should you wish to buy.

The harmonious, comfortable bedrooms lie along first-floor beamed corridors; downstairs there is a tiny cosy bar with stools and old English settles, open to hotel guests only. The restaurant is entered through a great barn door, but inside is extremely elegant, with marble floor, gilt fittings, high-backed chairs and a wealth of fresh flowers. The staff are all Italian and it enjoys a reputation as one of the best Italian restaurants in Germany.

Nearby Beethoven's house, 12thC Collegiate Church and Cloisters, Rhineland Museum.

53227 Bonn, Oberkasseler Str 10
Tel (0228) 440734
Fax (0228) 444400
Location in suburb of Beuel on E side of Rhine, exit Niederholtorf from A59; within grounds, with ample car parking
Meals breakfast, lunch, dinner
Prices rooms D-DD, with breakfast; meals DM28-48, children's DM20

Rooms 10 double (2 twin), 8 single, all with bath; all rooms have central heating, phone, TV, radio
Facilities breakfast room, TV room, bar, dining-room; terrace **Credit cards** AE, MC, V
Children very welcome
Disabled no special Facilities
Pets accepted **Closed** 4 weeks in Jul /Aug; 2 weeks at Christmas **Languages** English, French, Italian
Proprietor Barbara Bartel

Nordrhein-Westfalen

Manor house hotel, Dahlem-Kronenburg

Schloßhotel Das Burghaus

The cobbled streets of the idyllic medieval walled village of Kronenburg remain blissfully peaceful, thanks to its remote position in the unspoilt Eifel region. Das Burghaus is not a castle as such but was built as an official residence in 1776. Its severe façade, with thick whitewashed walls and grey-tiled roof, overlooks a courtyard; to the rear there is a narrow terrace and then the ground drops steeply away, opening up magnificent views.

   The entrance hall sets the tone of the public rooms – a worn flagstone floor, dark beams and heavy antique furniture. Dinner can be taken in the high-ceilinged but homely baronial hall or alternatively in the old kitchen, complete with original pots and pans, a huge walk-in fireplace and permanent smell of woodsmoke. The bedrooms are less impressive, with a hotch-potch of old-fashioned furniture and in some cases rather shabby decoration. The Hofers, who have been running the hotel for 15 years (it has been in the family for 150 years), admit that there is room for improvement. But any shortcomings are made up for by the beautiful setting and the relaxed, friendly welcome .

Nearby 'Eifel Route'; Zingsheim (10 km) – caves; Gerolstein (15 km) – wildlife park, archaeological museum.

53949 Dahlem-Kronenburg, Burgbering 1-4
Tel (06557) 265
Fax (06557) 1397
Location at end of narrow cobbled main street of hilltop village; with garden and car parking
Meals breakfast, lunch, dinner
Prices rooms D-DD with breakfast (children und free); Meals DM30-50
Rooms 8 double, 2 with bath, 6 with shower; 3 single with shower; 2 family rooms with bath; all rooms have central heati ng, TV, radio
Facilities sitting-room, dining-room, *Bierstube*, children's playroom; terrace
Credit cards DC, MC, V
Children very welcome
Disabled not suitable **Pets** accepted (DM7 per night)
Closed Tue **Languages** English, French, Swedish
Proprietor E D Hofer

Nordrhein-Westfalen

Country hotel, Hamminkeln-Marienthal

Haus Elmer

The brick-and-timber buildings now incorporated into the Haus Elmer, and the Elmer family's involvement with them, go back a long way, as Karl-Heinz Elmer's publicity handouts testify. Your first impression may not be one of great age – many of the wrinkles you might expect to find in an old building seem to have been neatly ironed out. But if so, it is in the interests of order, cleanliness and comfort, and a traditional decorative style prevails despite the modernisation and expansion.

This is a hotel which is thoroughly well run from every point of view. The food is richly satisfying – a view which is supported by the evident popularity of the restaurant. There are several traditionally welcoming sitting areas. The bedrooms make up in comfort what they may lack in character (the best are probably the ones recently created in one of the old buildings, with strikingly modern furniture combined with exposed beams). And the hotel has an equally neat flowery garden behind it.

This area, near the Dutch border, is prime bicycling country, and the hotel has its own stock of bikes for the use of guests.
Nearby cycling, golf; Xanten (10 km) – Roman town, archaeological park.

46499 Hamminkeln-Marienthal, An der Klosterkirche 12
Tel (02856) 9110
Fax (02856) 91170
Location in small village 15 km N of Wesel; with garden and ample car parking
Meals breakfast, lunch, dinner, snacks
Prices rooms DD-DDD, with breakfast; meals DM30-70
Rooms 20 double, 5 single, 6 apartments, all with bath; all rooms have central heating, phone, TV, radio
Facilities sitting-room, 3 dining-rooms, bar; terrace, bowling alley, bicycles
Credit cards DC, MC, V
Children welcome
Disabled one ground-floor room
Pets accepted in public rooms only **Closed** never
Languages English, French
Proprietor Karl-Heinz Elmer

Nordrhein-Westfalen

Converted castle, Isselburg

Wasserburg Anholt

Of all the *Wasserburgen* of north Germany, Anholt is one of the most impressive – a grand, rather severe red-brick building, with turrets and spires, floating on what amounts to a lake rather than a moat. The castle is open to the public – its interior has some impressive features, and it contains a major collection of paintings. The hotel occupies a separate part.

This is not the most personal of hotels, but you are more likely to be disappointed by a lack of style and antiquity than intimidated by an excess of elegance and formality – particularly in the bedrooms, some of which are no more than adequately comfortable (though others, such as the honeymoon tower-room, are impressively romantic).

The public areas are all attractive, in different ways. The ground-floor café is a highlight, leading out on to a wooden terrace built over the water. Upstairs is a very smart, dark-wood-panelled dining-room. Next to reception, a welcoming sitting-room with stripped-pine furniture and moat views. In the old stables, an all-wood bar serving snacks. Food in the main restaurant is as smart as the decoration, in the modern manner.

Nearby 'Swiss' park, St Pankratius church, Werth Windmill.

46419 Isselburg, Kleverstr 2
Tel (02874) 4290
Fax (02874) 4035
Location in countryside, 15 km W of Bocholt; grounds, garages, ample car parking
Meals breakfast, lunch, dinner, snacks
Prices rooms DD-DDDD, with breakfast; meals DM69-129
Rooms 21 double, 12 with bath, 9 with shower (2 twin); 6 single, 2 with bath, 4 with shower; 3 suites with bath; all rooms have central heating, phone, TV, radio; most have hairdrier, minibar **Facilities** dining-room, breakfast-room/café, bar, sitting-room; terraces, golf course, bicycles
Credit cards AE, DC, MC, V
Children welcome **Disabled** one ground-floor room, lift/elevator **Pets** in bedrooms only **Closed** 2-24Jan
Languages English, Dutch
Proprietor Heinz Brune

Nordrhein-Westfalen

Town restaurant with rooms, Lüdinghausen

Hotel Borgmann

Lüdinghausen is an unremarkable small town between the industrial Ruhr and Münster, in an area chiefly notable for its *Wasserburgen* – moated castles and manor-houses. Like so many German towns it has an old part with some charm, and it is here that the Borgmanns' little hotel is to be found: an exceptionally small establishment by German standards, with only seven bedrooms and no sitting-room apart from the bar – hence our classification of it as a restaurant-with-rooms.

It is a modest place, with simple furniture and tiled floors, but run with great care and pride (and a little bit of style) by the fourth generation of the Borgmann family. The building is a tall townhouse with sculptured gables, dating from the late 19th century, and the interior makes the most of exposed beams and other antique features. There is a shaded terrace, rather enclosed but very pretty, looking on to the old house next door. Bedrooms vary in style from the appealingly old-fashioned to the brightly modern.

The food is traditionally satisfying stuff, mainly 'vom Grill und aus der Pfanne', with special dishes for children.

Nearby Vischering Castle; Münster (25 km) – Mill Museum.

59348 Lüdinghausen, Münsterstr 17
Tel (02591) 91810
Fax (02591) 918130
Location in middle of old part of town, 28 km SW of Münster; with car parking
Meals breakfast, lunch, dinner
Prices rooms D-DD, with breakfast; meals DM18-35
Rooms 14 double, with bath; all rooms have central heating, phone, TV, minibar
Facilities dining-room, breakfast room, bar; terrace
Credit cards AE, DC, MC, V
Children welcome
Disabled not suitable
Pets accepted
Closed Easter; Sun, Mon until 18.00
Languages English
Proprietors Gitta and Werner Borgmann

Nordrhein-Westfalen

Town guest-house, Monschau

Haus Vecqueray

Our researches in Germany did not unearth many hotels or guest-houses undocumented by other guides, but here is one – a bed-and-breakfast guest-house set just off the main tourist track in the little picture-postcard town of Monschau. Like the other houses that the tourist comes here to see, it is tall, timbered and old – built in 1716, in the heyday of the Monschau cloth industry. Gisela has been running the guest-house since 1977 – a welcoming presence, entirely in harmony with the cosy house.

The bedrooms, which are reached up a narrow spiral staircase, are cottagey and captivating, with pretty curtains, polished antiques and rugs on wooden floors – and fine views over the roofs of Monschau. Showers have been accommodated with considerable ingenuity, but some of the rooms would nevertheless be rather cramped for two, so check what you are getting if possible.

The public areas are very limited: there is a tiny sitting area with fireplace off the entrance hall, and hearty breakfasts are served in a home-like little room with simple wooden chairs and old-fashioned wallpaper, and colourful rugs on a wooden floor. **Nearby** timbered houses; hiking, langlauf; Belgian border.

52156 Monschau, Kirchstr 5
Tel (02472) 3179
Fax (02472) 4320
Location next to church in tiny cobbled street of small town 60 km SW of Bonn; public car parking nearby
Meals breakfast
Prices rooms D, with breakfast; children under 6 free in parents' room
Rooms 10 double (3 twin), 2 single, one family room, all with shower; all rooms have central heating
Facilities breakfast room, sitting room
Credit cards DC, MC, V
Children welcome
Disabled not suitable
Pets accepted
Closed never
Languages English
Proprietors Gisela Vecqueray

Nordrhein-Westfalen

Country house hotel, Münster

Schloß Wilkinghege

Schloß Wilkinghege is a grand moated 18thC residence, which has been in the present owner's family for three generations. As you enter the lofty hallway you are immediately struck by the atmosphere of centuries past.

The house stands at the gates of the historic city of Münster, not far from a main road; but traffic noise is scarcely noticeable inside. The classical brick façade looks out on to a small formal garden containing a private chapel; to the back the windows have views of the moat and open countryside. The bedrooms in the main building are spacious, with heavy curtains and chandeliers and a mixture of solid old furniture and newer brass and glass pieces. Those in the converted stables and pheasant house tend more towards modern comfort, and a couple are designed in a strikingly effective modern style.

Dinner in the ballroom-sized dining-room, with its period furniture, heavy chandeliers, tapestries, oil paintings and huge gilt mirrors is rather like eating in a museum, although the reasonably priced menu and friendly service offsets any feeling of overwhelming grandeur.

Nearby cathedral, museum, walls, churches, amusement park.

48159 Münster, Steinfurter Str 374
Tel (0251) 213045
Fax 212898
Location in NW outskirts by city gates; with garden and ample car parking
Meals breakfast, lunch, dinner, snacks
Prices rooms DD-DDDD with breakfast; meals DM44-105
Rooms 12 double, 7 with bath, 5 with shower; 9 single, 3 with bath, 6 with shower; 13 suites with bath; all rooms have central heating, phone, hairdrier, TV, minibar, radio
Facilities sitting-room, 3 dining-rooms, conference room; terrace, tennis courts, 18-hole golf course
Credit cards AE, DC, MC, V
Children accepted **Disabled** no special facilities **Pets** small pets in bedrooms only (DM15 per night) **Closed** never
Languages English, French
Proprietor L Winnecken

Nordrhein-Westfalen

Farmhouse hotel, Münster-Handorf

Hof zur Linde

Hof zur Linde takes its name from the ancient lime tree standing beside the front door – one of many mature trees filling the park in which it stands, close to the river Werse. The building is an ancient half-timbered red-brick farmhouse. Some of its massive beams date from 1648, and a barely decipherable inscription in the stone gatehouse is evidence of its centuries-long history.

Otto Löfken, whose family have been running the hotel for several generations, is a consummate hotelier who will always find time to exchange a word with his guests. He is also passionate about hunting: the *Jagdstube* walls are covered with trophies and hunting scenes, and the game on the menu may come from his own bag. The atmospheric restaurant, where home-produced hams hang from beams above the fireplace, is full of rustic artefacts collected over the years. But the cuisine is anything but rustic – beautifully presented dishes are served by a team of experienced waiters under the attentive eye of Herr Löfken.

The bedrooms come in all shapes and sizes and each is furnished in its own distinctive style, ranging from local rustic through Chippendale and Victorian to strikingly modern.

Nearby Treasury, Prinzipalmarkt, Fine Arts museum, castle.

48175 Münster-Handorf, Am Handorfer Werseufer 1
Tel (0251) 32750
Fax (0251) 328209
Location in small village 7 km E of Münster; garages and ample car parking
Meals breakfast, lunch, dinner, snacks
Prices rooms DD-DDDD, with breakfast; meals from DM58
Rooms 27 double, 8 with bath, 19 with shower (one twin); 5 single, one with bath, 3 with shower, one with basin; 2 family rooms; 17 suites; all rooms have central heating, phone, TV, minibar, radio
Facilities dining-rooms, bar, conservatory; terraces
Credit cards AE, DC, MC, V
Children very welcome
Disabled access easy; some ground-floor rooms **Pets** not accepted **Closed** never
Languages English, French, Spanish
Proprietor Otto Löfken

Nordrhein-Westfalen

Converted castle, Petershagen

Schloß Petershagen

This riverside castle dating from the 14th century has been in the Hestermann family since the turn of the century and run by them as a hotel and restaurant for 25 years.

Despite the building's defensive role in the past, it is now as unintimidating as a castle could be, with its mellow stone, warm red-tiled roofs and painted shutters. And inside it is both elegant and welcoming. The main restaurant, richly furnished in pink, has been formed by enclosing a former terrace and has a soothing view across the gliding Weser. A highly regarded young chef is at work in the kitchen, producing imaginative modern creations alongside traditional dishes. The St Gorgonius Keller, in contrast, is medieval in decoration and cuisine. The small, peaceful sitting-room, too, is a cool, dark room with heavy furnishings.

Bedrooms have recently undergone a transformation and have now been brought up to a standard matching the elegance of the public rooms. The lush grounds are also a real asset, providing complete insulation from the noise of the nearby main road.

Nearby Beethoven's birthplace, Rhineland Museum.

32469 Petershagen 1, Schloßtr 5-7
Tel (05707) 346
Fax (05707) 2373
Location on banks of Weser, surrounded by meadows; in grounds, ample car parking
Meals breakfast, lunch, dinner
Prices rooms DD-DDD, with breakfast; meals DM55-115
Rooms 8 double, 5 with bath, 3 with shower; 3 single, one with bath, 2 with shower; one family room with bath; all rooms have central heating, phone, hairdrier, TV, mini-bar **Facilities** sitting-room, conservatory/dining-room; terrace, tennis court, swimming-pool **Credit cards** DC, MC, V **Children** welcome
Disabled not suitable **Pets** well-behaved dogs
Closed 3 weeks in early Jan
Languages English
Proprietors Rose-marie and Klaus Hestermann

Nordrhein-Westfalen

Converted castle, Schieder-Schwalenberg

Burghotel Schwalenberg

A night in the Burghotel Schwalenburg is quite an experience – it is a real old castle, with creaky corridors and dusty corners, suits of armour, well used antiques and a host of eccentric details. Its position is all you would expect of a 13thC fortress – perched high up, with magnificent views. The restaurant, a modern extension but decorated in keeping with the age of the castle, makes the most of it with a line of panoramic windows.

A glance at the extensive menu reveals the background of the owner. Olga Saul moved up from Stuttgart in 1971 to rescue the hotel from decline, and now her son heads the kitchen, which specializes in Swabian dishes. She is a jolly, motherly woman who greets her guests in a booming southern dialect.

The hotel is not the last word in style or comfort. The massive hallways contain a haphazard arrangement of treasures: life-size gilt statues of bishops, oil paintings and boars' heads mounted on the walls, and an enormous sofa with upholstery worn shiny by use. The spacious bedrooms contain a mixture of antiques (such as a carved wooden box-bed dating from 1605) and plain old-fashioned furniture.

Nearby Blomberg (5 km) – palace; Detmold (30 km) – castle.

32816 Schieder-Schwalenberg 2
Tel (05284) 5167
Fax (05284) 5567
Location on wooded hill above town 30 km E of Detmold; with gardens, garages and ample car parking
Meals breakfast, lunch, dinner, snacks
Prices rooms D-DDD; breakfast DM18.50; meals DM15-68, children half-price

Rooms 17 double (2 twin), 3 single, 4 family rooms, all with shower; all rooms have central heating, phone, TV, minibar, radio
Facilities dining-room, café, bar, conference room
Credit cards DC, MC, V
Children very welcome
Disabled no special facilities
Pets accepted **Closed** Jan and Feb **Languages** English, French, Italian
Proprietors Saul family

Nordrhein-Westfalen

Town inn, Stolberg

Altes Brauhaus Burgkeller

Stolberg is a town with industrial outskirts but a painstakingly rebuilt old core – and the oldest house (dating from 1594) forms part of this hotel. It rambles through several linked buildings and has been thoroughly modernized in parts. It retains plenty of charm, most notably in the beautifully beamed Ratsstube (in the oldest part), used as a second dining-room. The main dining-room, in contrast, has rather plush furniture and uninspired decoration. The cellar bar is done in a tasteful mix of modern and traditional styles, and outside is a courtyard-terrace by the adjacent river – the loudest noise to be heard in the rooms is that of water rushing over a weir. All the accommodation is in two-room apartments – modern, but very comfortable.

Despite the hotel's name (*Brauhaus* means brewery) the proprietor takes a particular interest in wine, and sells it by the case. Food is modern in style and excellent, without being wildly expensive.

The Burgkeller is run as a single operation with the modern Parkhotel, 5 minutes' walk away, and it is important to specify where you want to stay when booking.

Nearby old town, woods; Aachen (10 km) – treasury, cathedral.

52222 Stolberg, Klatterstr 8-12
Tel (02402) 12340
Fax ((02402) 123480
Location in cobbled pedestrian street by river, at foot of castle ruins; with terrace, and public car parking nearby
Meals breakfast, lunch, dinner
Prices rooms D-DDD, with breakfast; meals DM18.50-48.50
Rooms 22 double, 6 with bath, 16 with shower; 7 single, 5 with shower, 2 with basin; all rooms have central heating, phone, TV, minibar; most have hairdrier
Facilities breakfast room, hall, cellar bar, dining-room
Credit cards AE, DC, MC, V
Children welcome **Disabled** not suitable **Pets** accepted by arrangement **Closed** 24 Dec; 1 to 4 Jan **Languages** English and French **Proprietors** Marlis and Klaus Mann

Nordrhein-Westfalen

Town inn, Werne

Baumhove

This tall, picturesque, half-timbered house in the cobbled heart of old Werne is said to have been in the eponymous Baumhove family for over 500 years. Is this a record? Is it a fairy-tale? Does it matter? No: what matters is that the building itself clearly is of exceptional age, that its medieval atmosphere has been marvellously preserved, and that the Baumhove family are apparently determined to keep it that way.

The ground-floor is mainly given over to an extensive bar/dining-room divided into various cosy sections. It is all low, rough-beamed ceilings, brick walls and stone-flagged or tiled floors, with appropriately simple wooden furniture and rustic ornaments dotted about. An open staircase goes up to a slightly posher gallery area, and thankfully the breakfast room has now been brought up to the same standard . The bedrooms, reached along rather dark corridors, are mainly modern and fairly stylish, though a few have something of the downstairs atmosphere; some have views over the pedestrianized marketplace.

Food is traditional, robust and modestly priced.

Nearby Schloss Cappenberg – game reserve; Bockum Hövel – castle.

59368 Werne, Markt 2
Tel (02389) 2298
Fax (02389) 536223
Location in pedestrian square in middle of old town 12 km W of Hamm; with 3 garages **Meals** breakfast, lunch, dinner
Prices rooms D-DD with breakfast; meals from DM35; children's menu
Rooms 10 double, all with shower; 7 single, 4 with shower; all rooms have central heating, phone, TV
Facilities breakfast-room, dining-room, bar
Credit cards AE, DC, MC, V
Children welcome
Disabled lift/elevator
Pets accepted
Closed mid-July to early Aug; Sun 2pm to Mon 4pm
Languages English
Proprietors Baumhove family

Nordrhein-Westfalen

Country hotel, Westfeld-Ohlenbach

Waldhaus

New to the guide for 1999, the Waldhaus is a notably peaceful and very restful hotel situated on the fringe of a thickly wooded hillside in the mountainous Sauerland region between Kassel and Dusseldorf.

Until 1962, when it became a hotel, and began to expand, the Waldhaus was just that, a small wooden house almost entirely surrounded by trees. Today it is much larger, but retains the wooden, chalet-style look of the original, Inside, the public rooms are comfortingly old-fashioned, with homely touches such as idiosyncratic pieces of antique furniture, leather Chesterfields, sepia photographs, lace tablecloths and potted plants. There is a friendly welcome from the hotel's owners, the Schneiders.

Compared to the public rooms, bedrooms are more streamlined with pine furniture and floral fabrics. The food is well spoken of, using fresh local produce, and in warm weather you can enjoy a delicious breakfast on the terrace overlooking the woods and meadows. There is a pool, sauna and solarium, as well as mountain bikes to borrow, and in winter, given snow, you can ski cross-country from the door.

Nearby Schmallenberg (20 km); Marburg (60 km).

57392 Westfeld-Ohlenbach
Tel (02975) 840
Fax (02975) 8448
Location in isolated position, 3 km NE of Westfeld, 20 km NE of Schmallenberg
Meals breakfast, lunch, dinner
Prices rooms DD-DDD with breakfast; dinner from DM60
Rooms 40 double, 8 single, 2 suites, all with bath; all rooms have central heating, phone, hairdrier, TV, minibar

Facilities 2 dining-rooms, library; terrace, garden; sauna, solarium, tennis court, mountain bikes
Credit cards AE, DC, MC, V
Children welcome
Disabled rooms on ground floor, lift/elevator
Pets not accepted
Closed 8 Nov to 11 Dec
Languages English
Proprietor Schneider family

Nordrhein-Westfalen

Town inn, Wiedenbrück

Ratskeller Wiedenbrück

The amalgamated township of Rheda-Wiedenbrück does not look particularly appealing from the E34 autobahn that separates its two parts, but the old town of Wiedenbrück has streets lined by steep-roofed houses with timbered and decorated façades. One of them is the Ratskeller, dating from 1560 and beautifully restored – the colourful 'rear' façade looking on to the market-place most recently so. The hotel has been in the family of the rosy-cheeked Herr Surmann for five generations, and glows with family pride.

The main entrance faces in the opposite direction, on to a slightly noisy street; this side of the hotel is much newer, but built in traditional style. Inside, not surprisingly, it is the older parts that draw the visitor – the low-beamed dining-room and panelled bar that leads off it. But the modern breakfast room is light and pleasant, too. Bedrooms are relatively plain, with neutral decoration. But the furniture adds some character – a mixture of antique and reproduction, much of it in varnished pine and other light woods, some painted. The top-floor 'leisure area' is neatly done out.

Nearby Castle (Rheda); Münster (60 km) – cathedral, museums.

33378 Rheda-Wiedenbrück, Lange Strasse am Marktpl
Tel (05242) 9210
Fax (05242) 7256
Location in middle of historic town, 4 km from E34, 36 km NW of Paderborn; with ample car parking
Meals breakfast, lunch, dinner, snacks
Prices rooms DD-DDD with breakfast; meals DM28-110; children's menu
Rooms 20 double, 14 with bath, 6 with shower; 12 single with shower; 2 apartments with bath; all rooms have central heat ing, phone, hairdrier, TV, minibar
Facilities dining-room, breakfast room, bar; sauna, jacuzzi, roof terrace
Credit cards AE, DC, MC, V
Children welcome
Disabled lift/elevator **Pets** accepted **Closed** 23-25 Dec
Languages English
Proprietor Josef Surmann

Nordrhein-Westfalen

Converted castle, Attendorn

Burghotel Schnellenberg

A severe hilltop fortress dating from the 13th century, isolated amid forest. Grand inside, too, but not intimidating; elegant dining-rooms, a cosy cellar bar and romantic bedrooms – and the bonus of a leafy garden to laze in.

■ 57439 Attendorn **Tel** (02722) 6940 **Fax** (02722) 694169 **Meals** breakfast , lunch, dinner, snacks **Prices** rooms DD-DDDD with breakfast; meals from DM75 **Rooms** 42, all with bath, phone, TV, radio, minibar **Credit cards** AE, DC, MC, V **Closed** Christmas and 3 weeks Jan **Languages** English, French

Village hotel, Bad Laasphe-Feudingen

Landhotel Doerr

The Doerr family has been polishing its hotel-keeping operation for over a century, and the Landhotel fairly gleams as a result. Even the seminar rooms have the same mellow wooden pan-elling as the dining-room. Widely varying bedrooms.

■ 57329 Bad Laasphe-Feudingen, Sieg-Lahn Str 8 **Tel** (02754) 3081 **Fax** (02754) 3084 **Meals** breakfast, lunch, dinner **Prices** rooms DD-DDD with breakfast; meals from DM25 **Rooms** 37, all with bath or shower, central heating, phone, hairdrier, TV **Credit cards** DC, MC, V **Closed** never **Languages** English, some Dutch

Country hotel, Bad Laasphe-Glashütte

Jagdhof Glashütte

Over the decades the Dornhöfer family has transformed their simple country guest-house into a cossetting hotel which still retains the flavour of a hunting lodge. The swimming-pool is remarkable - built into the rock.

■ 57334 Bad Laasphe-Glashütte, Glashütter Str 20 **Tel** (02754) 399097 **Fax** (02754) 399222 **Meals** breakfast, lunch, dinner **Prices** rooms DM DD-DDDD with breakfast; meals from DM68 **Rooms** 29, all with bath or shower, central heating, phone, hairdrier, TV, minibar, radio **Credit cards** not accepted **Closed** never **Languages** English, French

Country inn, Bergneustadt

Rengser Mühle

Hidden away in wooded hills, the Vormstein's former mill is the quintessential charming, small hotel – good food is served in a pretty rustic dining room, a few delightful bedrooms, and a lush riverside garden in which to enjoy the home-made waffles.

■ 51702 Bergneustadt, Niederrengse 4 **Tel** (02763) 91450 **Meals** breakfast, lunch, dinner, snacks **Prices** rooms DD with breakfast; meals DM26-DM46 **Rooms** 4, all with bath or shower, central heating, phone, hairdrier, TV, minibar **Credit cards** AE, MC **Closed** restaurant only, Mon dinner, Tue **Languages** English, French

Nordrhein-Westfalen

City hotel, Bonn

Domicil

A refined, glossy hotel that may be short on charm but is long on style – glass, chrome and starkly monochromatic colour schemes predominate. Waiters wear waistcoats and bow-ties. A journalists' favourite.

■ 53111 Bonn, Thomas-Mann-Str 24 **Tel** (0228)729090 **Fax** (0228) 691207 **Meals** breakfast, lunch, dinner, snacks **Prices** rooms DD-DDDD buffet breakfast DM21, meals from DM30 **Rooms** 42 , all with central heating, telephone, hairdrier, TV, minibar, radio **Credit cards** AE, DC, MC, V **Closed** never **Languages** English, French

---

Village inn, Borken/Rhedebrügge

Grüneklee

Tucked away behind a line of hawthorn trees, the modest Grüneklee offers good food in pleasant surroundings – a sunny gard en terrace, a modest dining-room and a traditional *Bauernstube*. The bedrooms are attractively rustic.

■ 46325 Borken 1/Rhedebrügge, Rhedebrügger Str 16 **Tel** (02872) 1818 **Meals** breakfast , dinner **Prices** rooms D-DD with breakfast; meals from DM40 **Rooms** 5, all with bath or shower, central heating, phone, TV **Credit cards** AE, MC, V **Closed** Jan; Mon, Tue **Languages** English

---

Village hotel, Dahlem-Kronenburg

Eifelhaus

The bedrooms and dining-room of this cottagey hotel might not be anything to write home about, but its splendid position – perched on a hillside on the edge of a cobbled medieval hamlet – certainly is. Rustic furnishings, splendid breakfasts. "Everthing is perfect," according to a recent visitor from Holland.

■ 53949 Dahlem-Kronenburg, Burgbering 12 **Tel** (06557) 295 **Meals** breakfast, lunch, dinner **Prices** rooms D with breakfast; meals DM15-35 **Rooms** 19, all with bath or shower, central heating **Credit cards** not accepted **Closed** Jan; Wed **Languages** English

---

Town hotel, Dormagen

Hotel Hottche

A much-expanded guest-house, retaining a warm and welcoming ambience in its several, low-ceilinged, wood-panelled dining-rooms and bars; well-known for its excellent cuisine and run by the friendly Pesch family.

■ 41539 Dormagen 1, Krefelder Str 14-18 **Tel** (02133) 2530 **Fax** (02133) 10616 **Meals** breakfast, lunch, dinner **Prices** rooms DD-DDD with breakfast; meals DM30-50 **Rooms** 56, all with bath or shower, central heating, phone, TV, minibar **Credit cards** AE, DC, MC, V **Closed** Christmas and New Year **Languages** English, French, Italian, Spanish

Nordrhein-Westfalen

Converted castle, Dorsten-Lembeck

Schloßhotel Lembeck

It is easy to see why the tourists flock here: Lembeck is a moated, fairy-tale castle (and museum) set in vast, beautiful grounds. Meals are served on the café terrace (fine views) or in the cellar restaurant. Only ten bedrooms, book early.

■ 46286 Dorsten 12-Lembeck **Tel** (02369) 7213 **Fax** (02369) 77370 **Meals** breakfast, lunch, dinner **Prices** rooms D-DD with breakfast; meals from DM42 **Rooms** 10, all with bath or shower, central heating, phone, TV, radio **Credit cards** AE, DC, MC, V **Closed** Mon, Thu, Fri until 4.30 p.m. **Languages** English, French

Town hotel, Duisburg

Mühlenberger Hof

A rustic oasis in the heavily industrialized Ruhr – the beamed restaurant is decorated in country style; most bedrooms have pretty wooden furniture. Attractive beer garden in courtyard.

■ 47229 Duisburg 14-Rheinhausen, Hohenbudberger Str 88 **Tel** (02065) 41565 **Fax** (02065) 41342 **Meals** breakfast, lunch, dinner **Prices** rooms D-DD with breakfast; meals DM30-60 **Rooms** 11, all with shower, central heating, phone, minibar **Credit cards** MC **Closed** restaurant only, Mon **Languages** English

City hotel, Düsseldorf

Hotel Fischerhaus

Peacefully positioned near the yacht club and in easy reach of the commercial part of town, Peter and Gisela Nöthel's modern hotel may lack conventional charm but, with its grey and white 'colour' scheme, does not lack style. Excellent cooking.

■ 40547 Düsseldorf 11, Bonifatiusstr 35 **Tel** (0211) 597979 **Fax** (0211) 5979759 **Meals** breakfast, dinner, snacks **Prices** rooms DD-DDDD; breakfast DM9.50, dinner DM100 **Rooms** 39, all with central heating, phone, TV, minibar, radio **Credit cards** AE, DC, MC, V **Closed** restaurant Sun, Mon (not during trade fairs) **Languages** English, French, Spanish

Town hotel, Düsseldorf-Oberkassel

Hotel Hanseat

An immaculate townhouse just over the Rhine from the city and with something of the grace and style of a smart English country house. Bedrooms are simply yet tastefully furnished; public areas are peaceful and comfortable.

■ 40545 Düsseldorf 11-Oberkassel, Belsenstr 6 **Tel** (0211) 575069 **Fax** (0211) 589662 **Meals** breakfast **Prices** rooms DD-DDDD with breakfast **Rooms** 37, all with shower, central heating, phone, TV, minibar, radio **Credit cards** AE, DC, MC, V **Closed** Christmas to New Year **Languages** English, French

Nordrhein-Westfalen

Lakeside hotel, Essen

Parkhaus Hügel

Built by Krupp as a casino, this patrician house has been run as a hotel by the Imhoffs for three generations. French windows lead from the smart dining-rooms on to the almost equally smart terrace, with country views.

■ 45133 Essen 1, Freiherr-vom-Stein Str 209 **Tel** (0201) 471091 **Fax** (0201) 444207 **Meals** breakfast, lunch, dinner **Prices** rooms DD with breakfast; meals from DM40 **Rooms** 13, all with shower, central heating, phone, TV **Credit cards** AE, DC, MC, V **Closed** Christmas Eve **Languages** English, Italian

---

Town hotel, Essen-Kettwig

Résidence

The young Bühlers cosset their guests in this smoothly-run, headily expensive Michelin-starred restaurant. With its small, stylish bedrooms, the pristine white villa, surrounded by a leafy landscaped garden, is hidden away in a quiet southern suburb.

■ 45219 Essen-Kettwig, Auf der Forst 1 **Tel** (02054) 8911 **Fax** (02054) 82501 **Meals** breakfast, dinner, snacks **Prices** rooms DD-DDDD with breakfast; meals from DM50, menu from DM150 **Rooms** 18, all with bath, central heating, phone, TV, minibar, radio **Credit cards** DC, MC, V **Closed** one week at New Year, 3 weeks in summer **Languages** English, French

---

Converted castle, Essen-Kettwig

Schloß Hugenpoet

An imposing moated castle, now a grand and sumptuous hotel. Bedrooms are spacious and dotted with antiques; public rooms are b oldy decorated and furnished in magnificent style, with little baronial gloom.

■ 45219 Essen-Kettwig 18, August-Thyssen-Str 51 **Tel** (02054) 12040 **Fax** (02054) 1204 50 **Meals** breakfast, lunch, dinner **Prices** rooms DDD-DDDD with breakfast; meals DM115-155 **Rooms** 25, all with bath, central heating, phone, hairdrier, TV, minibar, radio **Credit cards** AE, DC, MC, V **Closed** 1 week Jan, 24 Dec **Languages** English, French

---

Town hotel, Hagen Haspe

Hotel Union

Not far from the Köln-Hannover *autobahn*, in an otherwise unappealing area on the fringe of the Ruhr basin, sits this immaculately restored art nouveau house, with harmonious furnishings and muted decoration. Bistro-bar.

■ 58135 Hagen-Haspe, Kölner Str 25 **Tel** (02331) 4730 **Fax** 47315 **Meals** breakfast, lunch, dinner **Prices** rooms DD-DDD; meals from DM60 **Rooms** 22, all with bath or shower, central heating, phone, TV, radio, minibar; 6 apartments **Credit cards** AE, DC, MC, V **Closed** 24 Dec to 6 Jan **Languages** English, French, some Swedish

Nordrhein-Westfalen

Country hotel, Heiligenhaus

Waldhotel

There is much to like about this steep-roofed house, refurbished with taste and confidence in modern style. Attractive terrace from which to enjoy the tranquility of surrounding woodland.

■ 42579 Heiligenhaus, Parkstr 38 **Tel** (02056) 5970 **Fax** (02056) 59760 **Meals** breakfast, lunch, dinner **Prices** rooms DD-DDDD; breakfast DM17, meals DM42 **Rooms** 32, all with bath or shower, central heating, phone, TV, minibar, radio **Credit cards** AE, MC, V **Closed** 24 Dec; restaurant only, Sun **Languages** English, French, Spanish, Italian

---

Country hotel, Hilchenbach-Vormwald

Siebelnhof

A compelling combination: a smartly run traditional-style house in a peaceful setting (in the Rothaargebirge nature reserve) with ambitious (Michelin-starred) cooking. Handsome public rooms, some rather dreary bedrooms.

■ 57271 Hilchenbach-Vormwald, Vormwalder Str 54 **Tel** (02733) 89430 **Fax** (02733) 7006 **Meals** breakfast, lunch, dinner **Prices** rooms DD with breakfast; meals DM50-150 **Rooms** 12, all with central heating, phone, radio; all have TV, minibar **Credit cards** AE, DC, MC, V **Closed** 2 weeks in summer, one week Jan **Languages** English

---

City hotel, Köln

Atrium

Iloona Loock-Löffler's slick 'designer' hotel is close to the Rhine, about 4km upstream from the city centre – quiet, and not too inconvenient. Restrained colour schemes, with omnipresent black woodwork and furniture.

■ 50996 Köln, Karlstr 2-10 **Tel** (0221) 393045 **Fax** (0221) 394054 **Meals** breakfast, lunch, dinner **Prices** rooms DD-DDDD with breakfast; meals from DM 28 **Rooms** 68, all with shower, central heating, phone, hairdrier, TV, minibar, radio **Credit cards** AE, DC, MC, V **Closed** never **Languages** English, French

---

Restaurant with rooms, Köln

Bitzerhof

Rustic little *Weinstube* distracting visitors from its suburban surroundings with tumbling greenery around the cobbled terrace and old farm tools on the walls of the restaurant. Light, comfortable bedrooms.

■ 50997 Köln 50, Immendorfer Hauptstr 21 **Tel** (02236) 61921 **Fax** (02236) 62987 **Meals** breakfast, lunch, dinner **Prices** rooms DD with breakfast; meals from DM28 **Rooms** 3, all with shower, central heating, phone, hairdrier, TV, radio **Credit cards** AE, MC **Closed** never **Languages** English, French, Italian

Nordrhein-Westfalen

Town hotel, Köln

Hotel Viktoria

Just off the left bank of the Rhine (some rooms have views), about a mile downstream from the central Deutzer Brucke, this turn-of-the-century villa has been stylishly furnished in modern style with art nouveau features. Splendid breakfasts.

■ 50668 Köln, Worringer Str 23 **Tel** (0221) 7200476 **Fax** (0221) 727067 **Meals** breakfast **Prices** rooms DD-DDDD, with breakfast **Rooms** 47, all with bath or shower, central heating, phone, TV, minibar, radio **Credit cards** AE, DC, MC, V **Closed** Christmas Day **Languages** English, French, Italian, Spanish

---

Country hotel, Lage-Hörste

Haus Berkenkamp

A modest, neat, timber-framed house with beautifully kept lawned gardens, run by the friendly Berkenkamp family. The interior is a comfortable and informal but not very stylish blend of old and new.

■ 32791 Lage-Hörste, Im Hesskamp 50 **Tel** (05232) 71178 **Meals** breakfast, lunch, dinner **Prices** rooms D-DD with breakfast; meals DM18-24 **Rooms** 17, all with bath or shower, central heating **Credit cards** not accepted **Closed** never **Languages** German only English, French, Italian, Spanish

---

Country hotel, Langenfeld

Hotel Gravenberg

Amid the maze of motorways between Köln and Düsseldorf is Fritz Lohmann's peaceful oasis – partly timbered, partly tile-hung outside, extravagantly ornamented in rustic style inside. Comfortable bedrooms, but lacking in style.

■ 40764 Langenfeld, Elberfelder Str 45 **Tel** (02173) 23061 **Fax** (02173) 22777 **Meals** breakfast, lunch, dinner **Prices** rooms DD-DDD with breakfast; meals DM45-50 **Rooms** 41, all with shower, central heating, phone, TV, minibar, radio **Credit cards** AE, DC, MC,V **Closed** Sun dinner and Mon **Languages** English, French

---

Manor house hotel, Lindlar

Schloß Georghausen

This tall, gracious manor house is set amid parkland which attracts golfers and anglers. The Kröngen family manage the difficult trick of catering for them while preserving the atmosphere of a private residence. In the hall, a four-poster bed quirkily serves as a bar.

■ 51789 Lindlar, Georghausen 8 **Tel** (02207) 2561 **Fax** (02207) 7683 **Meals** breakfast, lunch, dinner **Prices** rooms DD with breakfast; meals DM65 **Rooms** 13, all with bath or shower, central heating, phone; some rooms with TV **Credit cards** AE, DC, MC, V **Closed** restaurant only, Mon **Languages** English

Nordrhein-Westfalen

Country hotel, Lübbecke

Quellenhof

This well kept modern house presents a familiar picture: dull but admirably comfortable bedrooms above welcoming and expensively furnished dining-rooms and bars. The terrace overlooks a large pond, apparently containing trout.

■ 32312 Lübbecke, Obenfelder Allee 1 **Tel** (05741) 34060 **Fax** (05741) 340659 **Meals** breakfast, lunch, dinner **Prices** rooms D-DD with breakfast; meals from DM30 **Rooms** 24, all with bath or shower, central heating, phone, TV, radio **Credit cards** DC, MC, V **Closed** Fri; 2 weeks Jan; restaurant only, 2 weeks in summer **Languages** English

---

Town hotel, Moers-Repelen

Wellings Hotel zur Linde

An ancient inn (overlooked by an eponymous lime tree) plus a new hotel wing providing spacious and comfortable rooms – a strong combination. Various bars and dining-rooms, and a busy brick-paved *Biergarten*.

■ 47445 Moers-Repelen, An der Linde 2 **Tel** (02841) 73061 **Fax** (02841) 71259 **Meals** breakfast, lunch, dinner **Prices** rooms DD-DDD with breakfast; meals from DM40 **Rooms** 30, all with bath or shower, central heating, phone, hairdrier, TV, minibar, radio **Credit cards** AE, DC, MC, V **Closed** 24 Dec **Languages** English, French

---

Country house hotel, Möhnesee

Haus Delecke

A grand, perhaps slightly sterile country house in a beautiful position right by the Möhnesee (a reservoir), and with a large terrace from which to enjoy the view. Spacious, elegantly furnished bedrooms; excellent food and wine.

■ 4733 Möhnesee, Linkstr 10-14 **Tel** (02924) 8090 **Fax** (02924) 80967 **Meals** breakfast, lunch, dinner **Prices** rooms DD-DDD with breakfast; meals from DM43 **Rooms** 25, all with bath or shower, central heating, phone, TV, minibar, radio; some have hairdrier **Credit cards** AE, MC, V **Closed** Jan **Languages** English, French

---

Town house hotel, Monschau

Burghotel Monschau

Many visitors return year after year to this tall town house in the medieval heart of Monschau and it is easy to see why: both Herr Hoffmann-Bähr and his rather old-fashioned hotel have bags of character. Expect beams, winding staircases and antiques.

■ 52156 Monschau **Tel** (02472) 2332 **Meals** breakfast, lunch, dinner **Prices** rooms D with breakfast; meals DM10-30 **Rooms** 13, all with central heating; 7 rooms have shower, 3 rooms have TV **Credit cards** not accepted **Closed** Nov, Jan to mid-Feb; restaurant only, Wed **Languages** English, French

Nordrhein-Westfalen

Town house hotel, Monschau

Haus Rolshausen

This friendly five-storey guest-house is a pleasant base for exploring the old town of Monschau. The house is over 400 years old, but it has neat, modern bedrooms. Vaulted wine cellars for sitting, narrow beamed room for breakfast.

■ 52156 Monschau, Kirchstr 33 **Tel** (02472) 2038 **Meals** breakfast, lunch, dinner **Prices** rooms D-DD with breakfast; meals about DM25 **Rooms** 19, most with shower, central heating, phone, radio; some rooms have TV **Credit cards** AE, MC **Closed** Mon **Languages** English

---

Converted farmhouse, Münster-Wolbeck

Thier-Hülsmann

Not much of the farmhouse remains inside this tall gabled building, which has been converted by Clemens Hülsmann with unabashed enthusiasm, using new brick, old beams and vibrant splashes of colour. Modern bedrooms in adjoining annexe.

■ 48167 Münster-Wolbeck, Münsterstr 33 **Tel** (02506) 2066 **Fax** (02056) 3403 **Meals** breakfast, lunch, dinner **Prices** rooms D-DD with breakfast; meals DM25-76 **Rooms** 37, all with bath, central heating, phone, TV, minibar, radio; some hairdriers **Credit cards** AE, DC, MC, V **Closed** restaurant only, Sat, Sun; 3 weeks summer **Languages** English

---

Country hotel, Schmallenberg

Störmann

It is immediately obvious from the immaculate tile-hung, flower-decked exterior that this hotel is lovingly cared for by its long-standing eponymous owners. Rustic public rooms in main hotel; modern and rather characterless extension has valley views.

■ 57392 Schmallenberg, Weststr 58 **Tel** (02972) 4055 **Fax** (02972) 2945 **Meals** breakfast, lunch, dinner **Prices** rooms D-DDD with breakfast; meals from DM25 **Rooms** 37, all with bath or shower, central heating, phone, TV, hairdrier, radio **Credit cards** AE, DC, MC, V **Closed** Sun evening; 20-27 Dec; 3 weeks March **Languages** English, French

---

Country hotel, Selm-Cappenberg

Kreutzkamp

No elegant, curvaceous antiques, no trace of interior design: this plain, gabled, brick-built house is resolutely traditional. Two splendidly old-fashioned dining-rooms, one with a glorious coffered ceiling. Neat, comfortable bedrooms.

■ 59379 Selm-Cappenberg, Cappenberger Damm 3 **Tel** (02306) 5889 **Fax** (02306) 5880 **Meals** breakfast, lunch, dinner **Prices** rooms DD with breakfast; meals from DM25 **Rooms** 15, all with bath or shower, central heating, phone, TV, radio **Credit cards** AE, DC, MC, V **Closed** Mon **Languages** English, some French

Nordrhein-Westfalen

Town inn, Warendorf

Im Engel

Warendorf is where the Olympic riding committee meet, so the Duke of Edinburgh is only one of this hotel's illustrious past guests. Some traces of the rustic inn of 1545 remain, but rigorous refurbishment has lent a blandness to most of the rooms.

■ 48231 Warendorf 1, Brünebrede 35-37 **Tel** (02581) 93020 **Fax** (02581) 62726 **Meals** breakfast, lunch, dinner **Prices** rooms D-DDD with breakfast; meals DM38-95 **Rooms** 24, all with central heating, phone, hairdrier, TV, minibar, radio **Credit cards** AE, DC, MC, V **Closed** restaurant only, 3 weeks Jan & Jul; Thu **Languages** English, French

---

Converted castle, Wassenberg

Burg Wassenberg

Not exactly a feudal fortress, but a handsome 1,000-year-old house retaining many original features alongside the modern conveniences – including a grand fireplace. Bedrooms, recently refurbished, vary in style, food is sophisticated and modern.

■ 41849 Wassenberg, Kirchstr 17 **Tel** (02432) 4044 **Fax** (02432) 20191 **Meals** breakfast, lunch, dinner **Prices** rooms D-DDD meals DM32-50 **Rooms** 28, all with bath or shower, central heating, phone, TV, radio **Credit cards** AE, DC, MC, V **Closed** 2 weeks Jan **Languages** English, French, Spanish, Portuguese

---

Suburban hotel, Wesel

Waldhotel Tannenhäuschen

The Hetzel family are justifiably proud of their elegant hotel set in its own extensive, wooded grounds. The interior is lavish – chintzy fabrics, plush carpets, antique and reproduction furniture – as is the food.

■ 46487 Wesel, Am Tannenhäuschen 7 **Tel** (0281) 61014 **Fax** (0281) 64153 **Meals** breakfast, lunch, dinner, snacks **Prices** rooms DD-DDD; breakfast DM20, meals DM29-45 **Rooms** 46, all with bath or shower, central heating, phone, TV, radio **Credit cards** AE, DC, MC, V **Closed** never **Languages** English, French

---

Country hotel, Winterberg

Berghotel Astenkrone

A lot of money has gone into this ritzy retreat – fortunately, most of it spent with taste. Richly traditional panelled dining-rooms and smart, spacious bedrooms.

■ 59955 Winterberg-Altastenberg, Astenstr 24 **Tel** (02981) 8090 **Fax** (02981) 809198 **Meals** breakfast, lunch, dinner, snacks **Prices** rooms DD-DDD with breakfast **Rooms** 43, all with bath or shower, central heating, phone, TV, radio, minibar, hairdrier **Credit cards** AE, DC, MC, V **Closed** never **Languages** German only

Rheinland-Pfalz

Area introduction

Hotels in Rheinland-Pfalz

Mention the Rheinland-Pfalz to a vintner, and his nose will twitch, for this is the area that produces more wine than anywhere else in the country, and some of the best – Deidesheim, Bad Dürkheim, Forst and Wachenheim all come from here. It is a fertile region of sloping vineyards, where the Rhine valley is at its widest; the German Weinstrasse (Wine Road) stretches from Schweigen on the French border, and ends at Bockenheim to the west of Worms.

The *Kur* resort of Bad Bergzabern, in the mountainous Haardt region, lies half-way along the Weinstrasse; work off any over-indulgence with a massage at the Petronella (Tel (06343) 1075, fax 5313, 48 rooms).

Further north at Neustadt an der Weinstrasse is the Tenner (Tel (06321) 654, fax 69306, 38 rooms) a hotel garni set in parkland, with views over the protected Palatinate Forest, which extends over 650 square miles of good hiking country.

Climbers head for the Eifel region, where Idar-Oberstein is situated in a volcanic gorge which contained agate and mineral deposits, and is still a centre today for gem cutting and polishing. Stay at the friendly Handelshof, preferably in a room at the back (Tel (06781) 31011, fax 31057, 15 rooms), or head north to Kirn, where the Parkhotel offers modern comforts in a traditional villa set in pretty grounds (Tel (06752) 3666, fax 3667, 18 rooms). For total peace, the modern Forellenhof Reinhartsmühle is situated in a wooded valley, overlooking a large lake (Tel (06544) 373, fax 1080, 30 rooms). At Guldental is one of Germany's most renowned restaurants, the Val d'Or; it has no rooms, but the next-door Kaiserhof, also a restaurant, has seven modestly priced ones (Tel (06707) 8746); the two establishments are run by branches of the same family.

Still in the Eifel, north of Trier, Bitburg is an old brewing town. Under the auspices of a preservation society, the old brewery of Simonbräu has been turned into a small, simple hotel with good food (Tel (06561) 3333, fax 3373, 7 rooms).

Mainz, on the region's eastern edge, is the capital of the Land, and Germany's largest wine market. We can recommend the peacefully situated Am Lerchenberg, which is family-run and has far-reaching views over the city (Tel (06131) 73001, 53 rooms), or the Favorite Parkhotel, surrounded by city parks and with a pleasing garden terrace (Tel 82091, fax 831025, 46 rooms).

Further up the Rhine at Boppard, the Klostergut Jakobsberg is in a superb location. Offering squash, tennis, riding, clay pigeon shooting, it is let down by functional rooms, but its popularity is not affected. (Tel (06742) 3061, fax 3069, 110 rooms).

This page acts as an introduction to the features and hotels of Rheinland-Pfalz, and gives brief recommendations of good hotels that for one reason or another have not made a full entry. The long entries for this 'Land' – covering the hotels we are most enthusiastic about – start on the next page. But do not neglect the shorter entries starting on page 91: these are all hotels that we would happily stay at.

Rheinland-Pfalz

Restaurant-with-rooms, Bad Neuenahr-Heppingen

Zur Alten Post

In previous editions of our guide, we have described Hans-Stefan and Gabi Steinheuer's establishment at Heppingen thus: "come here for Hans-Stefan Steinheuer's impressive cooking, his even more impressive wine list, be guided to a comfortable bed for the night and then enjoy a perfect breakfast the next morning. Bliss".

There are two restaurants to choose from, in adjoining buildings. The more informal is the Poststuben, serving regional dishes with a creative twist. Steinheuers Restaurant is an altogether smarter, more elegant affair, where you can explore Hans-Stefan's aromatic new German cooking and his wine list of more than 400 bottles. In contrast, the hotel's six bedrooms come as quite a surprise, being very different with ultra-modern furniture and fittings which display a penchant for the clean line and the curve, and impressive state-of-the-art bathrooms. In 1998 the Steinheurs acquired a building across the road, where there are now four new suites and a breakfast room.

Zur Alten Post has linked up with several other hotels and restaurants in the region to which you can walk; your luggage will be brought to each new destination to await your arrival.
Nearby Roman villa; Bonn (30 km).

53474 Bad Neuenahr-Heppingen, Landskronerstrasse 110
Tel (02641) 7011
Fax (02641) 7013
Location on B266, 1 km W of Bad Neuenahr
Meals breakfast, lunch, dinner
Prices rooms DD-DDDD with breakfast; meals from DM60
Rooms 6 double, 4 suites, all with bath; all rooms have central heating, phone, TV, minibar; hairdrier; suites have fax
Facilities breakfast room, sitting-room
Credit cards AE, DC, MC, V
Children welcome
Disabled lift to suites
Pets not accepted
Closed restaurant only; Tues, Wed lunch
Languages English, French
Proprietors Hans-Stefan Steinheuer

Rheinland-Pfalz

Town inn, Bernkastel-Kues

Zur Post

Bernkastel is one of the main tourist towns on the Mosel and is not short of accommodation. It has no really outstanding hotel, but one of the smartest and most convenient is the Post. It is a modest 19thC building, fronting the main road along the valley, with shutters and geraniums at the windows, and steps up to to the front door.

Within, the welcome from Frau Rössling is professional but warm, and the furnishings in keeping with the age and style of the house. Recent refurbishments have left the bedrooms modern but slightly characterless, a lack that is more than made up for by the cheerful atmosphere in the bright, wood-panelled *Post Stüberle*. This serves as an all-day and evening meeting point and is certainly more welcoming than the formal main restaurant – where people tend to sit if there is no space in the *Stüberle*. For family groups, the hotel has a selection of interesting apartment-type rooms in an annexe next door.

Our inspector was slightly disconcerted to find himself sharing his bed with a wine-cork; the fact that he remained favourably disposed to the Post is testimony to its basic appeal.

Nearby 17thC market place, fountain; Landshut Castle (3 km).

54463 Bernkastel-Kues, Gestade 17
Tel (06531) 2022
Fax (06531) 2927
Location on main riverside road through town; with ample car parking
Meals breakfast, lunch, dinner
Prices rooms D-DD with breakfast (children under 3 free in parents' room); meals DM20-40
Rooms 42 double, 8 with bath, 34 with shower; one family room with bath; all rooms have central heating, phone, TV, mini bar; hair-drier on request
Facilities dining-room, bar, sauna, solarium
Credit cards AE, DC, MC, V
Children very welcome
Disabled access easy
Pets accepted
Closed Jan
Languages English
Proprietors Rössling family

Rheinland-Pfalz

Town hotel, Cochem

Alte Thorschenke

Most visitors to the town of Cochem, on the Mosel, probably photograph this old inn (dating from the 14th century) before they do anything else – it is right in front of you as you leave the main car parking area. Its façade is picture-postcard stuff, with pretty gables and towers, and to one side part of the old wall which used to surround the medieval town.

The interior of the Alte Thorschenke has the atmosphere and lived-in feel of a truly old building. If you have been lucky enough to secure a bedroom in the front part of the hotel (there are only a few) you will climb a wonderful, Gothic wooden spiral staircase from the club-like reception-cum-sitting area and proceed along creaking corridors to such delights as the Napoleon suite – a lovely spacious room furnished with an enormous four-poster and other antiques. There are more bedrooms in the rear part of the hotel – newer and generally less interesting, but with antiques, although a recent visitor felt they needed some refurbishment.

In the high-ceilinged dining-room, a varied menu is presented on parchment-style paper, with lots of regional fish and game dishes and home-grown Mosel. Breakfast is an impressive buffet.
Nearby Castle; Eltz (15 km) – castle.

56812 Cochem, Brückenstr 3
Tel (02671) 7059
Fax (02671) 4202
Location by bridge in middle of town; with 7 garages and ample public parking
Meals breakfast, lunch, dinner, snacks
Prices rooms D-DDD with breakfast; meals DM35-68
Rooms 38 double, 20 with bath, 11 with shower; 5 single, 3 with bath; all have central heating, phone, radio, hairdrier, TV, minibar
Facilities dining- room, reception, wine bar; terrace
Credit cards AE, DC, MC, V
Children welcome
Disabled lift/elevator
Pets accepted in bedrooms only (DM7 per night)
Closed 5 Jan to 15 Mar; restaurant only, Wed in winter **Languages** English, French, some Spanish, Russian **Managers** Walther and Annegret Kretz

Rheinland-Pfalz

Chalet hotel, Cochem

Weißmühle

Visitors to the Mosel and Rhine valleys pass seemingly endless hotels on the main roads, most of them uncomfortably close to the traffic or railway lines. If your idea of perfection is something a little quieter, look no further than this secluded backwater. As you wind along the lane to the Weißmühle, the only sound to disturb the silence is the chuckle of the little Endert stream which once boasted 24 mills along its banks. Once there, you are completely surrounded by forest.

In this setting the Weißmühle's Alpine-style exterior seems perfectly appropriate, but its conspicuous modernity inside comes as something of a disappointment. Bedrooms are functional, but most have a balcony and views down the valley towards Cochem.

Locally, the Weißmühle is known for its trout specialities (you can catch your own in a pond behind the hotel). Meals can be taken in the beautifully furnished restaurant, or on the terrace while you soak in the magical setting.

As a base to retreat to after a hard day of castle visits, river cruises and wine-tastings, the Weißmühle is unbeatable.

Nearby Castle; Eltz Castle (15 km); Nürburgring – motor racing.

56812 Cochem, Enderttal
Tel (02671) 8955
Fax (02671) 8207
Location in peaceful wooded valley, 2 km NW of Cochem; within grounds, with ample car parking and 5 garages
Meals breakfast, lunch, dinner, snacks
Prices rooms DD-DDD with breakfast; meals from DM25
Rooms 30 twin, 6 single, all with shower; all rooms have central heating, phone, TV, minibar
Facilities dining-rooms, sitting-room, coffee-shop, bar, bowling alley; terrace; sauna, solarium **Credit cards** DC, EC, V **Children** welcome
Disabled not suitable
Pets accepted (DM10 per night) **Closed** never
Languages English
Proprietors Gerhartz and Zimmer families

Rheinland-Pfalz

Manor house hotel, Daun

Kurfürstliches Amtshaus

Although this hotel markets itself through the Gast im Schloss consortium, first impressions are not so much of a castle as of a town hall – no surprise to German-speakers, who will know that its name translates roughly as 'Princely Official House'. But it has the impressive hilltop position and long views (enjoyable from the terrace) of a once-important fortress, and public areas full of grand antique furniture and an interesting collection of clocks.

Günter Probst enjoys publicity, and one of his many special leaflets promotes his star possession – the 'Best-known bed in Germany', slept in by over 50 visiting heads of state when it was in government accommodation in Bonn (it was lengthened for De Gaulle, strengthened for Brezhnev).

The Graf Leopold restaurant is an atmospheric setting for the 'new German cuisine with an Italian tendency', which is competently executed and supported by an excellent wine list. There is an attractive heated indoor swimming-pool, hewn from volcanic rocks.

Nearby summer 'toboggan' run, game park, mineral baths; crater lakes and springs in the Eifel massif.

54550 Daun, Auf dem Burgberg
Tel (06592) 3031
Fax (06592) 4942
Location on hill in middle of village; with garden and ample car parking
Meals breakfast, lunch, dinner, snacks
Prices rooms DD-DDD with breakfast; meals DM50-115
Rooms 25 double, 8 with bath, 17 with shower; 17 single, 4 with bath, 13 with shower; all rooms have central heating, phone, hair-drier, TV, minibar, radio
Facilities dining-room, sitting-room, swimming-pool, sauna, steam bath; terrace
Credit cards DC, MC, V
Children very welcome
Disabled access easy; lift/elevator **Pets** accepted (DM10 per night) **Closed** first 2 weeks Jan **Languages** English, French, Dutch
Proprietor Günter Probst

Rheinland-Pfalz

Luxury inn, Deidesheim

Deidesheimer Hof

Before he lost the election in September 1998, Chancellor Kohl liked to entertain important guests at this substantial, traditional inn at the centre of the pretty village of Deidesheim, on the German Wine Route. VIPs may be well served here – and past guests have included Margaret Thatcher and Mikhail Gorbachev – but the inn has an informal side to it too, especially on the flowery terrace which fronts the three-sided market square, and in the wood-panelled *weinstübe*. The Relais & Château hotel, formerly a bishop's residence, is owned by the winemakers Hahn, a family-run group which includes a chain of wine restaurants. Gerümpel and Goldbächel are two excellent local names to look for on the extensive wine list.

As might be expected, order and cleanliness prevail at the Deidesheimer Hof, although service can at times be slow. Bed rooms are pretty, traditionally furnished, relatively spacious and thoroughly comfortable. As well as the more informal Weinstübe St Urban, which serves excellent regional dishes – including Kohl's favourite, *saumagen*, or stuffed pig's paunch – there is a more serious, expensive gourmet restaurant, Schwarzer Hahn.
Nearby Bad Dürkheim, Pfälzerwald nature park (8 km).

67146 Deidesheim, Am Marktplatz 1
Tel (06326) 96870
Fax (06326) 7685
E-mail Deidesheimer HofHotelbet.GmbH@t-online.de
Location in village centre, 23 km SW of Mannheim; parking
Meals breakfast, lunch, dinner
Prices rooms DD-DDDD; breakfast DM20; dinner from DM80
Rooms 18 double, 2 suites, all with bath; all rooms have central heating, phone, TV, minibar, radio, hairdrier,
Facilities dining-rooms, sitting-room, breakfast room; terrace
Credit cards AE, DC, MC, V
Children accepted
Disabled no special facilities
Pets by arrangement
Closed first week Jan
Languages English, French,
Proprietor Anita Hahn

Rheinland-Pfalz

Chalet hotel, Dreis

Waldhotel Sonnora

Renowned for its Michelin two-star restaurant, the Sonnora makes a friendly, comfortable and (perhaps surprising considering the expense of the food) moderately priced place in which to stay. Owned by father and son, Vinzenz and Helmut Thieltges (who is the head chef, in charge of the gleaming steel and brass-railed kichen), the hotel is in the style of an alpine chalet, with wooden balconies. Breakfast is taken in a pretty beamed room with windows dressed in yellow floral curtains. The restaurant is a classical affair, with brocade chairs, white table linen and crystal chandliers. Large-paned windows look out on to the garden. The latter is evidently a source of pride to the Thieltges family, and lovingly maintained, although you might find the coy statues, bridge, benches, lamp post, arches and arbours irritatingly artful, expecially given the unspoilt meadows and wooded hills which surround the property.

The bedrooms are much more straightforward: white walls, colourful pictures, spotless white linen on the beds, simple wooden tables and chairs, shared balconies. There are two glamorous suites which are very good value.

Nearby Eifel massif; Wittlich (8 km); Trier (30 km).

54518 Dreis
Tel (06578) 406
Fax (06578) 1402
Location in in own grounds, between Salmtal and Dreis, 8 km SW of Wittlich;ample car parking
Meals breakfast, lunch, dinner
Prices rooms DD-DDDD with breakfast; dinner from DM145
Rooms 16 double, 2 single, 2 suites, all with bath; all rooms have central heating, phone, TV, hairdrier
Facilities dining-room, sitting-room, breakfast room; terrace
Credit cards AE, DC, MC, V
Children welcome
Disabled no special facilities
Pets accepted
Closed never
Languages English, French
Proprietors Thieltges family

Rheinland-Pfalz

Romantik Hotel Alte Vogtei

This historic half-timbered hotel (dating from the mid-17thC) is in a small village surrounded by the wooded valleys, hills and streams of the Westerwald, east of Bonn and the Rhine – not a prime tourist area, but one which invites exploration.

Timber dominates the interior as well as the exterior, with a strong supporting cast of other traditional materials; ancient ovens, sideboards and utensils employed over the years have been lovingly preserved and now decorate the public rooms. The decorative scheme is simple but effective: light walls, dark-wood beams and furniture, plain, warm-toned fabrics. The older bedrooms in the main body of the hotel are simply furnished with antique country furniture; the light, modern rooms overlooking the garden are slightly anonymous, but still comfortable (and more spacious).

The kitchens are supervised by Markus Wortelkamp, son of the house. His three-year apprenticeship in France and England has influenced his highly regarded cuisine, which depends heavily on local ingredients.

Nearby Marienstatt (25 km); Bonn (50 km); Brühl castle (55 km).

57577 Hamm/Sieg, Lindenalle 3
Tel (02682) 259
Fax (02682) 8956
Location in middle of small village, which is surrounded by woods, on B265, 63 km E of Bonn; with garden, garages and car parking
Meals breakfast, lunch, dinner
Prices rooms D-DD with breakfast; meals DM19-75

Rooms 14 double, 2 single, all with bath; all rooms have central heating, telephone, hairdrier, TV, minibar, radio
Facilities dining-room, bar; terrace
Credit cards AE, DC, MC, V
Children welcome
Disabled no special facilities
Pets accepted **Closed** 20 Jul to 10 Aug **Languages** English, French **Proprietors** Wortelkamp family

Rheinland-Pfalz

Country hotel, Holzappel

Herrenhaus zum Bären

Once the official residence of the Count of Holzappel – a county-state created by a grateful Emperor at the conclusion of the Thirty Years War in the mid-17th century – the 'Gentleman's House' has made a captivating little hotel. Outside, it is emphatically rustic – extravagantly timbered, with simple tables and chairs on a little terrace beneath pollarded trees. Inside, country furniture and hunting trophies are to be found in one of the dining-rooms, but do not dominate: this is a hotel rather than an inn, and the atmosphere is that much more sophisticated.

In the Herrenhaus itself there are 10 double rooms, all at the top end of the hotel's quoted price range. With their mixture of furnishing styles – heavy leather chairs, elegant antique or reproduction tables, smooth carpets – they are not for period-purists; but they are convincingly individual and exceptionally comfortable, and the best are notably spacious. Bathrooms are smartly marble-tiled. The other, cheaper rooms in the nearby Goethehaus are, not surprisingly, simpler.

Food is moderately ambitious, mostly successful.

Nearby hiking, watersports; Limburg (10 km) – old town, cathedral; Runkel (15 km) – village and castle.

56379 Holzappel, Am Alten Markt 15
Tel (06439) 7014
Fax (06439) 7012
Location in middle of village 16 km SW of Limburg; with garden and car parking
Meals breakfast, lunch, dinner
Prices rooms DD-DDDD, with breakfast; meals DM50-120
Rooms 18 double, 16 with bath, 1 with shower (3 twin); 2 single with bath; all rooms have telephone, TV and radio; some rooms have minibar
Facilities dining rooms, conference room; garden terrace **Credit cards** AE, DC, MC, V **Children** welcome
Disabled access easy
Pets well-behaved dogs only
Closed Jan
Languages English
Proprietors Karl-Heinz & Helga Falk

Rheinland-Pfalz

Converted mill, Horbruch im Hunsrück

Historische Schloßmühle

Well worth the effort it may take to find in the lush countryside between the Rhine, Mosel and Nahe, this welcoming old mill house offers, in the words of an enthusiastic German reporter, 'an atmosphere which is exceedingly restful, pleasant and delightful'. The thick walls, the water wheel and stream remind visitors of the building's working history (it was built in 1804, and ground grain for almost a century and a half), but it was successfully transformed into a hotel around thirty years ago.

However, what we previously described as not a particularly smart place is evolving into a very smart place indeed, even to a change of name from Bergmühle to the grander sounding Schloßmühle. This is not to say that the welcoming home-like warmth, the books and paintings which originally so attracted us have gone; it is more a fashionable smoothing out of the edges. Bedrooms and bathrooms remain thoughtfully furnished.

Our widely travelled reporter rates the cuisine 'excellent in every respect, equalling many of the finest French restaurants'. The comparison is not accidental; there is a pronounced French accent to Rüdiger Liller's regionally based cooking.

Nearby Bernkastel-Kues (15 km) – wine-tasting, market square.

55483 Horbruch im Hunsrück
Tel (06543) 4041
Fax (06543) 3178
Location in valley, one km from village of Horbruch, off the B327, 12 km SW of Morbach; with garden and ample car parkin g
Meals breakfast, dinner
Prices DD-DDD with breakfast; meals DM39-120
Rooms 9 double, one suite, all with bath; all rooms have central heating, phone, TV, minibar, radio
Facilities dining-room, breakfast room, sitting-room, bar; terrace
Credit cards AE, MC, V
Children welcome
Disabled access difficult
Pets not accepted
Closed restaurant only, Mon, lunch Tue-Fri
Languages English, French
Proprietors Anneliese and Rüdiger Liller

Rheinland-Pfalz

Village hotel, Kallstadt

Weinkastell 'Zum Weißen Roß'

The eye of the passer-by on the *Deutsche Weinstraße* is sure to be caught by the oldest part of this rambling roadside hotel – its upper storeys, half-timbered and decorated, jutting out over the mellow stone of the ground-floor.

The interior is not quite so quirky, having been thoroughly refurbished in recent times, but the flavour of the old building has been retained. In the main dining-room, crisply moulded arches bear on massive pillars. In the Gutsherren-Stube, used for breakfast as well as evening drinking, the walls and ceiling are pine-panelled, even if the panelling does conceal downlighters. The bedrooms' decoration is rather bland in comparison, although the furniture is handsome. There is a big four-poster in the honeymoon room; for less romantic occasions there is the 'Alcove Room', where you sleep foot-to-foot, with curtains to keep you separately cosy.

Norbert Kohnkes' cooking is reportedly over-ambitious at times, but is in general well above average. Jutta oversees the front of house with a smile.

Nearby wine-tasting, giant cask; Mannheim – Elector's residence, Jesuit Church.

67169 Kallstadt, an der Weinstr 80-82
Tel (06322) 5033
Fax (06322) 8640
Location in middle of small town, 26 km W of Mannheim; with public parking nearby
Meals breakfast, lunch, dinner
Prices rooms DD with breakfast; meals DM40-150
Rooms 13 double, 3 with bath, 7 with shower; all rooms have central heating, phone, TV, radio
Facilities dining-room, *Stube*
Credit cards AE, MC
Children welcome
Disabled no special facilities
Pets welcome **Closed** 4 weeks Jan/Feb, one week Jul/Aug; restaurant only Mon and Tue
Languages English, French
Proprietors Jutta and Norbert Kohnke

Rheinland-Pfalz

Converted castle, Oberwesel

Burghotel Auf Schönburg

On a steep wooded spur high above the Rhine, the Schönburg has the situation of a fairy-tale castle; and a castle it is, of sorts, with part of it built over 1,000 years ago. But the building no longer conforms to fairy-tale norms: much of the hotel is contained in a red-painted Gothic construction between the towers.

Happily, the interior holds no disappointments, offering a subtle blend of comfort and romance. In the bedrooms, any traces of medieval gloom are banished by tasteful decoration and polished antiques. Each room is different in style: some tiny, some large, some (in one of the old towers) round. Some give breathtaking views of the Rhine, but others face the hills. The candlelit dining-rooms are small, each with only six or seven tables, decorated with fresh flowers. The emphasis in the kitchen is on freshness, the major influence regional.

The engaging Hüttls take tremendous pleasure in running their hotel personally, and the majority of their staff, although young, have been with them for some time. With three children of their own, they know how to cater for families.

Nearby ramparts, medieval altarpieces in Liebfrauenkirche, wine-tasting, boat-trips on Rhine; Lorelei rock (5 km).

55430 Oberwesel
Tel (06744) 93930
Fax (06744) 1613
Location on hill overlooking Rhine, 2 km from Oberwesel; with public car parking
Meals breakfast, lunch, dinner, snacks
Prices rooms DD-DDDD with breakfast; meals DM44-145
Rooms 17 double, 11 with bath, 6 with shower (9 twin); 3 single with shower; 2 suites with bath; all rooms have central heating, phone, hairdrier, TV, minibar, radio
Facilities 3 dining-rooms, small library, sitting-room; courtyard, terrace
Credit cards AE, DC, MC, V
Children welcome
Disabled no special facilities
Pets not accepted
Closed Jan to Mar; restaurant only, Mon **Languages** English, French, Italian
Proprietors Wolfgang & Barbara Hüttl

Rheinland-Pfalz

Town inn, Oberwesel

Römerkrug

There is no shortage of attractive-looking old inns along the Rhine valley, but all too often what lies behind the façade is disappointingly ordinary. Here, in the small town of Oberwesel, is an exception.

This charming inn (dating from the 15th century) is situated in the tiny market square with a small terrace area around the doorway, surrounded by similar, wonderful, old half-timbered buildings – with the vine-clad slopes of the Rhine as a backdrop. Once inside, you are left in no doubt about the authenticity of the five-hundred-year-old house. Much of the interior is unaltered; any renovations and improvements have been undertaken with care, and there is a refreshing lack of excessive ornamentation. The overall impression – in the bedrooms as well as the dining-room and *Marktstube* – is of warmth and simple comfort. Food is conventionally satisfying.

The hotel remains by German standards very small – any temptation to enlarge it has mercifully been resisted thus far. The Matzner family have recently joined the 'Gast im Schloss' group; let us hope this does not indicate a change of heart.

Nearby Rhine boat-trips, wine-tastings.

55430 Oberwesel, Marktpl 1
Tel (06744) 8176
Fax (06744) 1677
Location in small cobbled square in heart of town, on B9 21 km N of Bingen; with ample car parking
Meals breakfast, lunch, dinner
Prices rooms D-DD with breakfast; meals DM36-62
Rooms 7 double, 4 with bath, 3 with shower (all twin); all rooms have central heating, phone, hairdrier, TV
Facilities dining-room, *Stube;* street terrace
Credit cards AE, MC, V
Children welcome
Disabled no special facilities
Pets accepted
Closed end Dec to mid-Feb; restaurant only, Wed
Languages English, French
Proprietors Matzner family

Rheinland-Pfalz

Castle hotel, Stromberg

Stromburg

Just off the A61, not far from the Rhine in Guldental stands the castle of Stromburg, now the fiefdom of chef Johann Lafer, and a luxurious Relais & Château hotel. Heavily restored and rather dull – save for the disproportionately tall tower which looks like a stranded lighthouse – the present building is a 19thC reconstruction of the castle first built there in the 11thC, although it was destroyed in 1689. The small town of Stromberg lies in the heart of the Nahe wine region. Protected by hills to the north and west, it acts as a sheltered balcony, 243 m above sea level.

The *raison d'être* is the food. You can choose between the formal surroundings of the Val d'Or restaurant (no characteristics of a castle here) where Herr Lafer and his team deliver luxurious and very expensive cuisine *à la mode* along with a suitably extensive wine list, or the rustic ambience of the Turmstübe (tower inn) which serves hearty regional dishes.

In keeping with the decoration in the public areas, bedrooms are calm and luxurious, if somewhat anonymous. They are spacious and thoughtfully equipped, as are the bathrooms. Best of all is the suite at the top of the tower – if you can afford it.
Nearby Rhine; Koblenz (50 km); Worms (50 km).

55442 Stromberg
Tel (06724) 93100
Fax (06724) 931090
E-mail johannlafer@germany.net
Location in Stromberg, just off A61; ample car parking
Meals breakfast, lunch, dinner
Prices rooms DD-DDDD breakfast DM29; dinner from DM85
Rooms 10 double, 3 single, 1 suite, all with bath; all rooms

have central heating, phone, hairdrier, TV , radio, CD player, minibar, hairdrier
Facilities dining-rooms, bar, meeting room
Credit cards AE, DC, MC, V
Children welcome
Disabled no special facilities
Pets accepted
Closed never
Languages English, French
Proprietors Johann Lafer

Rheinland-Pfalz

Town inn, Bacharach

Altkölnischer Hof

Half-timbered family-run inn, dating from the 11thC, conveniently set on main square of old town. Traditional atmosphere in large business-like restaurant and cosy bar; some bedrooms functional, others prettier but small.

■ 55422 Bacharach, Am Marktpl **Tel** (06743) 1339 **Fax** (06743) 2793 **Meals** breakfast, lunch, dinner, snacks **Prices** rooms D-DD **Rooms** 19, all with bath or shower, central heating, phone, hairdrier, TV, minibar **Credit cards** AE, DC, V **Closed** Nov to Apr **Languages** English

Riverside restaurant with rooms, Balduinstein

Zum Bären

Although his family has been here since 1827, Walter Buggle is a self-taught cook; he aims high, and charges accordingly. Two splendid dining-rooms – one with *Kachelofen*, the other with hand-carved bookcases.

■ 65558 Balduinstein, Bahnhofstr 24 **Tel** (06432) 81091 **Fax** (06432) 83643 **Meals** breakfast, lunch, dinner **Prices** rooms D-DD with breakfast; meals from DM55 **Rooms** 10, all with bath or shower, central heating, phone, hairdrier, TV, radio **Credit cards** AE, MC, V **Closed** 3 weeks in Feb; restaurant only Tue **Languages** English

Riverside guest-house, Beilstein

Haus Lipmann

Owned by the Lipmanns since 1795, this friendly little *Weinstube* offers simple accommodation in an idyllic village. A vine-covered terrace overlooks Mosel and hillside vineyards; the wood-pan-elled 'Cavalier' dining-room is delightful in winter.

■ 56814 Beilstein, Marktplatz 3 **Tel** (02673) 1573 **Meals** breakfast, lunch, dinner, snacks **Prices** rooms DD with breakfast; meals DM25-40 **Rooms** 5, all with shower, central heating, TV **Credit cards** not accepted **Closed** mid-Nov to mid-Mar **Languages** English, French

Town wine tavern, Bernkastel-Kues

Doctor-Weinstuben

Renovated old inn at heart of Mosel wine town (an excellent touring centre) – dreary outside, but jolly, traditional public areas within; impersonal modern bedrooms around pretty flowered court. Friendly and helpful staff.

■ 54470 Bernkastel-Kues, Hebegasse 5 **Tel** (06531) 6081 **Fax** 6296 **Meals** breakfast, lunch, dinner **Prices** rooms D-DD with breakfast **Rooms** 15, all with central heating, phone **Credit cards** AE, DC, MC, V **Closed** Jan, Feb and Mar; restaurant only Tue **Languages** English, French

Rheinland-Pfalz

Town inn and water-mill, Braubach

zum Weißen Schwanen

Next to the old walls of the small town of Braubach is this modest half-timbered old inn, run with good humour by Erich Kunz. The public areas are gloriously rustic, but the most charming bedrooms are nearby in an even older water-mill, with its machinery still in place.

■ 56338 Braubach, Brunnenstr 4 **Tel** (02627) 559 **Meals** breakfast, dinner Price s rooms D-DD, with breakfast; meals from DM30 **Rooms** 16, all with shower, central heating, phone, TV **Credit cards** AE, MC, V **Closed** restaurant only, 3 weeks Jul; Wed **Languages** English

---

Modern chalet hotel, Darscheid/Vulkaneifel

Kucher's Landhotel

Archetypal sweet young things Heidi and Martin Kucher run an attractive gourmet restaurant with spotless bedrooms above, all at affordable prices. Pretty garden and terrace overlook surrounding Eifel hills.

■ 54552 Darscheid/Vulkaneifel, Karl-Kaufmann-Str 2 **Tel** (06592) 629 **Fax** ((06592) 36 77 **Meals** breakfast, lunch, dinner, snacks **Prices** rooms DM60-120 with breakfast; meals D **Rooms** 14, all with bath or shower, central heating, phone, TV, radio **Credit cards** AE, MC **Closed** January; restaurant only, Mon, Tue lunch **Languages** English

---

Country hotel, Dudeldorf

Zum alten Brauhaus

The seventh generation of the Servatius family now run this former brewery. Rooms are furnished with old family portraits and inherited pieces. Guests idling in the leafy garden are spied on by a pair of rococo statues perched on the pavilion.

■ 54647 Dudeldorf, Herrengasse 2 **Tel** (06565) 2057 **Fax** (06565) 2125 **Meals** breakfast, lunch on request, dinner **Prices** rooms DD-DDD with breakfast; meals DM15-85 **Rooms** 15, al l with bath, central heating, phone, hairdrier, TV, radio **Credit cards** AE, DC, MC, V **Closed** end-Dec to end-Jan; restaurant only, Wed **Languages** English

---

Village inn, Kaiserslautern-Hohenecken

Burgschänke

A straightforward but appealing whitewashed inn, with a cosy pub-style bar with an open log fire for cooler days, and a sunny beer garden. Bedrooms are stylishly simple, with hand-crafted furniture. A visitor was enchanted by the pictures, plants and ornaments, but not by the chimes of the church clock.

■ 67661 Kaiserslautern 32-Hohenecken, Schlossstr 1 **Tel** (0631) 56041 **Meals** breakfast, lunch, dinner **Prices** rooms D-DD with breakfast; meals from DM26 **Rooms** 15, all with shower, central heating, phone, TV **Credit cards** AE, DC, MC, V **Closed** never **Languages** English

Rheinland-Pfalz

Village hotel, Kirchen-Katzenbach

zum Weißen Stein

The Stählers' 17thC miners' pub was adventurously extended in the 1960s and 1970s, and offers the familiar ingredients: public rooms bursting with character and bedrooms sadly lacking in it; plenty of space, though, and views.

■ 57548 Kirchen-Katzenbach, Dorfstr 50 **Tel** (02741) 62085
Fax (02741) 62581 **Meals** breakfast, lunch, dinner, snacks
Prices rooms D-DD with breakfast; meals from DM19.50 **Rooms** 31, all with shower, central heating, phone, radio; most have TV, minibar
Credit cards AE, DC, MC, V **Closed** one week mid-Jan
Languages Dutch, English, French

City hotel, Koblenz

Hotel Brenner

The unprepossessing exterior of this modern hotel makes the elegant, ornate interior – gilt mouldings and richly patterned rugs – something of a surprise. So is the hotel's secluded leafy garden in the heart of a large city.

■ 56068 Koblenz, Rizzastr 20 **Tel** (0261) 915780 **Fax** (0261) 9157855
Meals breakfast **Prices** rooms DD-DDD with breakfast **Rooms** 25, all with bath or shower, central heating, phone, TV, minibar, radio; some have hairdrier **Credit cards** AE, DC, MC, V **Closed** 3 weeks at Christmas **Languages** English

Village inn, Landau-Birkweiler

St Laurentius Hof

The Tarjans' little wine-village inn has been given the rustic treatment and is properly flower-decked, beamed and quaint. Rustic food, such as suckling pig, is served in the vine-hung inner courtyard, especially on weekend 'party nights'.

■ 76831 Landau-Birkweiler, Hauptstr 21 **Tel** (06345) 8945
Fax (06345) 7029 **Meals** breakfast, lunch, dinner **Prices** rooms D-DD with breakfast; meals from DM35 **Rooms** 12, all with central heating, minibar, radio; some have phone, TV **Credit cards** MC, V **Closed** Mon, Tue lunch **Languages** English, Hungarian, French

Hillside hotel, Trier

Hotel Petrisberg

A modern building set on a wooded hill with magical views over Trier. Some of the bedrooms have murals or painted ceilings, and wood carvings; suites in the small, attractive annexe. Cosy sitting-rooms and a buffet breakfast in the airy dining-room.

■ 54296 Trier, Sickingenstr 11-13 **Tel** (0651) 41181 **Fax** (0651) 73273 **Meals** breakfast, snacks **Prices** rooms D-DD with breakfast **Rooms** 24, 3 with bath, 21 with shower, 1 single, 5 family rooms; all with central heating, phone, TV **Credit cards** not accepted **Closed** never **Languages** English, French, some Spanish **Languages** English

Rheinland-Pfalz

Villa Hügel

Solid, neat, white-painted villa dating from 1914, in leafy suburb close to centre of historic Trier. The more modern bedroom extension provides a rooftop terrace for views and sunbathing. Tasteful furnishings. Indoor pool, sauna and solarium.

■ 54295 Trier, Bernhardstr 14 **Tel** (0651) 33066 **Fax** (0651) 37958 **Meals** breakfast, afternoon snacks Mon-Fri **Prices** rooms D-DDD with breakfast **Rooms** 34, all with bath, central heating, phone, TV, radio, hairdrier, minibar **Credit cards** AE, DC, MC, V **Closed** never **Languages** English

---

Scheid

You can try Hubert Scheid's cakes and tarts at his café-pâtisserie in nearby Trier, but for the full benefit of his classical French cuisine (Michelin-starred) you must come a few miles up the Mosel. Bedrooms are functional, in smart modern style.

■ 54332 Wasserliesch, Reinigerstr 48 **Tel** (06501) 13958 **Fax** (06501) 13959 **Meals** breakfast, lunch, dinner **Prices** rooms D-DD with breakfast; meals DM95-115 **Rooms** 13, all with shower, central heating; TV in some **Credit cards** AE, DC, MC, V **Closed** 2 weeks in Feb; restaurant only Mon, Tue lunch **Languages** French, some English

Saarland

Hotels in Saarland

It is tempting to overlook Saarland, a not-at-all glamourous little state tucked into the south-western corner of Rheinland-Pfalz, on the border with France. It is rich in coal, and dominated by heavy industry as a result – at least in the basin around Saarbrücken, the only sizeable city. Saarbrücken has no really distinguished hotels, and certainly no notable small ones; best in town is probably the 110-room Bauer Rodenhof, slightly out of the centre (Tel (0681) 41020, fax 43785). Bear in mind that our recommendation in Saarlouis is only a few miles down the Saar valley. In that same direction, but not quite so far down the valley, is Schwalbach, where the Mühlenthal (Tel (06834) 5017, 25 rooms) has been recommended to us.

North-west of Saarbrucken in Neunkirchen is one of the state's five notable restaurants, the Hostellerie Bacher, where Margarethe Bacher leads a highly competent and apparently all-female kitchen; it is a smart establishment, with four reasonably priced bedrooms above (Tel (06821) 31314).

Restaurant with rooms, Tholey

Hotellerie Hubertus

The kitchen is the heart of this place, offering beautifully presented meals which you can eat in the smart, formal dining-room with its coved ceiling, or in the more rustic Marktstube. Bedrooms are light and comfortable.

■ 66636 Tholey, Metzer Str 1 **Tel** (06853) 2404 **Fax** (06853) 30601 **Meals** breakfast, lunch, dinner **Prices** rooms D-DD with breakfast; meals DM25-95 **Rooms** 9, all with bath or shower, central heating; some have phone, TV **Credit cards** AE, DC, V **Closed** restaurant only Mon, Thu lunch, Sun dinner, **Languages** English, French

This page acts as an introduction to the features and hotels of Saarland, and gives brief recommendations of good hotels that for one reason or another have not made a full entry – as well as incorporating our one short entry for the 'Land'.

Reporting to the guide
The *Charming Small Hotel Guides* are greatly strengthened by reports from readers. Please write and tell us about your experiences of small hotels, guest-houses and inns, whether good or bad, whether listed in this edition or not. As well as Germany, we are interested in Britain and Ireland, Italy, France, Spain, Portugal, Austria and the United States. Particularly helpful reporters earn a free copy of the next edition of the guide concerned. And we are always on the lookout for recruits to our team of inspectors; some undertake trips especially for inspection purposes, while others combine hotel inspections with their own travels.

Saarland

Altes Pfarrhaus Beaumarais

Old Parsonages, Vicarages and Rectories are the staple diet of a guide to charming small hotels in Britain; in Germany they are distinctly rare – and in this case, at least, the German variety has little in common with the British. With 36 rooms, it is naturally not the last word in intimacy; and in terms of style, it is more severe and less home-like than a British visitor might expect.

The building was an aristocrat's summer villa before being used as a vicarage. The proprietors describe it as late-baroque, but there is none of the exuberant decoration that the label usually implies. On the contrary, the house (converted to a hotel in 1985) is stylishly plain: outside, white shutters against cream walls; inside, again, predominantly cream-coloured walls and fabrics, and furnishings which verge on the spare. This is particularly true of the spacious bedrooms – though even here there are just enough splashes of colour to make the decorative scheme seem clearly deliberate rather than negligent. The public areas are less restrained, with the occasional ornament, even. The dining-room has a small modern conservatory extension; there is no dining-terrace, but a very appealing courtyard *Biergarten*.

Nearby Saarlouis – old town; Merzig (10 km) – steam railway.

66740 Saarlouis 5, Haupstr 2-4
Tel (06831) 6383
Fax ((06831) 62898
Location in suburb 3 km W of Saarlouis, following Wallerfanger Str; with terrace and car parking
Meals breakfast, lunch, dinner
Prices rooms DD-DDD, with breakfast; meals DM60-90
Rooms 27 double, 24 with bath, 3 with shower; 7 single, 3 with bath, 4 with shower; 2 family rooms with bath; all rooms have central heating, phone, TV, minibar, radio
Facilities breakfast room, dining-room; conservatory, beer garden
Credit cards AE, DC, MC, V
Children very welcome
Disabled access easy; 7 ground-floor rooms
Pets accepted
Closed over Christmas
Languages English, French
Manager Eva Krause

Saarland

Villa Fayence

Although the main reason for visiting this grandly elegant, pink-washed villa is its restaurant, do not pass up the opportunity of spending a night in one of its luxurious bedrooms – furnished with flair by Suzanne and Bernhard Michael Bettler, and the best of them extravagantly spacious.

In winter, guests are encouraged to have an aperitif by the fire in the baroque drawing room, in summer in the conservatory overlooking the park; you are thus given ample time to consider the menu – no mean affair. The picture windows of the 'Wintergarten' restaurant share the parkland view.

Having temporarily withdrawn from the running of the kitchens, Bernhard is now back again. Inspiration is drawn from over the nearby French border: a mille-feuille of duck breasts and foie-gras, almond ice surrounded by orange 'soup', for example. The wine list, of course, is equal to the menu and none of these luxuries comes cheap. However, it is well worth opening the purse strings when you visit Villa Fayence, and lashing out, to be pampered in style by two such practised hosts.

Nearby Rehlingen (5 km) – caves and ruined castle.

66798 Wallerfangen, Hauptstr 12
Tel (06831) 96410
Fax (06831) 62068
Location in village 4 km W of Saarlouis; extensive grounds and ample car parking
Meals breakfast, lunch, dinner
Prices rooms DD-DDD with breakfast; meals DM68-105
Rooms 4 double, one with bath, 3 with shower (3 twin); all rooms have central heating, phone, hairdrier, TV, radio
Facilities restaurant and bistro, sitting area
Credit cards AE, DC, MC, V
Children welcome **Disabled** not suitable **Pets** not accepted **Closed** restaurant only, Sun eve, Mon
Languages English, French
Proprietor Bernhard Michael Bettler

Hessen

Hotels in Hessen

Hessen – the only state in our Central Germany region – is not high on the agenda of the tourist, but like most regions of Germany offers rewards to the explorer – including some glorious old towns and popular areas of natural beauty – the Waldeck region in the north-east, for example. The brothers Grimm were born at Hanau, east of Frankfurt, and an associated fairy-tale industry has sprung up, involving a fairy-tale road running north into Niedersachsen and on via Hameln (as in Pied Piper) to Bremen.

Frankfurt is one of Germany's most dynamic cities, and its financial capital, and naturally is equipped mainly with big, glossy business hotels. We have several detailed entries in and around the city, but also a couple of alternatives to mention here. A few miles to the east of Frankfurt in Mühlheim is the smart and very comfortable Landhaus Waitz, run with personal attention despite its 75 rooms, and offering excellent food (Tel (06108) 6060, fax 606488).

Further out in the same direction, the simpler Burg-Mühle at Gelnhausen has also been recommended to us (Tel (06051) 82052, fax 820554, 33 rooms). The attention of gourmets may instead turn north-east of the city, to Maintal, the location of Ludwig and Doris Hessler's eponymous Michelin-starred restaurant and four associated rooms (Tel (06181) 492951, fax 45029).

Fulda is a small town to the north-west, near the old border, that has an interesting Baroque core. A slightly cheaper alternative to the Goldener Karpfen (page 108) has been recommended to us – the 70-room Kurfürsten, occupying an 18thC house (Tel (0661) 70001, fax 77919).

Marburg, directly north of Frankfurt, is one of Hessen's real highlights, with a splendid Gothic church (reputedly Germany's first). If we had to pick a hotel within easy reach of the city it would be a toss-up between the Fasanerie, at Gisselberg (Tel (06421) 7039, fax 77491, 35 rooms), and the jolly, family-oriented Dammühle at Wehrshausen (Tel (06421) 31007, fax 36118, 20 rooms).

Kassel, in the extreme north, is a sizeable city with some interesting sights but a dearth of appealing hotels. Closer to the city than our Emstal recommendation (page 107) is the pleasantly set Schloßhotel Wilhelmsthal at Calden (Tel (0561) 30880, fax 3088428) – not to be confused with the actual Schloß Wilhelmsthal a mile or two away, which is a mildly interesting house in pretty gardens. To the west of Kassel, near the border with Nordrhein, the Rathaus in the small town of Korbach is recommended (Tel (05631) 50090, fax 500959).

This page acts as an introduction to the features and hotels of Hessen, and gives brief recommendations of good hotels that for one reason or another have not made a full entry. The long entries for this 'Land' – covering the hotels we are most enthusiastic about – start on the next page. But do not neglect the shorter entries starting on page 107: these are all hotels that we would happily stay at.

Hessen

Mansion hotel, Eltville-Hattenheim

Kronen Schlösschen

Within easy reach (about half an hour's drive) of Frankfurt city centre and its airport, and only a few kilometres from Weisbaden and Mainz, Kronen Schlösschen makes a convenient haven for the executive traveller, in peaceful surroundings. A new entry to our guide, it contrasts strongly with our other recommendation, Zum Krug, in the same cobbled wine town of Hattenheim. Whilsts the former is a simple, atmospheric *weinstübe*, Kronnen Schlösschen is full of swags and drapes, marble and velvet, with three function rooms (one with a lovely tiled stove, another with an evocative mural on the walls). It has its idiosyncracies, both in the interior decoration and in the architecture. All the rooms and suites are differently decorated, some in light modern style, some more old-fashioned using dark reds and deep blues; all have polished antique pieces and ritzy marble bathrooms. The exterior is rather whimsical, white-painted with grey slate roofs, onion-shaped domes capping towers and pretty stepped gables. The house is surrounded by an attractive garden, with a shaded terrace for summertime. The hotel's two restaurants, one gourmet, one 'bistro' are well thought of.
Nearby wine-tasting, walks, boat trps on the Rhine.

65347 Eltville-Hattenheim, Rheinallee
Tel (06723) 640
Fax (06723) 7663
Location between Weisbaden and Rüdesheim, just W of Eltville, in its own grounds; ample parking
Meals breakfast, lunch, dinner
Prices rooms DDD-DDDD, breakfast DM24; dinner from DM60
Rooms 13 double, 1 single, 4 suites, all with bath; all rooms have central heating, phone, TV, radio, CD player, minibar, hairdrier
Facilities dining-rooms, sitting-room, bar, meeting rooms; terrace
Credit cards AE, DC, MC, V
Children welcome
Disabled no special facilities
Pets accepted **Closed** never
Languages English, French,
Proprietors Hufnagel-Ullrich family

Hessen

Wine-village inn, Eltville-Hattenheim

Zum Krug

Set in the middle of the pretty wine-growing region of the Rheingau, this timber-panelled and painted *Weinstube*-with-rooms – dating from 1720 but carefully renovated in 1986 – is hung with flowers and surrounded by the cobbled streets of Hattenheim. The dark-green exterior and decorative wrought iron are immediately eyecatching. The interior is just as attractive, with a wood-panelled dining-room, massive green-tiled stove, and stained-glass windows illustrating (as you might expect) a wine-imbibing theme.

Underlining the fact that this is a serious wine-drinking establishment, there is a special gourmet menu for DM75, which includes an appropriately chosen glass of *sekt* or other locally produced wine with each of the four courses, finishing with a glass of vintage port.

Like the food, the bedrooms are perhaps secondary in a place with such a focus on wine, but they are entirely adequate – cosy, simply decorated with handsome traditional furniture and pretty flowered materials, in keeping with the tranquil atmosphere of the hotel and its surroundings.

Nearby wine-tasting, walks, boat trips on the Rhine.

65347 Eltville-Hattenheim, Hauptstr 34	have central heating, telephone, TV, radio
Tel (06723) 2812	**Facilities** dining-room, TV room
Fax (06723) 7677	
Location in middle of village, 14 km SE of Wiesbaden; with car parking	**Credit cards** AE, DC, MC, V
	Children welcome
	Disabled access difficult
Meals breakfast, lunch, dinner, snacks	**Pets** accepted
	Closed 3 weeks in Jan, 2 weeks in Jul; restaurant only, Sun evening, Mon
Prices rooms DD with breakfast; meals from DM25	
Rooms 9 double, one single, all with shower; all rooms	**Languages** English
	Proprietor Josef Laufer

Hessen

Hotel Westend

You could hardly expect a sharper contrast than that between the peaceful, sober elegance of this little hotel *garni* on the one hand and the thrusting pace and modern style of surrounding central Frankfurt – and most of its hotels –,on the other.

It is an old-fashioned place, in the nicest sense – giving every indication of having been preserved in a time-warp since the 18thC. Candle-style light fittings and gilt-framed oil-paintings set the tone throughout. The elegant furniture has been accumulated rather than specified, although some of the pieces are more interesting than they are functional. Bedrooms are comfortable, the small sitting-rooms more like those of a gracious private house than a hotel. But for many visitors (or at least those lucky with the weather) the Westend's crowning glory is the leafy walled garden, where tables are set out for breakfast. Cold snacks are available at the hotel in the evening.

Sadly, our latest inspection bore witness to busy workings in front of the hotel preparatory to the erection of an office block. One negative reader's report on the Westend recently, too: further comments please.

Nearby Goethe's house, Senckenberg Museum.

60325 Frankfurt 1,
Westendstr 15
Tel (069) 746702
Fax (069) 745396
Location in residential district, 5 minutes' walk N of main station; walled garden, private car parking
Meals breakfast
Prices rooms DD-DDDD, with breakfast
Rooms 9 double, one with bath, one with shower, 7 with basin; 11 single, 4 with bath, 7 with basin; all rooms have centr al heating, phone, TV; most rooms have minibar
Facilities 3 sitting-rooms; terrace
Credit cards AE, DC, MC, V
Children tolerated
Disabled not suitable
Pets accepted
Closed Christmas to New Year **Languages** English, French, Polish, Turkish, Spanish, Serbo-Croat
Proprietors E and C L Mayer

Hessen

Hotel Hohenhaus

In the comparative hotel rankings of which German travel and gastronomic magazines are so fond, the Hohenhaus is generally to be found in the top 20. So it is perhaps not surprising that we had such difficulty persuading Günther Haderecker to give us any information about his hotel; after all, his rooms are 95% full year-round with no help from us.

The Hohenhaus has an attractive, peaceful setting in wooded, hilly countryside near the old East German border, close (but not too close) to the E40 motorway, making it well placed to cash in on the much increased traffic between east and west. Although the building is not new, this is very much a 'designer' hotel, with newness thrust upon it – clean lines, natural materials and ethnic patterns stylishly combined, as in a Habitat showroom. There is a great deal of glass, bringing the countryside indoors. But in the dining-room, in particular, traditional styles are maintained. There are some marvellously spacious bedrooms, with a less conspicuously modern feel.

Achim Schwekendiek has won awards for his eclectic cooking. **Nearby** walking; Eisenach (15 km) – Bach's birthplace, Wartburg castle.

37293 Herleshausen 7, Holzhausen
Tel (05654) 680
Fax (05654) 1303
Location in countryside 2 km N of A4, exit Wommen, 15 km NW of Eisenach; in grounds; ample car parking
Meals breakfast, lunch, dinner, snacks
Prices rooms DD-DDDD; breakfast DM25; meals DM85-150
Rooms 17 double, 12 with bath, 5 with shower; 9 single with shower; all rooms have central heating, phone, hairdrier, TV, radio **Facilities** sitting-room, 2 dining-rooms, bar, conference room; indoor swimming-pool, sauna, tennis, horse-riding **Credit cards** AE, MC, V **Children** tolerated **Disabled** one ground-floor room **Pets** in bedrooms only **Closed** never **Languages** English, French **Proprietor** Günther Haderecker

Hessen

Converted castle, Hofgeismar

Dornröschenschloß Sababurg

For the last hundred years this romantic 14thC fortress-turned-hunting-lodge has been prefixed 'Sleeping Beauty Castle'; it may or may not have been the inspiration for the fairy-tale told by the Brothers Grimm, but Sababurg is now the centrepiece of a 'Fairy-Tale' industry. Having travelled along the Fairy-Tale Road, guests can be welcomed by Sleeping Beauty, and then buy mementoes in the gift shop. Add to this the fact that the parkland contains a zoo (albeit of an unconventional kind), and you would be justified in writing Sababurg off as a theme park.

But you could not be more wrong. In a part of the old castle the Koseck family have created a thoroughly civilized and tasteful hotel, which they run with care and thoughtfulness, and once the daytime crowds ebb away, all is peace and seclusion. There is none of the medieval gloom that you might fear; bedrooms (named since the 16thC after animals) are stylishly furnished, with lovely fabrics – the few rooms up in the tower being particularly romantic – and give glorious views of the park shared by some of the tables in the dining-room. The cooking is richly impressive, with the emphasis on local game.

Nearby walks; Münden (10 km) – 14thC bridge.

34369 Hofgeismar, Hofgeismar-Sababurg
Tel (05671) 8080
Fax (05671) 808200
Location in woods, 10 km N of Munden, E of Hofgeismar; with park, large garden and ample car parking
Meals breakfast, lunch, dinner, snacks
Prices rooms DDD-DDDD with breakfast; meals from DM45

Rooms 17 double, one single, all with bath; all rooms have central heating, phone, hairdrier, radio
Facilities drawing-room, dining-room, theatre; roof terrace, horse-riding, zoo
Credit cards AE, DC, MC, V
Children very welcome
Disabled not suitable
Pets welcome **Closed** mid-Jan to mid-Feb **Languages** English
Proprietors Koseck family

Hessen

Country house hotel, Kelkheim

Schloßhotel Rettershof

This four-square stone-built pile looks every inch the Victorian country house, and would be equally at home in the Scottish highlands as here in the Taunus mountains. It stands on an ancient estate which traces its origins back to a 12thC monastery, and which would have been split up for sale in the 1980s had the local council not intervened and bought the whole property.

Given this background it would be surprising if the Rettershof were notably intimate or personal, and it is not. But neither is there much of the civic institution about it – the sitting-rooms are pleasantly clubby, the dining-rooms elegantly calm with pink fabrics against warm wooden panelling, and the kitchen capable of impressive results. Some of the bedrooms are in the main house – traditionally elegant in style – while others are in an inconspicuous modern extension, with rather anonymous fitted furniture; all are spacious and comfortable.

The informal wooded garden leads off to various other estate buildings, including riding stables and a café-restaurant call Zum fröhlichen Landmann – The Happy Squire.

Nearby cloisters, town hall; Kronberg (5 km) – ruined castle, medieval old town; Bad Soden (5 km) – spa town.

65779 Kelkheim
Tel (06174) 29090
Fax (06174) 25352
Location in wooded countryside on B455 5 km NE of Kelkheim, 19 km NW of Frankfurt; in grounds with ample car parking
Meals breakfast, lunch, dinner, snacks
Prices rooms DD-DDD, with breakfast; meals DM35-90
Rooms 34 double, 3 with bath, 31 with shower; one single with shower; all rooms have central heating, phone, T V, minibar, radio
Facilities 3 dining-rooms, sitting-room; terrace, tennis, horse-riding, bowling alley, sauna, whirlpool, solarium
Credit cards AE, DC, MC, V
Children welcome **Disabled** wheelchair; ground-floor room **Pets** accepted **Closed** never; restaurant, Sun, Mon
Languages English, French
Proprietor Hans Baumann

Hessen

Schloßhotel Kronberg

There may be older *Schloßhotels* than this, but there are few more impressive: an imposing stone-and-slate mansion, all pointed towers and stepped gables, built at the end of the 19th century by Queen Victoria's eldest daughter, the Empress Frederick – mother of Kaiser Wilhelm II.

Such a house could easily be a gloomy and intimidating place; the great delight of Kronberg is that it is not. Despite the high ceilings, gilt picture frames, ornate chandeliers, polished antique furniture and regal provenance, the atmosphere is that of a comfortable, even welcoming, lived-in house. Partly this is because much of the furniture has been chosen for comfort rather than antiquity or appearance; partly because the decoration, except in the grand set-piece rooms, is light and stylish.

It is set in a magnificent park, ringed by mature and exotic trees – embracing a major golf-course as well as a rose garden.

Of course, this is not a cheap hotel, but for what you get, it is by no means unreasonably expensive. The cooking is as polished and impressive as the antiques.

Nearby walks, medieval old town; Grosser Feldberg (10 km) – panorama; Königstein (10 km) – 16thC fortress.

61476 Kronberg, Hainstr 25
Tel (06173) 70101
Fax (06173) 701267
Location at N edge of small town, 17 km N of Frankfurt; in grounds; car parking
Meals breakfast, lunch, dinner, snacks
Prices rooms DDD-DDDD; breakfast DM30; meals DM60-135
Rooms 27 double (3 twin), 24 single, 7 suites, all with bath; all rooms have central heating, phone, hairdrier, TV, mini bar, radio
Facilities dining-rooms, bar, sitting room with open fire, library, salon, conference room; Italian garden, 18-hole golfcourse **Credit cards** AE, DC, MC, V **Children** welcome
Disabled no special facilities
Pets accepted **Closed** never
Languages English, French
Managers Gerhard Köhler and Sönke Tuchel

Hessen

Converted castle, Spangenberg

Schloß Spangenberg

Visitors to this 13thC hilltop *Schloß* will find everything they expect in a romantic old castle, from the surrounding moat to the wooden drawbridge and crenellated gate house. However, this is no fusty monument to a past age, but a living hotel converted with some style whilst retaining its castle origins.

But there is no denying that the chief attraction of Spangenberg (as of so many *Schloßhotels*) is the setting, the tranquillity and the views – in this case shared by some of the rooms but best enjoyed from the narrow café-terrace outside the walls, which catches the afternoon and evening sun. The bedrooms are spacious, full of character and interestingly varied, the best probably being those in the family apartment in the gatehouse, with one four-poster bedroom and one split-level one.

The refurbished dining-room has authentically thick walls, with cherry wood furniture and floral curtains, and the deep set windows overlook wooded hills. Venison is a speciality and can be tried in pastry or with mushrooms, cranberries and asparagus. There is also a 'Schloss Spangenberg' five-course menu.

Nearby Klosterstrasse; Melsungen (10 km) – town hall, half-timbered houses.

34286 Spangenberg
Tel (05663) 866
Fax (05663) 7567
Location on top of hill above village, 36 km SE of Kassel; with terrace and car parking
Meals breakfast, lunch, dinner
Prices rooms DD-DDD with breakfast; meals from DM49
Rooms 24 twin, 4 with bath, 20 with shower; 2 single with shower; one family room with shower; all rooms have central he ating, phone, hairdrier, radio; most rooms have TV **Facilities** dining-room, sitting areas, conference rooms, wine bar
Credit cards AE, DC, MC, V
Children welcome
Disabled no special facilities
Pets accepted (DM8 per night) **Closed** Jan, 2 weeks in summer; restaurant only, Sun evenings **Languages** English, French **Manager** Wilfried Wichmann

Hessen

Town hotel, Bad Hersfeld

Zum Stern

The obvious place to stay (or eat) in this spa town: a neat flower-decked old hotel on the marketplace. Cosy panelled dining-rooms and good cooking. Bedrooms have individual themes. Swimming pool and sauna.

■ 36251 Bad Hersfeld, Linggpl 11 **Tel** (06621) 1890 **Fax** (06621) 189260 **Meals** breakfast, lunch, dinner **Prices** rooms DD-DDD **Rooms** 45, all with bath, central heating, phone, TV, radio, minibar, hairdrier **Credit cards** AE, DC, MC, V **Closed** restaurant only, Fri lunch and early Jan **Languages** German only

---

Town villa, Bad Karlshafen

Haus Schöneck

The cool, almost austere, white-painted rooms and apartments suit the restrained style of this turn-of-the-century villa. Mature trees shelter gravelled terraces which surround the house, and gazebos and grottos dot the rolling landscaped gardens. Indoor swimming-pool. Barbecue.

■ 34381 Bad Karlshafen, C D Stunzweg 10 **Tel** (05672) 925010 **Fax** (05672) 925011 **Meals** breakfast **Prices** rooms D-DD with breakfast; **Rooms** 18, all with bath or shower, central heating, phone,TV, minibar **Credit cards** AE, DC, MC, V **Closed** never **Languages** English

---

Country hotel, Biebertal-Königsberg

Berghof Reehmühle

A pretty hotel, creeper-covered and painted. The windows of the simple dining-room offer marvellous panoramic views over the flowery garden and surrounding countryside. Rustic bedrooms with sloping ceilings and flower-painted furniture.

■ 35444 Biebertal-Königsberg, Bergstr 47 **Tel** and **Fax** (06446) 360 **Meals** breakfast, lunch, dinner **Prices** rooms D-DD with breakfast; meals DM20-50 **Rooms** 8, all with central heating, phone, TV **Credit cards** MC **Closed** 2 weeks mid-Aug; restaurant only, Mon **Languages** English

---

Country guest-house, Emstal-Sand

Grischäfer

Well, country guest-house and butcher's, actually. This collection of rustic buildings is only a few miles south-west of bustling Kassel, but in another world. Beams dominate inside and out, with solid carved furniture to match.

■ 34308 Bad Emstal, Kasseler Str 27 **Tel** (05624) 354 **Fax** (05624) 8778 **Meals** breakfast, lunch, dinner **Prices** rooms D-DD with breakfast **Rooms** 17, all with shower, central heating, phone **Credit cards** not accepted **Closed** Mon **Languages** English, French, Spanish

Hessen

Country house hotel, Fischbachtal-Lichtenberg

Landhaus Baur

An ambitious country restaurant in its own grounds, which has grown into a hotel – though food remains the main attraction . Bedrooms, with luxury bathrooms, are decorated in Laura Ashley style in the main house and contemporary furnishings in the new wing. Swimming-pool.

■ 64405 Fischbachtal-Lichtenberg, Lippmannweg 15 **Tel** (06166) 8313 **Fax** (06166) 8841 **Meals** breakfast, lunch, dinner **Prices** rooms DD-DDD with breakfast **Rooms** 10, all with central heating **Credit cards** AE, MC **Closed** 2 weeks Jan; Mon, and Thur half-day **Languages** English

City hotel, Frankfurt am Main

Hotel Palmenhof

A haven of comfort and peace in a frenetic city. Bedrooms are plush, done in soft colours, with a smattering of impressive antiques among contemporary pieces, as well as business facilities. Equally welcoming is the Bastei Restaurant for lunch and dinner.

■ 60325 Frankfurt am Main 1, Bockenheimer Landstr 89-91 **Tel** (069) 7530060 **Fax** (069)75300666 **Meals** breakfast, lunch, dinner **Prices** rooms DD-DDDD with breakfast; meals from DM39 **Rooms** 46, all with bath or shower, central heating, phone, hairdrier, TV, minibar **Credit cards** AE, DC, MC, V **Closed** end-Dec to Jan **Languages** English, French

Town hotel, Fulda

Goldener Karpfen

The 'Golden Carp' is a well-presented and welcoming tradition-al town hotel, much extended and refurbished in recent years. The cuisine is variable: simple dishes are reliable. Some glori-ously spacious bedrooms.

■ 36037 Fulda, Simplizius-Pl 1 **Tel** (0661) 70044 **Fax** (0661) 73042 **Meals** breakfast, lunch, dinner **Prices** rooms DD-DDDD with breakfast; meals DM30-80 **Rooms** 62, all with central heating, phone, hairdrier, TV, minibar, radio **Credit cards** AE, DC, MC, V **Closed** 24 and 31 Dec **Languages** English, French, Italian, Spanish

Suburban villa, Hanau

Hotel Birkenhof

A gracious post-war villa with landscaped gardens, in a residential area, and a short walk from the castle, church and restaurants. Its brightly coloured interior is comfortable and well-maintained by the omnipresent Frau Richter. Home-made jams and cakes.

■ 63456 Hanau 7-Steinheim, von Eiff-Str 37-41 **Tel** (06181) 64880 **Fax** (06181) 648839 **Meals** breakfast, dinner, snacks **Prices** rooms DD with breakfast **Rooms** 23, all with bath, central heating, phone, TV, radio, minibar **Credit cards** AE, MC, V **Closed** Christmas **Languages** English, Russian

Hessen

Country house hotel, Königstein im Taunus

Sonnenhof

A former summer residence of the Rothschilds' in Gothic hunt-ing-lodge style, set in its own 20-acre park only 20 minutes' drive from Frankfurt. Deeply comfortable and relaxing; recent refur-bishment has breathed new life into the place.

■ 61462 Königstein im Taunus, Falkensteinerstr 9 **Tel** (06174) 29080 **Fax** (06174) 290 875 **Meals** breakfast, lunch, dinner, snacks **Prices** rooms DD-DDD with breakfast **Rooms** 42, all with bath or shower, central heating, phone, TV, radio **Credit cards** AE, DC, MC, V **Closed** never **Languages** German only

---

Country hotel, Lich-Kloster Arnsburg

Alte Klostermühle

We might have called this a converted monastery, or mill, or brewery, since it is partly each of those – a cluster of buildings immersed in deciduous woods. Countless rustic dining-rooms, and beautifully antique-furnished bedrooms.

■ 35423 Lich **Tel** (06404) 91900 **Fax** (06404) 4867 **Meals** breakfast, lunch, dinner, snacks **Prices** rooms D-DDD with breakfast; meals DM22-46 **Rooms** 25, all with shower, central heating, phone, TV, radio; some have minibar **Credit cards** AE, DC, MC, V **Closed** Mon, Tue lunch **Languages** German only

---

Town hotel, Limburg an der Lahn

Hotel Zimmermann

This nondescript-looking hotel close to the pretty old heart of Limburg holds surprises inside: it is elegantly furnished with glowing antiques and rich fabrics, heavy gilt-framed pictures adorning the walls. Renovation was in progress in 1991.

■ 65549 Limburg an der Lahn, Blumenröder Str 1 **Tel** (06431) 4611 **Fax** (06431) 41314 **Meals** breakfast, dinner **Prices** rooms DD-DDD with breakfast; dinner from DM40 **Rooms** 30, all with central heating, phone, hairdrier, TV, minibar; some have radio **Credit cards** AE, DC, MC, V **Closed** 20 Dec to 6 Jan **Languages** English, French

---

Town villa, Nidda-Bad Salzhausen

Hotel Jäger

A convalescent home, converted in plush style with a rich over-designed gilt-and-glass interior. Softly co-ordinating colours dec-orate the elegantly modern bedrooms; some overlook the hand-some gardens at the rear. Luxury bathrooms.

■ 63667 Nidda, Kurstr 9-13 **Tel** (06043) 4020 **Fax** (06043) 402100 **Meals** breakfast, lunch, dinner **Prices** rooms DD-DDD with breakfast; meals DM70 **Rooms** 29, all with bath or shower, central heating, phone, TV, minibar **Credit cards** AE, DC, MC, V **Closed** never **Languages** English, French

Eastern Germany

Hotels in Eastern Germany

In this edition we continue to expand gradually our coverage of the old East. However, our sort of hotel is still a relative rarity in this part of Germany, with most of the investment made by big hotel chains. Glorious but decaying buildings ignored by the old regime have been bought for conversion to hotels with appeal to Western tastes, some with more success than others. Kempinski have been involved in a massive reconstruction of the old Taschenberg-palais in Dresden and have sensitively left the original façade intact. The new hotel opened in 1995, (Tel (06102) 50020) adding 213 bedrooms to help ease the city's chronic accommodation problems – in summer, barges are brought up river from Hungary to serve as temporary hostels. Other than the large Grand Hotel Kempinski in Dresden, we recommend Alpha, restored from an old house (Tel (06102) 5022441, 75 rooms).

Berlin, for so long an oasis of affluence and style in the desert of East Germany, is still predominantly a city of smart, big, modern hotels. Apart from our entries on the following pages, possibilities with a more personal touch include the very polished Seehof, in a convenient but quiet lakeside setting in the Charlottenburg district (Tel (030) 320020, 77 rooms); the Belvedere, a small villa in the residential area of Grünewald (Tel (030) 826 1077, 19 rooms); and the tasteful, modestly priced Pension Wittelsbach in Wilmersdorf (Tel (030) 876345, 37 rooms).

Away from Berlin, we know of a number of interesting possibilities, on which feedback would be welcome: just a 10-minute tram ride from Dresden centre is the little Pension Altriesnitz, rustic but with excellent modern facilities (Tel (0351) 423900, 7 rooms); perched on a hill-top at Konigstein, Landgasthof Müller has a homespun charm and a long verandah for lazy afternoons enjoying the river view (Tel (035022) 2794, 5 rooms); in Zeitz is the handsome and comfortable Villa Zeitz (Tel (03441) 713826; and finally, at Bârenfels, is the cosy Hotel Felsenberg (Tel (035052) 20450).

In this section we depart from the usual pattern of the book by treating the whole of Eastern Germany in a single chapter. The long entries, covering the hotels we are most enthusiastic about, start on the next page. But do not neglect the shorter entries starting on page 119. Additional suggestions for this chapter would be particularly welcome.

Eastern Germany

Town hotel, Bad Doberan

Kurhotel

Yes, it looks like a white barracks, yes, it's got 60 bedrooms, but the Kurhotel has something still singularly lacking in the East – style. Moreover, it has managed to avoid the atrocities so frequently carried out in the name of modernisation. Built in 1793 as a guest house for local duke Friedrich Franz von Mecklenburg, the building has been through several reincarnations over the years until given a restorative shot in the arm in the 1980's. Further refinements in 1992 created a hotel of some standing, well able to hold its own on the international market.

It will certainly appeal to lovers of the Laura Ashley school of interior decoration, with its English country fabrics and pastel colours, used to good effect in the airy bedrooms – those under the eaves are particularly impressive, with sloping ceilings accentuated by softly striped wallpapers.

Classical Biedemeier sets the scene in the public rooms downstairs; prints of Bad Doberan's long history hang on subtly coloured walls, adding character to the undoubtedly cheerful personality of the hotel. Warning: food is an area where improvements could happily be made. It is of the heavy regional variety.
Nearby 'Molli' Railway; Ahrenshoop (25 km) – painters' colony

18209 Bad Doberan, Am Kamp
Tel (038203) 3036
Location opposite park in middle of town, 10km E of Rostock; with ample public car parking
Meals breakfast, lunch, dinner, snacks
Prices rooms DD-DDD with breakfast; meals from DM25
Rooms 50 double (10 twin), 10 single, all with bath; all rooms have central heating, phone, hairdrier, TV, radio; most rooms have minibar
Facilities dining-room, restaurant, bar; terrace, sauna, solarium
Credit cards AE, MC, V
Children welcome
Disabled no special facilities
Pets small dogs only **Closed** 20 to 24 Dec **Languages** English, French **Proprietor** Horst Werner Metz

Eastern Germany

Landhaus Schlachtensee

A 'country house' indeed: although this pristine turn-of-the-century villa is in the middle of a city, it is set in an area of woods and lakes (including the eponymous Schlachtensee), away from the bustle of downtown Berlin yet only a short underground train-ride to the middle of the city.

Arranged on three floors, the rooms are rather anonymous, but comfortable and stylish – large, light and airy, done out in peaceful grey tones, with modern, elegant furniture, and slick lighting. Bathrooms too are modern and fully equipped. Three of the bedrooms have a balcony, six are on the ground floor and all are quiet.

Local artists' works hang spotlit on the white walls of the breakfast room, which also doubles as a reception room. It leads out on to the terrace overlooking the garden; breakfast is served out here on fine days. Like most Berlin hotels, the Schlachtensee is popular and reservations should be made at least a month in advance.

Nearby Kufürstendamm, Checkpoint Charlie, boat trips on Wannsee, Dahlem Museum, Charlottenburg Palace; excursions to other cities in what was East Germany.

14163 Berlin, Bogotastr 9
Tel (030) 809 9470
Fax (030) 809 94747
Location in quiet upmarket suburb of Zehlendorf, 10 km from Kudamm; with garden and limited car parking
Meals breakfast, snacks on demand
Prices rooms DD-DDD with breakfast
Rooms 16 double, 3 with bath, 13 with shower; 2 single, one family room, with shower; all rooms have central heating, te lephone, hairdrier, cable TV, minibar, radio
Facilities breakfast room with terrace; bicycles
Credit cards AE, MC, V
Children welcome **Disabled** not suitable **Pets** accepted, except in breakfast room
Closed never **Languages** English, French, Italian, Spanish **Proprietors** Jürgen Wasmann and Jürgen Rühle

Eastern Germany

Schlosshotel Vier Jahreszeiten

Hardly typical of our guide, the Schlosshotel Vier Jahreszeiten is one of the most luxurious you could hope to find anywhere, but its history, its relatively small number of rooms, its wooded setting in the elegant residential Grunewald district, and its opulent makeover by Karl Lagerfeld make it idiosyncratic enough to include – should you be able to afford it.

Now part of the Ritz-Carlton group, the hotel was built as a private palace in 1914 for aristocrat Walter von Pannwitz in late Baroque style, with a Renaissance style double-height great hall, a library with painted ceiling, a gallery designed for von Pannwitz's art collection, and other richly decorated salons. In 1994 it was completely restored, under the artistic direction of fashion guru Karl Lagerfeld, a friend of the new owners. Unless he is there himself, you can stay in his private suite, decorated with his own furniture and paintings. All the bedrooms and bathrooms are dreamily luxurious and superbly equipped. There are two restaurants, Le Jardin and the gourmet Vivaldi (very palatial), and two bars, one open air, one with open fire, as well as a cool white health centre. The whole place exudes high-living opulence.
Nearby Kurfuerstendamm; Tegel airport

Brahmsstrasse 10, 14193 Berlin
Tel (030) 895840
Fax (030) 8958400
Location in Grunewald, close to city centre; ample parking
Meals breakfast, lunch, dinner
Prices DDDD; breakfast DM26-38
Rooms 40 double, 12 suites, all with bath; all rooms have central heating, phone, fax, TV, video, PC jack, air conditioning, minibar, hairdrier, safe **Facilities** 2 dining-rooms, 2 bars; terrace; health centre, beauty salon; bicycles **Credit cards** AE, DC, MC, V **Children** welcome; under 12s free, sharing parents' room **Disabled** access possible **Pets** accepted **Closed** never **Languages** English, French, Italian **Manager** Reto G. Gaudenzi

Eastern Germany

Country inn, Klein-Briesen

Parkhotel "Juliushof"

Deep in the forest, with an atmosphere reminiscent of an old fairytale, the Juliushof looks just the place where a wolf might grab Red Riding Hood's granny and disappear. It is certainly not for those who favour the bright city lights; a former DDR hunting lodge, it will appeal to back-to-nature weekenders or sportsmen who enjoy hunting, shooting and fishing.

But don't worry about the comfort of the place as, despite its darkly rugged log-cabin look from outside, the Juliushof is a civilized place to stay. Within the hotel there are eight suites, each well-equipped with cloakroom, living room and fair-sized bathroom. A separate cabin nearby contains a further two double bedrooms and two single rooms. Colours are muted and furniture comfortable, if unexceptional.

A pardonable rash of rusticity breaks out in the dining room, where antlers and other trophies adorn the walls. The menu is, as would be expected, heavily weighted towards venison, wild boar, and locally caught trout, although salads do feature for the faint-hearted. No-one, however, can fail to appreciate the wonderful scent of the pines which surround the Juliushof.

Nearby fishing, walking.

14806 Klein-Briesen (Kreis Belzig)
Tel (033846) 40245
Fax (033846) 40245
Location in forest 20 km S of Brandenburg on B102; in grounds with ample car parking
Meals breakfast, lunch, dinner
Prices rooms DD with breakfast; meals from DM25
Rooms 2 double, 2 single, 10 suites, all with bath; all rooms have central heating, phone, TV, minibar
Facilities dining-room, breakfast room; terrace, fishing, shooting
Credit cards AE, MC
Children very welcome
Disabled ground-floor rooms
Pets tolerated
Closed never
Languages English
Proprietor W-J Stolte

Eastern Germany

Village hotel, Kloster Zinna

Alte Försterei

Part of a weavers' settlement built at the behest of Frederick the Great in 1764, Alte Försterei began life as a forester's lodge. In the 1960s, the Baroque building became flats, when in 1991 when two West Germans took over, restored it and opened it as a hotel. New to our guide, it has been warmly recommended by readers.

Heavy oak doors lead into the hall with its original polished stone floor. First impressions are of warmth and character, with antique carpets and furnishings, table lamps, plants, and birds in a cage, and an unobtrusive personal welcome to match. Bedrooms are on the upper floor, built into the Baroque hipped roof. Oak beams frame pastel walls in each of the rooms, decorated with rustic furniture, bright colours and friendly details. Bathrooms are mostly small, white-tiled and spotlessly clean.

Of the two restaurants, the elegant Friedrichs Stuben, offers fine regional cuisine featuring particularly good soups and sauces. The wine list is limited - try a white Elbling from Saxony. The pub-like 12 Mönche, housed in the former stables, offers a simpler, more solid menu and the chance to meet the locals. Service is helpful and friendly, if sometimes a little amateur.

Nearby Juterbög (4 km); Wittenberg (30 km).

14913 Kloster Zinna, Markt 7
Tel (03372) 4650
Fax (03372) 465222
Location in village, on B101 between Luckenwalde and Jüterbog, 64 km S of Berlin
Meals breakfast, lunch, dinner
Prices B&B DD-DDD
Rooms 15 double, 3 single, 2 suites, all with bath; all rooms have central heating, phone, TV, stereo, minibar

Facilities 2 dining-rooms, breakfast room, sitting-room, bar, meeting room
Credit cards V
Children welcome
Disabled no special facilities
Pets accepted
Closed never
Languages English, French
Proprietor Roland Frankfurth

Eastern Germany

Seaside resort hotel, Kühlingsborn

Apartmenthotel Röntgen

The smell of freshly baked bread is just one of many pleasant things about this innovative hotel which offers apartments for rent on a daily basis. The friendly Röntgen family, who own the adjoining café/restaurant, have an in-house bakery and provide free fresh rolls each morning to guests who want to make their own breakfasts. Otherwise, the café serves breakfast until 2 pm.

The apartments are pristine, painted in white, but made cosy with well-upholstered floral-patterened sofa and armchairs and patterned rugs on the polished wooden floor. The dining area has quality solid wooden tables and upholstered chairs. The bathrooms gleam with all-white tilings. Everything has been thought out with care since the Röntgens decided to renovate their 1908 property with the idea of letting people enjoy their own home comforts while on hoiday. They provide free indoor and outdoor games for children.

The bakery's selling area is a showplace, with royal red walls and fittings sporting the Röntgen monogram in gold, and it has a cosy fireplace and a sunny terrace; a long counter displays wonderful iced cakes and pastries.

Nearby Rostock museum, island tours, Bad Doberan cathedral.

18225 Kühlingsborn, Strandisstrasse 30A
Tel (038293) 7810
Fax (038293) 78199
Location next to the forest, 4 minutes' walk to the beach, one minute walk to the city centre; parking possible next to the hotel
Meals self-catering apartments; café/restaurant
Prices DD-DDD
Rooms 17 apartments, 3 one-room, 12 two-room, 2 three-room; all with kitchen, bath, phone, fax point, TV, radio
Facilities dining area, desk, seating area; refrigerator, freezer, dishwasher, stove
Credit cards AE, MC, V
Children very welcome
Disabled café has a specially designed WC **Pets** welcome
Closed never **Languages** English **Proprietors** Frank and Nina Röntgen

Eastern Germany

Town villa, Magdeburg

Residenz Joop

We get an unusually large number of letters recommending this charming old converted villa. One well-travelled reader comments: 'Without a hint of exaggeration, it compares favourably with any small hotel or inn I stayed in anywhere.'

Bernd and Ursula Joop restored this grand old house, which formerly belonged to the Swedish Consul, who was Mr Joop's grandfather. Their use of pale colours, such as ivory or cream for the subtly-striped wallpaper, adds to the feeling of space in the amply-sized bedrooms, which have large windows, mostly overlooking extensive, lush grounds. Bamboo cane chairs with pink and blue floral cushions give a summery feel, as do the modern prints on the walls. Sunny yellow is used in the bright breakfast room; a swathe of yellow fabric is draped over flounced lace curtains, and chandeliers reflect its era as a consulate Topped with a gingerbread-style top floor, the exterior of this white stucco and brick hotel looks cosily inviting and all the rooms are pristine and immaculately kept. The personal attention shown by the friendly, elegant Joops, who opened for business in 1993, further explains the rave reviews we have received.

Nearby Gothic cathedral, puppet theatre, locks, Harz mountains.

D-39112 Magdeburg, Jean Burger Strasse 16
Tel (0391) 62620
Fax (0391) 6262100
Location in a quiet residential neighbourhood of the city centre; ample car parking in the grounds
Meals breakfast
Prices DDD-DDDD
Rooms 16 double, 9 single; all rooms have bath or shower, central heating, phone, fax, minibar, satellite TV
Facilities sitting-room
Credit cards AE, DC, MC, V
Children welcome
Disabled no special facilities
Pets not accepted
Closed 20 Dec to 10 Jan
Languages English
Proprietors Bernd and Ursula Joop

Eastern Germany

Seehotel

The small village of Neukloster lies south of the old Hanseatic League towns of Rostock and Wismar, and, just outside the village, the Seehotel fringes the shore of the quiet Lake Neukloster. The original main house was built at the turn of the century in red brick, typical of the Mecklenburg region. After reunification, a pair of architects from West Berlin transformed it into an intimate hotel, rebuilding the old house, with a wood-deck terrace overlooking the orchard and the lake. A new thatched house sleeps parties of up to eight, with a hall for functions and exhibitions.

Modern simplicity is the keynot in the Seehotel, both in the light and airy dining-room and in the bedrooms. Our reporter describes light wooden furniture and occasional antique pieces fitting well into often limited spaces. Beds are comfortable, and bedside lighting ingenious. Televisions are tucked out of sight behind a small blue door in the wardrobe.

Breakfast is a health-conscious buffet, while lunch and dinner menus consists of mainly light dishes such as soups, salads and fish at very reasonable prices.

Nearby sailing, riding; Wismar (20 km).

23992 Nakenstorf bei Neukloster, Seestrasse 1
Tel & fax (038422) 25445
Location outside village, on lake Neukloster, 20 km SE of Wismar; parking
Meals breakfast, lunch, dinner
Prices DD; breakfast DM15
Rooms 12 double, 3 apartments sleeping up to 4, 1 suite sleeping up to 8; all with bath or shower; all rooms have central heating, phone, fax, TV, radio, hairdrier
Facilities sitting-room, dining-room, function room; terrace **Credit cards** MC
Children welcome
Disabled access difficult
Pets accepted
Closed Christmas; Jan to mid-Mar **Languages** English
Proprietor Gernot Nalbach

Eastern Germany

Country house hotel, Berlin

Forsthaus Paulsborn

A quirky and captivating hunting lodge, built in a grand style in the 19th century in magnificent wooded parkland by the Grune waldsee. Muted colour schemes, wrought iron light fittings and hunting trophies abound.

■ 14193 Berlin 33, Am Grunewaldsee **Tel** (030) 8138010 **Fax** (030) 8141156 **Meals** breakfast, lunch, dinner **Prices** rooms DD-DDD with breakfast; meals DM15-50 **Rooms** 10, all with bath or shower, central heating, phone, hairdrier, TV, minibar **Credit cards** AE, DC, MC, V **Closed** restaurant only, Monday **Languages** English, French, Italian

---

Town hotel, Berlin

Hecker's Hotel

A stylish and luxurious modern hotel, larger than usual for this guide, a few steps from the famous Ku'damm. Choice of bedrooms, classic or modern in design. Friendly, young staff.

■ 10623 Berlin 12, Grolmanstr 35 **Tel** (030) 88900 **Fax** (030) 8890260 **Meals** breakfast, lunch, dinner **Prices** rooms DDD-DDDD; breakfast DM20, meals DM35-60 **Rooms** 72, all with bath or shower, central heating, air conditioning, phone, hairdrier, TV, minibar, radio **Credit cards** AE, DC, MC, V **Closed** never **Languages** English, French, Italian, Spanish

---

Castle inn, Eisenach

Auf der Wartburg

Guests can ignore the no-parking signs and drive right up to this 11thC castle complex perched high on a forested hill. Admire the far-reaching views and then (before 7.00 pm if you want dinner) savour the gloomily historic atmosphere, undiminished by large, dark rooms furnished with a mix of modern and old.

■ 99817 Eisenach **Tel** (03691) 5111 **Fax** (03691) 5111 **Meals** breakfast, lunch, dinner **Prices** rooms DDD with breakfast **Rooms** 28, all with central heating, phone, TV **Credit cards** AE, MC **Closed** never **Languages** German only

---

Lakeside hotel, Groß-Nemerow

Bornmühle

Spectacularly situated in wooded parkland by Lake Tollense. Although newly-built in local farmhouse style – long and low with steeply pitched roof – sensitive handling gives a relaxed, rustic atmosphere. Bedrooms with lake views are worth the extra tariff.

■ 17094 Groß-Nemerow, Bornmühle 35 **Tel** (039605) 361 **Fax** (039605) 360 **Meals** breakfast, lunch, dinner **Prices** rooms DD-DDD with breakfast **Rooms** 42, all with shower, central heating, phone, minibar, radio **Credit cards** AE, DC, MC, V **Closed** never **Languages** English

Eastern Germany

Town inn, Heiligenstadt

Traube

Turrets and half-timbering highlight the exterior of this turn-of-the-century hotel on the main road out of town. The Kitter family's high standards extend from the spotlessly clean bedrooms to the kitchens. 'Food as good as any in Germany' according to a satisfied American visitor.

■ 91332 Heiligenstadt/Eichsfeld, Bahnhofstr 2 **Tel** (0306) 2253 **Fax** (039605) 360 **Meals** breakfast, lunch, dinner **Prices** rooms D with breakfast; meals from DM20 **Rooms** 11, all with bath or shower, central heating, phone **Credit cards** not accepted **Closed** never **Languages** German only

---

Seaside hotel, Heringsdorf

Diana

This graceful turn-of-the-century villa has shed the drabness of its most recent past and now looks more like the elegant home of the banker Bleichroder it once was. Suites with sea views in main hotel, simpler bedrooms in annexe. Luscious breakfasts.

■ 17424 Heringsdorf, Delbrückstr 14 **Tel** (038378) 31952 **Fax** (038378) 31953 **Meals** breakfast **Prices** rooms DD-DDDD with breakfast; children under 6 free **Rooms** 10, all with bath or shower, central heating, phone, hairdrier, TV, minibar, radio **Credit cards** AE, DC, MC, V **Closed** 1- 24 Dec **Languages** English, Spanish

---

Town hotel, Heringsdorf

Residenz Neuhof

On a peninsula curiously attached to Northern Poland, this former holiday home for union members has been slickly updated to suit Western tastes. Work off the meals served in the elegant Marron d'Or restaurant by a brisk walk to the nearby sea.

■ 17424 Heringsdorf, Kanalstr 7 **Tel** (038378) 32000 **Fax** (038378) 2943 **Meals** breakfast, lunch, dinner **Prices** rooms D-DDD with breakfast; children under 12, 50% reduction; **Meals** from DM 20 **Rooms** 35, all with shower, central heating, phone, TV **Credit cards** AE, MC, V **Closed** never **Languages** German only

---

Seaside hotel, Kühlungsborn

Residenz Waldkrone

A delicate touch has been used to revamp what was recently a works holiday home. Wicker, pastel prints and soft lighting lift this friendly hotel out of the ordinary run of eastern hotels. Its position by a sandy stretch of coastline adds to the attraction.

■ 18225 Kühlungsborn, Tannenstr 4 **Tel** (038293) 596 **Fax** (038293) 6187 **Meals** breakfast, lunch, dinner **Prices** rooms DD-DDDD with breakfast; meals from DM20 **Rooms** 21, most with bath or shower, all with central heating, phone, hairdrier, TV, radio **Credit cards** AE, MC, V **Closed** never **Languages** English

Eastern Germany

Country inn, Lichtenhain

Berghof Lichtenhain

Set in a national park, this little inn has spectacular views of the rock cliffs from its pretty, rustic restaurant. The rooms are basically furnished. There is a beer garden.

■ 01855 Kirnitzschtal, PT Lichtenhain, Am Anger 3 **Tel** (035971) 6512 **Fax** (035971) 6513 **Meals** breakfast, lunch, dinner **Prices** D with breakfast **Rooms** 21 double, with shower, TV (5 with central heating and phone, others with automatic electric heaters **Credit cards** not accepted **Closed** occasionally in winter

Village hotel, Moraas

Heidehof

Two squat brick and beamed cottages with neat thatching, one a *stube*, the other a hotel, newly converted and already popular, so worth booking in advance. Tranquil position beside village pond.

■ 19230 Moraas, Hauptstr 15 **Tel** (0855) 45238 **Fax** (0855) 45238 **Meals** breakfast, lunch, dinner **Prices** rooms D-DD with breakfast; meals from DM20 **Rooms** 10, all with bath or shower, central heating, TV **Credit cards** not accepted **Closed** never **Languages** English

Lakeside hotel, Netzen

Seehof

The position's the thing here, right on a large lake where guests can fish, sail or row – they will need to do something as it's a mite isolated. Inside, greys and browns do nothing to dispel the spartan atmosphere, but it is adequately comfortable.

■ 14797 Netzen, Am See **Tel** (03382) 807 **Fax** (03382) 842 **Meals** breakfast, lunch, dinner **Prices** rooms DD; breakfast DM14, meals from DM15 **Rooms** 32, all with bath, central heating, phone, TV, minibar, radio **Credit cards** MC, V **Closed** never **Languages** English

Country hotel, Potsdam

Schloß Cecilienhof

Turn-of-century country house with famous historical associations, now combining modernized hotel with museum. Interior retains old elegance; impressive views over surrounding gardens. Decent enough food.

■ 14469 Potsdam, Neuer Garten **Tel** (0331) 37050 **Fax** (0331) 22498 **Meals** breakfast, lunch, dinner **Prices** rooms DD-DDDD with breakfast **Rooms** 42, all with central heating, phone, hairdrier, TV, minibar, radio **Credit cards** AE, DC, MC, V **Closed** never **Languages** English

Eastern Germany

Converted woodcutter's lodge, Rügen

Baumhaus

The Oberhardt's have transformed this thatched 18thC lodge on the edge of Jasmund National Park into an ideally unpretentious base from which to study local fauna and flora. A new restaurant is being added to enhance the comfortable apartments.

■ 18551 Hagen auf Rügen **Tel** (038392) 22310 **Meals** breakfast **Prices** apartments DD with breakfast **Rooms** 8, all with bath, central heating, phone, TV, minibar **Credit cards** not accepted **Closed** 15 Nov to 15 Dec **Languages** German only

---

Lake town hotel, Waren

Hotel Ingeborg

Close to the harbour and the church, this pleasant hotel has been decorated with some flair, especially in the public rooms and café, popular with the locals. The white-walled bedrooms are a decent size and well-furnished with handsome wooden furniture.

■ 17192 Waren **Tel** (03991) 61300 **Fax** (03991) 613030 **Meals** breakfast **Prices** DD with breakfast **Rooms** 10 double, 17 single, 1 suite, all with shower, central heating, phone, TV, minibar **Credit cards** AE, DC, MC, V **Closed** never **Languages** English

---

Seaside hotel, Warnemünde-Diedrichshagen

Landhaus Frommke

This hotel has that pleasantly co-ordinated look which newly built hotels acquire if well designed. Pretty breakfast room, large well-furnished bedrooms; landscaped garden and an indoor swimming-pool; sauna, solarium and fitness room.

■ 18119 Warnemunde-Diedrichshagen, Stoltoraser Weg 3 **Tel** (0381) 5191904 **Fax** (0381) 5191905 **Meals** breakfast **Prices** DD-DDD **Rooms** 7 doubles, 1 single, 1 suite, all with shower, phone, central heating, TV, minibar **Credit cards** AE, DC, MC, V **Closed** never **Languages** English, Russian

---

Town hotel, Weimar

Amalienhof

This unusual hotel in 'Goethe's city' should have a friendly atmosphere: it's part of the Association of Christian Hotels, run in a 'Christian spirit', with 'a warm welcome extended to everyone'. The 1826 building was renovated in 1992 to create a stylish, comfortable modern ambience. Close to the historic city centre and Goethe's House.

■ Amalienstrasse 2, 99423 Weimar **Tel** (03643) 5490 **Fax** (03643) 549110 **Meals** breakfast **Prices** DD **Rooms** 29 (singles and doubles), 2 suites, shower or bath; one apartment; all with phone, TV **Credit cards** AE, MC, V **Closed** Never **Languages** German, English

Baden-Württemberg

Hotels in Baden-Württemberg

From Mannheim and Heidelberg in the north, down to Weil in the south-west and Konstanz in the south-east, Baden-Württemberg has the lion's share of Germany's scenic beauties. Land of cuckoo clocks, thatched farmhouses and dense pine forests, the famous Schwarzwald stretches for 170 km; hiking and skiing are the main attractions, and there is no lack of suitable simple accommodation – much of it covered in the entries that follow. Alternatives include the quaint Linde in Münstertal, just south of Freiburg, (07636) 447, fax 1632, 16 rooms), and the gourmet 18thC Hirschen in Sulzburg (Tel (07634) 8208, fax 6717, 7 rooms). There is also the Kloster Hirsau in Calw, mid-way between Baden-Baden and Stuttgart; once part of a Benedictine monastery, it is anything but austere now, and the food is good (Tel (07051) 5621, fax 51795, 42 rooms).

In the sandy north, close to the Rhine, the city of Karlsruhe is both an administrative and industrial centre, home of the Supreme Courts, as well as an important link in Germany's road and rail services; the Schloßhotel has been renovated to a high standard (Tel (0721) 35040, fax 3504413, 97 rooms).

Stuttgart, to the west, is the birthplace of Gottlieb Daimler and Carl Benz, and high on any car enthusiast's list is a visit to the city's motor museums. Finding a small hotel of equal prestige is nigh impossible, but the Wörtz zur Weinsteige is quietly situated, with delightful garden terrace, and is family run (Tel (0711) 245396, fax 6407279, 23 rooms), while in nearby Plieningen, the Traube is a family-run country inn, renowned for good food (Tel 458920, fax 4589220, 22 rooms); an alternative is the countrified Gaststätte zum Muckenstüble, (Tel 865122, 25 rooms).

The east of the region is simpler, flatter and less fortunate in its hotels than the west. Ulm, for example, has a famous cathedral, is of great commercial importance being on the Danube, and only one small hotel that we can recommend: the Ulmer Spatz (Tel (0731) 68081, fax 6021925, 36 rooms) – peaceful, yet central, with an outside terrace, and very reasonably priced. However, once the Bodensee (Lake Constance) is reached, not only does the climate become warmer, but also the search for accommodation easier; on the island of Reichenau, for example, the Hotel Seeschau has lovely views over the lake (Tel (07534) 257, fax 7894, 23 rooms).

The old university town of Heidelberg is compelling, but over-crowded in summer; further along the Neckar valley at quieter Schönau, the Pfalzer Hof is pleasant enough (Tel (06228) 8288, 13 rooms); to the north, the Watzenhof at Hemsbach (Tel (06201) 7767, fax 73777, 13 rooms) has a lovely position in a wooded valley.

This page acts as an introduction to the features and hotels of Baden-Württemberg, and gives brief recommendations of good hotels that for one reason or another have not made a full entry. The long entries for this 'Land' – covering the hotels we are most enthusiastic about – start on the next page. But do not neglect the shorter entries starting on page 145: these are all hotels that we would happily stay at.

Baden-Württemberg

Hotel Sonne

If you were to walk along the main street of this little spa town, the Sonne – half-timbered, immaculately kept, fronted by a flowery garden-terrace – would probably draw you on looks alone. If you knew the charm of the welcome that awaited within, there would be little reason for hesitation. This is hotel-keeping of the old style: a smile here, a friendly joke there, and a host of regular clients looking very happy to be comfortably installed once again.

Most of this feeling of warm well-being – not a common feature of spa hotels – is due to the owners, the Fischer family. But it is more than just a reflection of their personalities: their hotel is run with enormous care – fresh flowers, for example, are everywhere – and housekeeping standards are as high as you could wish.

Although the furniture and decorations are not remarkable, the public rooms are bright and welcoming, and the bedrooms are comfortable without being over-quaint. Some have very smart, modern bathrooms.

Nearby Kurpark; skiing, walks in Black Forest; Blauen – views across Rhine valley (5 km).

79405 Badenweiler, Moltkestr 4
Tel (07632) 75080
Fax (07632) 750865
Location in middle of small spa town, 35 km S of Freiburg; with gardens; garages, ample car parking
Meals breakfast, lunch, dinner
Prices rooms D-DDD with breakfast; meals DM30-65
Rooms 22 twin, 14 with bath, 8 with shower; 19 single, 5 with bath, 14 with shower; all rooms have central heating, phon e; most rooms have TV
Facilities dining-room, sitting-room, *Stube*; garden terrace **Credit cards** AE, DC, MC, V **Children** tolerated
Disabled not suitable
Pets not accepted
Closed mid-Nov to mid-Feb
Languages English, French
Proprietors Fischer family

Baden-Württemberg

Hotel Ritter

Durbach is a small wine-town – little more than a village, really – ringed by steeply sloping vineyards, a little way east of the Rhine. It is not notably picturesque, and would attract few visitors were it not for this exceptionally polished hotel. Recent expansions have made the Ritter uncomfortably large to be included here, but it does retain its small-hotel feel admirably.

The original half-timbered building is 400 years old, and has been run as a hotel by the Brunner family since the turn of the century. They have given it a sense of luxury that does not seem to conflict with its essentialy rustic style. Throughout the public areas – except in the stone-walled Ritter-Keller – you are surrounded by glowing wood and harmonious, traditional fabrics. There are traditional-style bedrooms in the main house, where one guest reported uncomfortable beds, but many visitors are seduced by the style and sheer space of the recently added, boldly designed apartments, with individual sunny terraces.

Food is another highlight of the Ritter – satisfying, traditionally based but fashionably presented dishes, earning Wilhelm Brunner a Michelin star.

Nearby walking, *Langlauf*, wine-tasting; Baden-Baden (25 km).

77770 Durbach, Talstr 1
Tel (0781) 93230
Fax (0781) 9323100
Location in middle of small town; with garages and ample car parking
Meals breakfast, lunch, dinner, snacks
Prices rooms D-DDD with breakfast; meals DM40-60
Rooms 48 twin with bath; 14 single with shower; all rooms have central heating, phone; most have hairdrier, TV, minibar, radio; some have air-conditioning
Facilities dining-room, bar, cellar bar; indoor swimming-pool, sauna
Credit cards AE, DC, MC, V
Children welcome
Disabled no special facilities
Pets accepted
Closed never
Languages English, French
Proprietor Wilhelm Brunner

Baden-Württemberg

Country house hotel, Friedrichsruhe

Wald & Schloßhotel Friedrichsruhe

This handsome country house, dating from the early 18thC has not made the most intimate hotel – it is rather stiff in its elegance, as well as being larger than our ideal. But there is no denying its widely recognized attractions.

Chief among these, perhaps, is the food. Lothar Eiermann may or may not be the best chef in Germany, but he is certainly a contender, applying modern thinking to traditional dishes and producing food to delight the eye and palate as a result. It is served with appropriate care in a plush, richly draped dining-room, candle-lit at night. Elsewhere in the complex of buildings there are less formal alternatives – a terrace surrounded by lawns, and a *Jägerstube* with the usual trophies.

Bedrooms and suites, in the main house and the hunting lodge, are spacious and deeply comfortable, with calm colour schemes – some of them reminiscent of an English country house.

This is of course not a cheap hotel; but for what you get, the prices are not outrageous.

Nearby cathedral; Sindringen (10 km) – steam paradise; Langenburg (30 km) – castle, motor museum

74639 Friedrichsruhe
Tel (07941) 60870
Fax (07941) 61468
Location in countryside NE of junction of A6 and A81, 50km N of Stuttgart; in large grounds with ample car parking
Meals breakfast, lunch, dinner, snacks
Prices rooms DD-DDDD with breakfast; meals DM125-195
Rooms 23 double; 6 single; 16 suites; all with bath or shower; all rooms have central heating, phone
Facilities dining-room, *Jägerstube*, conservatory, bar; indoor and outdoor swimming-pools, tennis court, 18-hole g olf course
Credit cards AE, DC, MC, V
Children welcome
Disabled lift/elevator; some adapted rooms
Pets accepted **Closed** never
Languages English, French
Manager Lothar Eiermann

Baden-Württemberg

Restaurant with rooms, Glottertal

Gasthaus zum Adler

The Glottertal is a lush, peaceful valley north-east of Freiburg, set in the hills of the southern Black Forest, with a number of small hotels and guest-houses dotted along its length.

What distinguishes this roadside guest-house is its restaurant. The menu is out of the ordinary, offering, for example, salad of dandelion leaves and grilled langoustine, home-produced black puddings, and asparagus done in several different ways. There is even a menu for child-gourmets.

The main restaurant is decorated in the local traditional style, but has not been done to death with unnecessary fancy trimmings. Walls have been kept white under a wood-panelled ceiling and large windows give a feeling of light. There is also another dining-room, cosy, colourful and less formal than the restaurant, with a choice of lighter dishes.

The Adler has been in private ownership throughout its 150-year history, and Frau Langenbacher takes pride in its distinctive provincial atmosphere. The renovated bedrooms are colourfully furnished, with individual touches giving each room some personality.

Nearby walking, skiing; various sights in Freiburg (15 km).

79286 Glottertal, Talstr 11
Tel (07684) 1081
Fax (07684) 1083
Location on valley road between Denzlingen and St Peter, NE of Freiburg; with garden and car parking
Meals breakfast, lunch, dinner, snacks
Prices rooms D-DD with breakfast; lunch DM15-38, dinner DM29-68
Rooms 10 double, 3 with bath, 6 with shower, one with basin; 3 single, one with shower, 2 with basin; 1 apartment; all rooms have central heating, phone, TV, minibar **Facilities** dining-room, conference room; terrace **Credit cards** DC, MC, V **Children** very welcome **Disabled** access difficult **Pets** accepted (DM10) **Closed** restaurant only, Tue **Languages** English, French **Proprietor** Stephanie Langenbacher

Baden-Württemberg

Stadtschänke

We would have liked to fill this book with places like the Stadtschänke – or 'Stadtschänke, historischer Gasthof Johannespfründe', to use its formal name. It is a tall half-timbered building, dating from 1434, overlooking the market-place of a small town in the heart of the wine-growing area of Württemberg. Winding cobbled streets surround the hotel.

There is still a medieval atmosphere about the small timbered rooms, decorated with tasteful simplicity. Downstairs, the furniture is rustic but the table linen crisp and pink. The few bedrooms are prettily furnished, with dried flowers and candlesticks giving a cosy feel, and firm modern beds ensuring a good night's sleep.

The smiling Sybille Könneke gave up her hairdressing business to help her husband, Hans, take over the hotel. He is a dedicated chef, and his cooking, influenced by his years spent in Sweden, has a bias towards fresh fish and local ingredients. Wine, too, plays an important role, with tastings encouraged. Helpful advice is gladly given to guests who wish to increase their knowledge of the area.

Nearby Ludwigsburg (10 km); Hessigheim rocks (10 km).

71723 Grossbottwar,
Hauptstr 36
Tel (07148) 8024
Location in market square, opposite town hall; take Mundelsheim exit from A81 N of Stuttgart; car parking in square
Meals breakfast, lunch, dinner
Prices rooms D-DD with breakfast; meals DM22.50-36.50

Rooms 3 twin, 2 single, all with shower; all rooms have central heating, TV; some rooms have telephone
Facilities dining-room, bar, terrace
Credit cards AE, DC, MC, V
Children welcome **Disabled** not suitable **Pets** accepted
Closed first week in Sep
Languages English, French, Swedish **Proprietors** Hans and Sybille Könneke

Baden-Württemberg

Lakeside villa, Hagnau am Bodendsee

Erbguth's Villa am See

Christine and Holgen Ergbuth are a talented couple who, with their daughter Sandra, have been hoteliers by Lake Constance for some time. Their first establishment, Ergbuth's Landhaus, was sold in 1995, but they kept the villa in the grounds, which used to be an annexe, although 'annexe' does not do it justice.

It is a delightful place, close to the shores of the lake, in grounds which run right down to the shore. In summer, a big attraction is breakfast in the garden followed by a swim. The building is essentially a refined, heavily gabled suburban villa, pristinely maintained; but the interior really marks it out. The style is an interesting mixture of the masculine and feminine, with pastel mauves, oranges and greens cropping up in rectangular patterns on carpets and bedspreads. The effect is clean and modern, quite sparse, but relieved by some eye-catching touches - for instance, an exotic plant on an unusual, bulky stand in a bathroom. Verandas are equipped with outdoor furniture and offer not-to-be forgotten views across the lake and to the Alps.

With just six bedrooms, you are assured a personal, but professional reception from the family.

Nearby skiing, walking, watersports.

88709 Hagnau am Bodensee,
Tel (07532) 43130
Fax (07532) 6997
Location in centre of town on edge of Lake Constance; with gardens and car parking
Meals breakfast, snacks
Prices rooms D-DDDD with breakfast; children under 4 free
Rooms 6 double; all rooms have central heating, phone, hairdrier, TV, minibar, radio
Facilities breakfast room; swimming in lake
Credit cards AE, DC, MC, V
Children welcome
Disabled easy access
Pets accepted
Closed Jan, Mar
Languages English, French
Proprietor Holger Erbguth

Baden-Württemberg

Village hotel, Häusern

Hotel Adler

Polished to its current state over almost a century and a half in the hands of the Zumkeller family, the Adler is now a shining example of a German speciality: the expanded and sophisticated country inn with its rustic origins still much in evidence despite the introduction of elegant furnishings, the addition of modern bedrooms and the development of ever more ambitious cooking.

There is mellow wooden panelling on the walls and ceiling in the dining-rooms, bar and sitting-rooms, and richly coloured Persian-style rugs on the tiled floors. The furniture is not orchestrated around any particular theme – it is a mixture of the comfortably traditional and the delicately antique; pictures, ornaments and flowers are distributed with care. The bedrooms, sadly, are relatively bland; but there is some compensation in their spaciousness.

The adventurous modern cooking of young Winfried Zumkeller already has a high reputation – though not all observers are quite as enthusiastic as Michelin, which awards a star. Simpler country food is served in the striking Chämi-Hüsle, centred on an island fireplace.

Nearby walking, skiing; St Blasien (5 km) monastery.

79838 Häusern, Fridolin Str 15
Tel (07672) 4170
Fax (07672) 417150
Location in village 58 km SE of Freiburg, just off B 500; garden, ample car parking
Meals breakfast, lunch, dinner
Prices rooms D-DD with breakfast; meals DM50-120
Rooms 22 double, 12 with bath, 10 with shower; 10 single 4 with bath, 6 with shower; 12 suites; all have central heating, phone, TV, minibar, radio; most have balcony **Facilities** sitting-room, dining-room, playroom; indoor pool, tennis, sauna **Credit cards** AE, DC, MC, V **Children** very welcome **Disabled** no special facilities **Pets** accepted **Closed** mid Nov to mid-Dec; restaurant only, Mon and Tue **Languages** English, French **Proprietors** Zumkeller family

Baden-Württemberg

Town hotel, Heidelberg

Hirschgasse

If Mark Twain could look out today from the quaint little windows of the Hirschgasse, where he once stayed, across the gliding river Neckar, he would still be able to recognize the view of old Heidelberg. Whether he would recognize his room is quite another matter: the hotel was totally refurbished in 1989 to create a series of delectable suites, all designed by Laura Ashley but each entirely individual. The Chinoiserie Suite has red lacquered walls, bamboo tables and Chinese lamps; the Rose Suite is decorated with pink frills, cherubs and Country Rose fabrics; the Blueberry Suite is richly club-like – and so on.

Herr Kraft supervised the renovations closely, ensuring that modern trappings were concealed within antique exteriors – no plastic-and-chrome televisions marring the elegance. This care carries through to the comforts that make a traveller feel pampered: in the bathrooms, hot water thunders from the taps, towels are thick and soft, soaps outsize.

The intimate little restaurant is called 'Le Gourmet', which sums it up. It is the best in town, and thus very popular; hotel guests have a degree of priority, but booking is still essential.
Nearby castle, Philosophers' Walk, museum.

69120 Heidelberg 1,
Hirschgasse 3
Tel (06221) 4540
Fax (06221) 454111
Location opposite old part of town, next to bridge, opposite castle; with car parking
Meals breakfast, dinner, snacks
Prices rooms DDD-DDDD; breakfast DM25; meals DM59-120

Rooms 20 suites, all with whirlpool bath; all rooms have central heating, telephone, hairdrier, TV, minibar, radio
Facilities dining-room
Credit cards AE, DC, MC, V
Children welcome **Disabled** no special facilities **Pets** not accepted **Closed** never
Languages English, French, Italian
Proprietor Ernest Kraft

Baden-Württemberg

Sassenhof

Hinterzarten is a pleasantly modest resort, without the bulk tourism and crowds of nearby Titisee. It has a novel feature for a Black Forest resort – a huge village green, English-style. And among the hotels scattered around the green is this welcoming little place – an undistinguished building of no particular style, but exceptionally welcoming within.

Beautifully furnished in an elegantly old-fashioned style – a long way from Black Forest rustic norms – and kept spotlessly clean by the ever-present Frau Pfeiffer, the Sassenhof is one of those rare hotels that manages to feel like a home. Bedrooms vary widely in size – some are apartment-like, others (particularly those up in the roof space) on the small side.

There is no restaurant, but the Sassenhof's situation in the hub of the village means you are never far from food – and such is the informality of the place that guests seem free to take snacks up to their room when hunger strikes. Breakfasts are a delight, served with great charm (and some classical music). Anything less than a hearty appetite causes great concern.

Nearby skiing, walking; Schauinsel (20km) – cable-car; Titisee (5 km) – lake.

79856 Hinterzarten, Adlerweg 17
Tel (07652) 1515
Fax (07652) 484
Location in middle of resort village; with garden and ample car parking
Meals breakfast
Prices rooms D-DD with breakfast
Rooms 5 double, 4 with bath, one with shower; 11 single with bath; 6 suites with shower; 4 holiday apartments; all rooms have central heating, phone, hairdrier, TV **Facilities** breakfast room, sitting-room, stube, indoor swimming-pool, sauna
Credit cards not accepted
Children welcome **Disabled** not suitable **Pets** accepted (DM10-15 per night depending on size) **Closed** mid-Nov to mid-Dec
Languages English, Spanish, French **Proprietors** Irmgard and Paul Pfeiffer

Baden-Württemberg

Country hotel, Kaisersbach

Schassberger's Ebnisee

This thriving country hotel (formerly known as Landhaus Hirsch) is a complex of chalet-style buildings in a woodland setting. It is not the last word in style or intimacy, but for many contented visitors presents a satisfying combination of attractive features, including a wide range of diversions – many deriving from its location close to the Ebnisee.

Interior designers should stay well away (or formulate proposals and present them for the Schassbergers' consideration). The sitting-room, in particular, is a triumph of function over fashion, supremely comfortable, but visually dreary. The bedrooms have rather more style, while losing nothing in comfort. Apart from the main dining-room, there is also a choice of two styles of eating: creative-classic cooking in the Hirschstube, Swabian specialities in the Flößerstube.

There is plenty to do around here, and the Schassbergers make sure that you know it: you are given a veritable guidebook explaining not only where to find table-tennis balls but also the routes of countless local walks and less-local drives.

Nearby *Langlauf*, hiking, fishing, boating, cycling; Welzheim (5 km) – animal park.

73667 Kaisersbach, am Ebnisee
Tel (07184) 2920
Fax (07184) 292204
Location in wooded countryside by lake, 40 km NE of Stuttgart; with garden, garages, ample car parking
Meals breakfast, lunch, dinner, snacks
Prices rooms DD-DDDD with breakfast; meals DM33-95
Rooms 29 double, 14 with bath, 15 with shower; 17 single with shower; 3 family rooms; all rooms have central heating, phone, hairdrier, TV, minibar, radio **Facilities** bar, sitting-room; terrace, indoor pool, tennis, squash, sauna
Credit cards AE, MC, V
Children very welcome
Disabled access easy; wheelchair; ground-floor rooms
Pets in bedrooms only **Closed** never **Languages** English, French, Italian **Proprietor** Iris & Ernst-Ulrich Schassberger

Baden-Württemberg

Seehotel Siber

The problem in describing this captivating place, open for business only since 1984, lies in knowing where to start. For many visitors, priority will go to Bertold Siber's *haute cuisine*, which is universally admired by the gourmet guides and not wildly expensive by gastronomic standards (especially at lunchtime, when there is a bargain menu).

But Herr Siber's house is also something of a gem – a late-19thC villa in a privileged position overlooking Lake Constance, with an elevated dining-terrace from which the lake view is best appreciated. The casino is next door, the middle of Konstanz a short walk.

The interior has been smartly renovated, with great attention to detail; ornamental display cabinets, for example, are integrated with the dark wooden panelling on the dining-room walls. The bedrooms are understated (or perhaps a trifle bland, to take a more critical view) but harmonious and polished, the best notably spacious with lake views.

Service is entirely appropriate to the ambience: attentive, but effortless.

Nearby surfing, swimming, sailing, diving.

78464 Konstanz, Seestr 25
Tel (07531) 63044
Fax (07531) 64813
Location on promenade in middle of resort, close to casino; with gardens and ample car parking
Meals breakfast, lunch, dinner, snacks
Prices rooms DDDD; breakfast DM35; meals DM28-170
Rooms 11 double, 10 with bath, one with shower; all rooms have central heating, air-conditioning, phone, TV, radio, mini bar, hairdrier, safe
Facilities restaurant, bar; lakeside terrace, roof terrace
Credit cards AE, DC, MC, V
Children tolerated
Disabled no special facilities
Pets small dogs accepted
Closed 2 weeks Feb
Languages English, French, Spanish, Swedish, Italian
Proprietor Bertold Siber

Baden-Württemberg

Town inn, Meersburg

Zum Bären

Hotel-keeping is in Michael Gilowsky's blood: the Hotel-Gasthof zum Bären has been in his family for five generations. But the inn's history goes back much further: although the date 1605 is written over the Renaissance entrance, the Bären was built in about 1250, and part of the ground floor and one of the two cellars are original; the archives even contain a bill dated 1456.

The inn is just what you would hope to find in a charming old lakeside town like Meersburg. Its location could not be bettered – right on the delightful market place. Outside flowers and climbing plants (a local speciality) all but cover the carved and painted decoration, with stepped gables towering above. Inside, the two dining-rooms are cosily rustic, with only a handful of tables in each, encouraging guests to share. Upstairs, there may be surprises: some of the rooms are rather grand, with ornately worked ceilings and colourful painted furniture, some plainer, though still carefully furnished. Michael Gilowsky (who has cooked abroad) prepares a changing menu of simple but satisfying dishes, including a range of fixed-price meals.

Nearby castle, Steigstraße, market-place; sailing on Lake Constance, walking.

88709 Meersburg, Marktplatz 11
Tel (07532) 43220
Fax (07532) 432244
Location by historic market-place in old part of lakeside town; with garaging for all cars (DM6.50)
Meals breakfast, lunch, dinner
Prices rooms D-DD with breakfast; meals DM18.50-35, children's meals DM12

Rooms 16 double, 3 single, 17 with shower, 2 with bath ; all rooms have central heating, phone, TV **Facilities** 2 dining-rooms **Credit cards** not accepted **Children** welcome **Disabled** access difficult **Pets** accepted **Closed** mid-Nov to mid-Mar; restaurant only, Mon, alsoTue in spring **Languages** English, some French **Proprietor** Michael Gilowsky

Baden-Württemberg

Country hotel, Münstertal

Spielweg

The Spielweg Romantik Hotel is at its core a warm and welcoming old *gasthof* which has been in the same family for five generations. Over the years, further bedrooms have been added in three adjacent buildings. The oldest of these, the Stammhaus, has fairly small but pretty and inexpensive bedrooms, while there are more contemporary and spacious rooms and suites in the Haus am Bach and Haus Sonnhalde, all with balcony. There are also well-stocked indoor and outdoor play areas for children, as well as an indoor and outdoor swimming-pool, and sauna and solarium.

Situated amongst rolling meadows and surrounded by wooded hills, Spielweg's main building is a two storey white-painted black-shuttered farmhouse which in summer is embellished by a profusion of flowers and large white parasols shading tables and chairs. Inside, beyond the lobby with its open fire, the cosy low-ceilinged dining-rooms are charmingly traditional, with panelled walls hung with pretty ceramics and pictures, and lit by lamps hanging low over linen-draped tables. Guests report that the kindly Fuchs family ensure an 'easy-going and relaxing atmosphere, ideas for eating well or just resting'.

Nearby walking; cycling; Freigburg (27 km).

79244 Münstertal,
Spielweg 61
Tel (07636) 7090
Fax (07636) 70966
Location in upper Münstertal, off A5 motorway, exit Bad Krozingen; ample parking
Meals breakfast, lunch, dinner
Prices rooms DD-DDDD with breakfast; dinner from DM80
Rooms 30 double, 9 single, 5 suites, all with bath; all rooms have central heating, phone, TV, radio, hairdrier
Facilities sitting-room, dining-rooms, playroom, meeting room; 2 swimming pools, sauna **Credit cards** AE, DC, MC, V **Children** welcome
Disabled ramps, lift **Pets** accepted (except in Haus Sonnhalde) **Closed** never
Languages English, French
Proprietor Hansjörg Fuchs

Baden-Württemberg

Converted castle, Niederstotzingen

Schloßhotel Oberstotzingen

This smartly renovated 700-year-old Wasserschloß – a manor-house rather than a fortress, in flat countryside near the marsh-flanked Danube – is clearly aiming at the business market, with its five high-tech conference rooms. But it also has attractions for the individual visitor.

Chief among them is the rich and tasteful furnishings of the bedrooms, of which there are a mere 17 (not many by the standards of thriving German hotels). The furniture is uniform – modern with traditional overtones – but the rooms are given individuality by careful choice of their bold, warm colour schemes. They vary in shape as well as size – some of the most attractive are in the little round tower.

The hotel's stylish dining-room – with candles and spotlights, traditional fabrics and rugs beneath a smoothly vaulted ceiling – operates under the name of Restaurant Vogelherd. Cooking is creative and satisfying, with a regional element, the choice including a daily-changing fixed-price menu. There is an unusually wide selection of wines by the glass.

Nearby golf, horse-riding, caves (locally and in Lone valley); Dilingen (20 km) – gilded hall.

89166 Niederstotzingen, Stettener Str 35-37
Tel (07325) 1030
Fax (07325) 10370
Location in countryside 120 km E of Stuttgart; in grounds with ample car parking
Meals breakfast, lunch, dinner
Prices rooms DDD with breakfast; children in parents' room free; meals DM50-90
Rooms 11 double, 2 with bath, 7 with shower; 4 single, one with bath, 3 with shower; 2 family rooms; all rooms have central heating, phone, hairdrier, TV, minibar, radio
Facilities dining-room, drawing-room, banqueting room, sun room; tennis, sauna
Credit cards AE, DC, MC, V
Children welcome **Disabled** no special facilities **Pets** in bedrooms only (damage deposit DM50) **Closed** never
Languages English, French
Manager Klaus Kranz

Baden-Württemberg

Country villa, Pfinztal-Söllingen

Villa Hammerschmiede

New to our guide, the Villa Hammerschmiede is a luxurious enclave at the northern edge of the Black Forest. The villa itself, a solid late-19thC mansion of red brick striped in stone, is no beauty, but it has been transformed into a sophisticated hotel with consummate skill (the work of Baden-Baden architect Elmar Scherzinger). The hotel is surrounded by its own large park, pleasant for strolls before dinner.

The Relais & Château hotel is an efficient family-run operation involving Norbert Schwalbe, his wife Barbara and his daughter and son-in-law. Recent guests have praised the smooth, helpful service, the pampering and 'beautifully lit' indoor pool, whirlpool and sauna complex, and the restaurant, for which chef Markus Nagy has been a Michelin star. 'You can regard us first and foremost as a restaurant with comfortable bedrooms to which to retire, or as a hotel which prides itself on its food,' say the owners. The main restaurant, is set in a large conservatory with a terrace for warm weather; or you can eat in the wine cellar from the same menu. Bedrooms are spacious, with luxurious marble bathrooms, stylishly furnished with modern Italian pieces. **Nearby** Black Forest; Karlsruhe (13 km).

76327 Pfinztal-Söllingen, Hauptstrasse 162
Tel (07240) 6010
Fax (0720) 60160
Location on the edge of village in own grounds, 9 miles (13 km) E of Karlsruhe; ample parking
Meals breakfast, lunch, dinner
Prices rooms DD-DDDD; breakfast DM23; dinner from D80

Rooms 24 double, 1 single, 1 suite, all with bath; all rooms have central heating, phone, TV, radio, minibar, hairdrier **Facilities** sitting-room ,bar, library, dining-room, terrace, pool, sauna, solarium, tennis court **Credit cards** AE, DC, MC, V **Children** welcome **Disabled** lift **Pets** accepted (DM12 per night) **Languages** English, French **Proprietors** Norbert Schwalbe family

Baden-Württemberg

Town hotel, Rottweil

Haus zum Sternen

In the middle of one of Germany's oldest and prettiest fortified towns, this hotel is one of Rottweil's oldest buildings, from the outside still looking today much as it must have done when it was built in the late 14th century. The place practically creaks with history, from the sublime roofing (a copybook example of Gothic carpentry) to the remarkable tracery above the Renaissance door and colourful 16thC paintings on the beams.

Although the hotel is fully equipped with every modern comfort, nothing mars the age-old feel of the place. Low beamed ceilings, plain fitted carpets and white walls are the tasteful backdrop to antique beds, tables and wardrobes – some elegant and polished, some handsomely rustic, some vividly painted; pretty silks and fabrics hang at the windows.

Dorothy Ehrenberger takes pride in being able to offer individual attention to each guest; she is ably assisted by Manfred Lang, her manager and chef, serving traditional Swabian food in the wine-bar and fashionably lighter meals in the restaurant. Together they run a tranquil hotel, a distinct cut above average.
Nearby Kapellenkirche (Gothic tower, church of the Holy Cross); Dreifaltigkeitsberg (20 km).

78628 Rottweil, Haupstr 60
Tel (0741) 53300
Fax (0741) 533030
Location in middle of ancient town, 100 km S of Stuttgart; with garages
Meals breakfast, lunch, dinner
Prices rooms D-DDD with breakfast; meals DM15-38
Rooms 6 twin, all with bath; 5 single with shower; one family room with bath; all rooms have central heating, telephone, hairdrier, TV, radio
Facilities dining-room, cellar bar; garden terrace
Credit cards AE, MC, V
Children welcome
Disabled not suitable
Pets accepted
Closed never
Languages English, French
Manager Julia Ehrenberger

Baden-Württemberg

Village hotel, Schönwald

Hotel Dorer

Although the ambition of many small hotels in Germany is to get bigger, nothing could be further from the minds of the charming Scherer family, owners of this beautiful little establishment. As the Dorer lies in the heart of the Black Forest, it is a pleasant surprise to discover that the interior is not filled with the wood carvings and cuckoo clocks that typify this area. Instead there are interesting antiques and elegant, understated furnishings set against plain panelling. Visitors are usually fascinated by the extraordinary old gramophone on the first floor; you may well pass it on your way to one of the supremely comfortable bedrooms. Their decoration, though rooted in tradition, is uncluttered, and careful consideration has been given to space and light. Most rooms give out on to either a balcony or shared terrace, from where you can enjoy the fabulous surroundings.

Diners will find the food interesting and well cooked by the master of the house, Herr Sherer, who is as keen to get away from the traditional menu of this region as from the typical decor. A recent visitor praises the comfort and friendly atmosphere here.
Nearby skiing, cycling; Furtwangen (10 km) – historical clock museum; Triberg (5 km) – waterfalls.

78137 Schönwald, Franz-Schubertstr 20
Tel (07722) 95050
Fax (07722) 950530
Location near heart of village, 56 km NE of Freiburg; garden, garages and ample car parking
Meals breakfast, lunch, dinner, snacks
Prices rooms D-DD; lunch and dinner DM30-60
Rooms 10 double, 3 with bath, 7 with shower; 5 single, 2 with bath, 3 with shower; 4 suites, all have radio, central heating, phone, cable TV
Facilities dining-room, sitting-room, solarium, beauty salon, indoor pool; garden, tennis court **Credit cards** AE, DC, MC, V **Children** welcome
Disabled not suitable **Pets** in bedrooms only (DM10/ night) **Closed** never
Languages English, French, Italian **Proprietors** Scherer and Cerasola family

Baden-Württemberg

Hotel zum Ochsen

This well planned hotel – mainly modern, although its origins go back to the end of the 18th century – is set in beautiful, open countryside in the heart of the Black Forest. Herr Martin, the smiling, bearded owner, has succeeded in creating a wonderful feeling of spaciousness, even in the more traditional parts of the hotel. The large windows help – along with the glass-roofed sitting-room and the glass-walled indoor pool, surrounded by greenery. And greenery, above all else, is what you are here for. The hotel's grounds extend into meadows and forest, making the scenery and walks of the Black Forest seem conveniently close at hand. Mountain bikes are available too.

Herr Martin's restaurant, much frequented by the locals, has a good reputation. The decoration is very traditional, with much use of wood. Bedrooms are comfortable but unremarkable in style; some are exceptionally spacious, with apartment-style sitting areas.

This is a very good alternative to some of the busier roadside or spa-town hotels of the region.

Nearby skiing, golf, walking; Furtwangen (10 km) – historical clock museum; waterfalls at Triberg (7 km).

78141 Schönwald, Ludwig-Uhland-Str 18
Tel (07722) 1045
Fax (07722) 3018
Location in meadows outside village; within grounds, with garages, ample car parking
Meals breakfast, lunch, dinner, snacks
Prices rooms D-DDD with breakfast (discounts for children); meals from DM33
Rooms 28 double, one single, 4 family rooms, all with bath; all rooms have central heating, phone, hairdrier, TV, mini bar
Facilities dining-room, sitting-room, conservatory, indoor pool, solarium; terraces, tennis, fishing
Credit cards AE, DC, MC, V
Children very welcome
Disabled not suitable
Pets dogs in bedrooms only (DM15) **Closed** never
Languages English, French
Proprietor Horst A Martin

Baden-Württemberg

Ochsen Post

From the outside, this is a village inn in the classic mould – red and green shutters at the windows, flowers billowing beneath and a half-timbered façade in keeping with its rural surroundings. The interior of the Ochsen Post is essentially as traditional as its exterior, with plenty of old wood – some painted, some polished – in the public rooms. But it is that little bit smarter than you expect, with the hand of the interior designer in evidence here and there.

The explanation is that this is not simply an inn but a Michelin-starred restaurant noted for its *nouvelle*-but-satisfying, regionally based cuisine (for example, ragout of fresh morels, fillet with noodles in a vodka and pepper sauce). A stylish, crisply furnished conservatory accommodates the many diners it attracts. Upstairs, the interior designer has been confined more or less to the opulent bathrooms; the bedrooms have plain walls (some timbered) and floors, and are furnished with a mixture of antiques and solid reproductions.

Although set in lush meadowland, the village has hills nearby, and a Gothic church containing art treasures.

Nearby Gothic church; Pforzheim (15 km); Black Forest.

75333 Tiefenbronn, Franz-Josef-Gall-Str 13
Tel (07234) 8030
Fax (07234) 5554
Location in middle of village, 16 km SE of Pforzheim; with ample car parking
Meals breakfast, lunch, dinner
Prices rooms D-DD with breakfast; meals DM38-47
Rooms 14 double, 7 with bath, 7 with shower; 5 singles with shower; all rooms have central heating, phone, minibar, radi o; most rooms have TV
Facilities dining-room, conservatory
Credit cards AE, D, MC, V
Children welcome
Disabled no special facilities
Pets accepted (DM10 per night)
Closed restaurant only, Mon, Sun
Languages English
Proprietor Regine Weis

Baden-Württemberg

Village inn, Überlingen-Andelshofen

Johanniter Kreuz

Here is a prime example of a family enterprise which has expanded and matured over the years without losing touch with its origins. It was first opened as the village guest-house of Andelshofen by the grandfather of the current proprietor, Egon Liebich, who took over from his father in 1976. Now, the son of the family is studying hotel catering, while the daughter Sabine looks after reception.

Despite expansion to add bedrooms – most recently in the separate, elegantly furnished Haus Luisenhöhe, opened in 1991 – the place remains intimate in scale and atmosphere. It is essentially a two-storey black-and-white timbered building, but some of the most attractive rooms (for those who don't mind sloping ceilings) have been accommodated in the roof-space. Furnishings are rustic, decorations plain, with a little bit of style in evidence. Downstairs, beams and white walls again set the tone, with crisply laid tables adding a touch of elegance. There is an open fire for winter, and French windows looking on to the garden – in fine weather you would eat on the sunny terrace. Regionally based food, with fish specialities.

Nearby water sports, golf, riding, tennis, Minster, Moat Walk.

88662 Überlingen-Andelshofen, Johanniterweg 11
Tel (07551) 61091
Fax (07551) 67336
Location in rural suburb to N of town, 3 km from Lake Constance; gardens, ample car parking
Meals breakfast, lunch, dinner
Prices rooms D-DDD with breakfast; meals DM25-60
Rooms 20 double with bath; 5 single with shower; one family room with shower; all have central heating, phone, TV
Facilities dining-room, sitting-room, bar, playroom; garden terrace
Credit cards AE, DC, MC, V
Children welcome **Disabled** access easy **Pets** accepted by arrangement **Closed** never
Languages English
Proprietors Egon and Jutta Liebich

Baden-Württemberg

Schweizer Stuben

'A culinary village nestled in the beautiful countryside of the River Main valley, surrounded by meadows and cornfields,' says the brochure. It is a fair summary of a rather unusual establishment which has grown from a single chalet-style hotel-and-restaurant building in 1971 to half a dozen buildings spread around an informal park, with several tennis courts in the middle.

Diners are spoilt for choice: this is perhaps the only hotel in Germany (certainly the only one in this book) with three restaurants that individually merit plaudits from the gourmet guides. Ambitious French cuisine, widely recognized as among the best in Germany, is served in the original, warmly panelled Schweizer Stuben; Swiss specialities can be tried in the cosily rustic Schober; and there are Italian delicacies to be savoured in Taverna la Vigna.

There is an equally wide choice of rooms, suites and apartments in the original hotel, in another chalet known as Villa Schweizer Stuben and in two long, low chains of buildings known as the Landhaus. All are impressively tasteful and comfortable, many with rustic touches complementing the smart furnishings.
Nearby cathedral, ruined castle

97877 Wertheim-Bettingen, Geiselbrunnweg 11
Tel (09342) 3070 **Fax** 307155
Location in fields close to river Main, 5km NE of Wertheim, off A3 30km W of Würzburg; car parking
Meals breakfast, lunch, dinner, snacks
Prices rooms DDD-DDDD with breakfast; meals DM60-200
Rooms 33 double, all with bath; all rooms have central heating, phone, TV, radio, minibar, hairdrier **Facilities** 3 dining-rooms; indoor and outdoor tennis, pitch-and-putt, saunas with solarium, steam bath, outdoor heated pool, bicycles **Credit cards** AE, DC, MC, V **Children** welcome **Disabled** some ground-floor rooms
Pets accepted by arrangement **Closed** never
Languages English, French
Proprietor Adalbert Schmitt

Baden-Württemberg

Town hotel, Albstadt-Ebingen

Hotel Linde

Kurt Hettler's unfailing eye for detail extends throughout his neat hotel – half-timbered outside, panelled and polished inside. Some opulent bedrooms. The kitchens specialize in lobster and attract high praise.

■ 72458 Albstadt 1, Untere Vorstadt 1 **Tel** (07431) 53061 **Fax** (07431) 53322 **Meals** breakfast, lunch, dinner **Prices** rooms D-DD with breakfast; meals DM22-98 **Rooms** 23, all with bath or shower, central heating, phone, hairdrier, TV, minibar **Credit cards** V **Closed** Christmas to Jan; 3 weeks Jul/Aug; restaurant only Sat and Sun **Languages** English, French

Town hotel, Asperg

Adler

An old half-timbered building with a glossy modern extension, the whole interior cleverly joined to make a smart hotel, yet still retaining family-run atmosphere. Indoor pool, sauna and conference rooms ensure a nucleus of business guests.

■ 71679 Asperg, Stuttgarter Str 2 **Tel** (07141) 26600 **Fax** ((07141) 266060 **Meals** breakfast, lunch, dinner **Prices** rooms DD-DDD with breakfast; meals DM35-90 **Rooms** 65, all with bath or shower, central heating, phone, hairdrier, TV, minibar, radio **Credit cards** AE, DC, MC, V **Closed** never **Languages** English, French

Town hotel, Asperg

Landgasthof Lamm

The industrial-style conservatory on the side of this modest hotel has done nothing for its appearance, but it does allow the cheerful Herbert Wiessert to accommodate an increasing flow of diners. There are stone-and-wood *Stuben* for traditionalists.

■ 7144 Asperg, Lammstr 1 **Tel** (07141) 62006 **Fax** (07141) 660162 **Meals** breakfast, lunch, dinner, snacks **Prices** rooms D-DD; meals from DM35 **Rooms** 18, all with bath or shower, central heating, phone, TV, radio, hairdrier **Credit cards** AE, DC, MC, V **Closed** Mon; restaurant only 3 weeks Jul **Languages** English, some French

Manor house hotel, Bad Rappenau

Schloß Heinsheim

Elegantly furnished manor house with large grounds, and the reception and restaurant housed in converted stable yard. Conference facilities create a business atmosphere on weekdays.

■ 74906 Bad Rappenau, Gundelsheimer Str 36 **Tel** (07264) 1045 **Fax** (07264) 4208 **Meals** breakfast, lunch, dinner, snacks **Prices** rooms DD-DDDD with breakfast **Rooms** 40, all with bath or shower, central heating, phone, TV, minibar, radio **Credit cards** AE, DC, MC, V **Closed** 22 Dec to 1 Feb **Languages** English, French

Baden-Württemberg

Spa hotel, Bad Überkingen

Bad-Hotel

This 400-year-old hotel is far removed from the spa-hotel norm – steep-roofed and half-timbered outside, suavely done out in an austere modern style inside (with the exception of the unconvincingly rustic *Jagdstube*). Free tennis and spa pool.

■ 73334 Bad Überkingen, Badstr 12 **Tel** (07331) 3020 **Fax** (07331) 30220 **Meals** breakfast, lunch, dinner **Prices** rooms DD-DDD with breakfast; meals DM30-45 **Rooms** 20, all with central heating, phone, hairdrier, TV, minibar, radio **Credit cards** AE, DC, MC, V **Closed** one week end Dec ; 6 weeks mid-Jan to end Feb **Languages** English

---

Suburban hotel, Baden-Baden

Bocksbeutel

A smart modern hotel among vineyards and orchards on the southern outskirts of Baden-Baden. The dining rooms are elegant, with handsome panelling, and Reiner Springmann's cooking is ambitious. His wife, Christa, is the driving force.

■ 76534 Baden-Baden 11, Umweger Str 103 **Tel** (07223) 58031 **Fax** (07223) 60808 **Meals** breakfast, lunch, dinner **Prices** rooms D-DD with breakfast; meals from DM40 **Rooms** 10, all with bath or shower, central heating, phone, radio; some have TV **Credit cards** AE, DC, MC, V **Closed** Mon **Languages** English, French

---

Country guest-house, Baden-Baden-Neuweier

Gasthaus zum Lamm

A recent visitor and her family was well satisfied with this welcoming guest-house. Bedrooms are simply decorated, with painted headboards. You can choose to eat in the dining-room amid antique farm implements, or outside on the leafy terrace.

■ 76534 Baden-Baden, Mauerbergstr 34 **Tel** (07223) 57038 **Fax** (07223) 52612 **Meals** breakfast, lunch, dinner **Prices** rooms D-DD with breakfast; meals from DM22 **Rooms** 12, all with bath or shower, central heating, phone, radio **Credit cards** AE, DC, MC, V **Closed** Jan to mid-Feb; restaurant only, Wed & Thu **Languages** English, French

---

Town villa, Badenweiler

Villa Hedwig

Pristine "Arts & Crafts" *hotel garni* on no-through road overlooking the Kurpark. The Dietz family pride themselves on their cuisine, served to the sounds of tasteful classical music. No traffic is allowed in Badenweiler between the hours of 1.30 and 2.30 pm.

■ 79410 Badenweiler, Römerstr 10 **Tel** (07632) 220 **Fax** (07632) 820031 **Meals** breakfast, dinner, snacks **Prices** rooms DD-DDD with breakfast; meals DM25-45 **Rooms** 15, all with shower, central heating, phone, satellite TV, radio **Credit cards** MC **Closed** 1-25 Dec, first 3 weeks Jan; restaurant only, Thu **Languages** English, French

Baden-Württemberg

Country hotel, Baiersbronn-Mittteltal

Lamm

The Klumps have done more than their share to support the local timber industry, incorporating massive beams and arches into their highly traditional hotel at every opportunity. Bedrooms have less character, but beautiful views.

■ 72270 Baiersbronn-Mittteltal **Tel** (07442) 4980 **Fax** (07442) 49878 **Meals** breakfast, lunch, dinner **Prices** rooms D-DD; meals from DM40 **Rooms** 44, all with bath or shower, central heating, phone, TV, radio **Credit cards** AE, DC, MC, V **Closed** never **Languages** English, French

Country hotel, Binzen

Mühle

Hansjörg Hechler's old mill has become a sophisticated, well designed hotel, blending antiques with richly patterned fabrics in glowing colours. Good food in the beamed garden-restaurant.

■ 79589 Binzen, Mühlenstr 26 **Tel** (07621) 6072 **Fax** (07621) 65808 **Meals** breakfast, lunch, dinner **Prices** rooms D-DDD with breakfast; meals from DM35 **Rooms** 22, all with bath or shower, central heating, phone, TV, radio; some have minibar **Credit cards** AE, DC, MC, V hotel only **Closed** 2 weeks Feb; restaurant only, Sun, national holidays **Languages** English, French, Italian

Country hotel, Blaufelden

Gasthof zum Hirschen

Small, certainly, but charming? Well, no – that is the last word you would apply to Manfred Kurz's glossy inn. The dining-room, retains some signs of age, but elsewhere the modernization has been relentless. Enjoy the rich Michelin-starred cooking.

■ 74572 Blaufelden, Haupstr 15 **Tel** (07953) 1041 **Fax** (07953) 1043 **Meals** breakfast, lunch, dinner **Prices** rooms D-DDD breakfast DM18; meals from DM30 **Rooms** 12, all with bath or shower, central heating, phone, hairdrier, TV, minibar **Credit cards** not accepted **Closed** Jan; restaurant only, Mon; Sun eve, Oct-Mar **Languages** English, French, Spanish

Chalet hotel, Breitnau

Kaiser's Tanne-Wirtshus

Situated on the main road between Breitnau and Hinterzarten, a bright, modern chalet, filled with kitsch. Family run, with oodles of bonhomie – zither concerts, grill evenings, and so on. Not for the reclusive, although a new room has been added for guests.

■ 79874 Breitnau, Am Wirbstein **Tel** (07652) 1551 **Fax** (07652)1507 **Meals** breakfast, lunch, dinner, snacks **Prices** rooms D-DDDD with breakfast; meals DM30-45 **Rooms** 36, all with bath, central heating, phone, TV, minibar, radio; some rooms with hairdrier **Credit cards** not accepted **Closed** never **Languages** English

Baden-Württemberg

Restaurant with rooms, Bühl

Grüne Bettlad

A 300-year-old black-and-white timbered house in the town centre with a flowery courtyard. The colourful dining room may be too elaborate, but the French-influenced cooking is not. Romantic, prettily decorated bedrooms.

■ 77815 Bühl, Blumenstr 4 **Tel** (07223) 24238 **Fax** (07223) 24247 **Meals** breakfast, lunch, dinner **Prices** rooms DD-DDD with breakfast **Rooms** 6, all with bath or shower, central heating, phone, TV, minibar **Credit cards** AE, MC, V **Closed** 22 Dec to mid-Jan, 2 weeks in summer; restaurant only, Sun & Mon **Languages** English

---

Town hotel, Bühl

Wehlauer's Badischer Hof

A handsome 17thC house named after its famous chef, Peter Wehlauer. Restrained decoration, with some starkly modern furnishings in bedrooms. There is a pleasant waterside terrace where meals can be served.

■ 77815 Bühl, Haupstr 36 **Tel** (07223) 23063 **Fax** (07223) 23065 **Meals** breakfast, lunch, dinner, snacks **Prices** rooms DD-DDDD with breakfast **Rooms** 25, all with bath or shower, central heating, phone, TV, radio, minibar, hairdrier **Credit cards** AE, DC, MC, V **Closed** restaurant only, 2 weeks Jan; Sun, Mon **Languages** German only

---

Converted watermill, Büsingen

Alte Rheinmühle

An ancient, beautifully restored mill with the Rhine lapping at its feet, open log fires, tasteful decoration, good food in a beamed room overlooking the river. Fredy Wagner's prices are in Swiss Francs – to lessen the immediate impact of the bill?

■ 78266 Büsingen, Junkerstr 93 **Tel** (07734) 6076 **Fax** (07734) 6079 **Meals** breakfast, lunch, dinner **Prices** rooms D-DDDD with breakfast; meals DM75-120 **Rooms** 14, all with bath or shower, central heating, phone **Credit cards** AE, DC, MC, V **Closed** mid-Dec to mid-Jan **Languages** English, French, Italian

---

Town hotel, Eberbach am Neckar

Altes Badhaus

A new owner continues the brilliant combination of traditional simplicity and ultra-modern sophistication – quaint, beamed bedrooms with hi-tech lighting. Food is equally exciting: dinner in the elegant restaurant, breakfast in the vaulted basement.

■ 69412 Eberbach am Neckar, Am Lindenplatz 1 **Tel** (06271) 92300 **Fax** (06271) 923040 **Meals** breakfast, lunch, dinner **Prices** rooms DD with breakfast; meals DM10-96 **Rooms** 13, all with bath or shower, central heating, phone, TV, minibar, radio **Credit cards** AE, MC, V **Closed** Mon **Languages** English, French

Baden-Württemberg

Country inn, Eberbach-Brombach

Haus Talblick

This old timbered inn enjoys a secluded situation in the beautiful Odenwald valley – great walking country. Simple rooms and a jolly, locally renowned restaurant serving good country fare and game specialities.

■ 69730 Eberbach-Brombach **Tel** (06272) 1451 **Fax** (06272) 3155 **Meals** breakfast, dinner **Prices** rooms DD, with breakfast **Rooms** 5, some with shower; all with central heating , radio **Credit cards** not accepted **Closed** Jan, Jul; restaurant only Wed, Thurs; lunch Mon to Sat **Languages** German only

---

Country inn, Ehrenkirchen

Gasthaus zur Krone

A traditional whitewashed inn with blue painted shutters and flower-filled window boxes. It is on the *Badischer Weinstrasse*, and the Kiefer's wine tastings are as worth savouring as their wholesome food.

■ 79238 Ehrenkirchen, Herrenstr 5 **Tel** (07633) 5213 **Fax** (07633) 83550 **Meals** breakfast, lunch, dinner **Prices** rooms D, with breakfast **Rooms** 9, some with shower; all with central heating **Credit cards** DC, MC, V **Closed** 3 weeks Jul, 2 weeks Feb; restaurant only Tue, Wed lunch **Languages** German only

---

Country hotel, Emmendingen 12-Maleck

Park-Hotel Krone

The 'park' (that is, garden with pond) is one of the attractions, as are the resident flamingoes, the handsomely furnished bed rooms, and the reliable food, served in an elegant room with murals. Elsewhere, the decorative style is bizarre.

■ 79312 Emmendingen 12-Maleck, Brandelweg 1 **Tel** (07641) 8496 **Fax** (07641) 52576 **Meals** breakfast, lunch, dinner **Prices** rooms D-DD with breakfast; meals DM38-140 **Rooms** 18, all with bath or shower, central heating, phone, hairdrier, TV, minibar, radio **Credit cards** AE, DC, MC, V **Closed** Mon **Languages** English, French

---

Country hotel, Enzklösterle

Enztalhotel

Let's be clear: the Enztalhotel has about as much visual charm as an airport concourse. But the setting is splendid, and inside the hotel could not be more different: gleaming wooden panelling, harmonious fabrics – and a cheerful family welcome.

■ 75337 Enzklösterle, Freudenstädter Str 67 **Tel** (07085) 180 **Fax** (07085) 1642 **Meals** breakfast, lunch, dinner **Prices** rooms DD-DDD with breakfast; meals DM40 **Rooms** 49, all with bath or shower, central heating, phone, TV, radio **Credit cards** MC, V in restaurant only **Closed** 10-2 0 Dec; restaurant only, Wed, Thur **Languages** English, French

Baden-Württemberg

Town hotel, Ettlingen

Erbprinz

A traditional hotel with a restaurant and wine bar, now in the hands of Dieter and Claire Marschall. Sombre hues in the dining-room, lighter and brighter furnishings in the spacious bedrooms.

■ 76257 Ettlingen, Rheinstr 1 **Tel** (07243) 3220 **Fax** (07243) 16471 **Meals** breakfast, lunch, dinner, snacks **Prices** rooms DD-DDDD with breakfast; meals DM45-100 **Rooms** 47, all with bath or shower, central heating, phone, TV, minibar, radio; most have hairdrier **Credit cards** AE, DC, MC, V **Closed** restaurant only, Mon **Languages** English, French

---

Country chalet, Feldberg-Bärental

Adler

This delightful chalet is just what we have looked for and rarely found – a small old house, tastefully furnished and immaculately kept by the Wimmer family. The irony is that they do not wish to appear in this guide. Beautiful setting, too.

■ 79868 Feldberg-Bärental, Feldbergstr 4 **Tel** (07655) 1242 (07655) 1228 **Meals** breakfast, lunch, dinner **Prices** rooms D-DD with breakfast; meals DM45-62 **Rooms** 14, all with bath or shower, central heating, phone, TV, minibar, radio **Credit cards** DC, MC, V **Closed** never **Languages** English

---

Town hotel, Freiburg im Breisgau

Zum Roten Bären

A hotel since 1120 – perhaps Germany's oldest – with a smartly modernized interior behind an interesting old, painted façade, in a central position in the old town. Traditional restaurant serving regional food.

■ 79098 Freiburg im Breisgau, Oberlinden 12 **Tel** (0761) 387870 **Fax** (0761) 3878717 **Meals** breakfast, lunch, dinner, snacks **Prices** rooms DD-DDDD **Rooms** 25, all with bath or shower, central heating, phone, TV, radio **Credit cards** AE, DC, MC, V **Closed** never **Languages** English, French

---

Wine tavern with rooms, Freiburg im Breisgau

Oberkirchs Weinstuben

The *Weinstube* itself is hard by Freiburg's fantastic minster, a warmly welcoming panelled tavern serving satisfying food. There are rooms here, but many are in a separate and, although newly updated, less atmospheric building around the corner.

■ 79098 Freiburg im Breisgau, Münsterplatz 22 **Tel** (0761) 31011 **Fax** (0761) 31031 **Meals** breakfast, lunch, dinner **Prices** rooms DD-DDD; meals DM40 **Rooms** 27, all with bath or shower, central heating, phone, TV **Credit cards** AE, MC, V **Closed** Sun, Christmas, Jan **Languages** English, French

Baden-Württemberg

Country hotel, Freudenstadt

Langenwaldsee

Deep in the woods a mile or two west of the *Kurort* of Freudenstadt, this well run traditional hotel on a small lake is great for sporty types, with a full-size swimming-pool next door. Some beautiful antique features. Muted modern bedrooms.

■ 72250 Freudenstadt, Strassburger Str 99 **Tel** (07441) 2234 **Fax** (07441) 4191 **Meals** breakfast, lunch, dinner **Prices** rooms D-DD; meals from DM25 **Rooms** 53, all with bath or shower, central heating, phone, hairdrier, TV, radio **Credit cards** DC, MC, V **Closed** early Nov to mid-Dec **Languages** English, French, Italian, Spanish

---

Town hotel, Freudenstadt

Hotel Schwanen

The Bukenberger family have run this modest, spick-and-span little hotel – handily placed between the station and the central park – for over 40 years. Pleasant terrace area – and for a garden, the family has a *Landhaus* across town. Much liked by an American visitor.

■ 72250 Freudenstadt, Forststr 6 **Tel** (07441) 91550 **Fax** (07441) 915544 **Meals** breakfast, lunch, dinner **Prices** rooms D-DD with breakfast; meals DM30 **Rooms** 17, all with shower, central heating, phone, TV **Credit cards** MC, V **Closed** Thu **Languages** French, some

---

Country hotel, Gaggenau-Moosbronn

Mönchhof

This substantial half-timbered house, built for a master glass-blower in the 18th century, was restored in the early 1980s to great effect. There are beams and tiled floors downstairs, cosy rustic bedrooms upstairs. Iceland ponies available for hire.

■ 76571 Gaggenau-Moosbronn **Tel** (07204) 619 **Fax** (07204) 1256 **Meals** breakfast, snacks **Prices** rooms D-DD with breakfast; meals from DM22 **Rooms** 16, all with shower, central heating **Credit cards** DC **Closed** Mon; 22 Dec to 20 Jan **Languages** English

---

Chalet hotel, Glottertal

Hotel Hirschen

Gilded wooden carvings, antique chests and painted ceilings blend happily in the cosy downstairs rooms of this Black Forest chalet. In the bedrooms, a different story – leather armchairs, built-in melamine cupboards and coffee tables.

■ 79286 Glottertal, Rathausweg 2 **Tel** (07684) 810 **Fax** (07684) 1713 **Meals** breakfast, lunch, dinner **Prices** rooms D-DDD with breakfast; meals DM30-50 **Rooms** 53, all with bath or shower, central heating, phone, TV, minibar; some have hairdrier **Credit cards** MC, V **Closed** restaurant only, Mon **Languages** English, French

Baden-Württemberg

Chalet hotel, Glottertal

Hotel Hirschen

Gilded wooden carvings, antique chests and painted ceilings blend happily in the cosy downstairs rooms of this Black Forest chalet. In the bedrooms, a different story – leather armchairs, built-in melamine cupboards and coffee tables.

■ 79286 Glottertal, Rathausweg 2 **Tel** (07684) 810 **Fax** (07684) 1713 **Meals** breakfast, lunch, dinner **Prices** rooms D-DDD with breakfast; meals DM30-50 **Rooms** 53, all with bath or shower, central heating, phone, TV, minibar; some have hairdrier **Credit cards** MC, V **Closed** restaurant only, Mon **Languages** English, French

---

Town hotel, Hagnau am Bodensee

Der Löwen

This pretty timbered 17thC house does not enjoy a lakeside setting, but does have a private foreshore only five minutes away – and the compensation of a lush little garden (with pond) and terrace. Light, pine-furnished bedrooms.

■ 88709 Hagnau am Bodensee, Hansjakobstr 2 **Tel** (07532) 6241 **Fax** 9048 **Meals** breakfast, dinner, snacks **Prices** rooms D-DD with breakfast; meals from DM35 **Rooms** 17, all with bath or shower, central heating, phone; some have TV, radio **Credit cards** not accepted **Closed** end Oct to end Mar; Wed **Languages** English, some French

---

Manor house hotel, Haßmersheim-Hochhausen

Schloß Hochhausen

Occupying part of the family seat of the Graf von Helmstatt, this old-fashioned hotel has large bedrooms furnished in Biedemeier, open fires in the public rooms; meat and vegetables for the table come from the surrounding deer-park and garden.

■ 74855 Haßmersheim-Hochhausen **Tel** (06261) 893142 **Meals** breakfast, lunch, dinner **Prices** rooms D-DD with breakfast, meals from DM35 **Rooms** 18, all with bath or shower, central heating **Credit cards** not accepted **Closed** Jan, Feb **Languages** English, French

---

Town hotel, Heidelberg

Perkeo

Well modernized, popular hotel on main street of Heidelberg's traffic-free old town. Impersonal but smart and roomy bedrooms, and helpful staff. Beer garden and panelled restaurant under separate management.

■ 69117 Heidelberg, Haupstr 75 **Tel** (06221) 14130 **Fax** (06221) 141337 **Meals** breakfast **Prices** rooms DD **Rooms** 25, all with bath or shower, central heating, phone, TV, radio, minibar **Credit cards** AE, DC, MC, V **Closed** Christmas and New Year **Languages** English

Baden-Württemberg

Town villa, Heilbronn

Park Villa

Two neighbouring villas set in mature gardens combine to make one hotel. Bedrooms are spacious and comfortable; all that is lacking is a bit of flair in the decoration.

■ 74074 Heilbronn, Gutenbergstr 30 **Tel** (07131) 95700 **Fax** (07131) 957020 **Meals** breakfast **Prices** DD-DDD with breakfast **Rooms** 25, all with bath, central heating, phone, TV, minibar, radio **Credit cards** AE, DC, MC, V **Closed** Christmas **Languages** English, Spanish

---

Town inn, Heitersheim

Krone

Nothing to jar the eye in this softly coloured inn. Even the 300-year-old cellar with its coved ceiling has been given the feminine touch with fringed hanging lamps and lacey tablecloths.

■ 79423 Heitersheim, Hauptstr 7 **Tel** (07634) 51070 **Fax** (07634) 510766 **Meals** breakfast, lunch, dinner **Prices** rooms D-DD with breakfast; meals from DM30 **Rooms** 25, all with bath or shower, central heating, phone, hairdrier, TV, radio; most have minibar, balcony **Credit cards** V **Closed** restaurant only, Tue, Wed lunch **Languages** English, French

---

Country hotel, Hinterzarten

Hotel Reppert

A comfortable, friendly hotel run by the third generation of Repperts, in an idyllic situation overlooking a small lake, surrounded by woods and meadows and on the edge of a popular village. Steeply pitched roofs and flowery balconies without, surprising plush elegance within.

■ 79856 Hinterzarten, Adlerweg 21-23 **Tel** (07652) 12080 **Fax** (07652) 120811 **Meals** breakfast, dinner, snacks **Prices** D-DDD; suites DDDD with breakfast; meals DM25-65 **Rooms** 34, all with bath or shower, central heating, phone, hairdrier, cable TV, radio, safe **Credit cards** AE, DC, MC, V **Closed** Nov **Languages** English, French, Spanish, Italian, Flemish

---

Country hotel, Horben bei Freiburg

Zum Engel

A rustic, four-storey building, with a flowery garden and shady terrace, set in beautiful, hilly countryside. Previously uninspiring bedrooms have all been refurbished in suitably provincial style.

■ 79289 Horben-Langackern **Tel** (0761) 29111 **Fax** (0761) 290627 **Meals** breakfast, lunch, dinner, snacks **Prices** D-DD with breakfast **Rooms** 22, all with shower, central heating, phone, TV, radio **Credit cards** MC, V **Closed** restaurant only, Mon **Languages** English

Baden-Württemberg

Country inn, Isny-Großholzleute

Adler

The Gasthof Adler is the picture of rustic charm, inside and out – its yellow-washed walls abundantly decorated with riding scenes. But the bedrooms are over the road in Ulrich Zürn's modern chalet-style *Kurhotel* – comfortable but bland.

■ 88316 Isny-Großholzleute **Tel** (07562) 2041 **Fax** (07562) 55299 **Meals** breakfast, lunch, dinner **Prices** rooms D-DD with breakfast; meals from DM30 **Rooms** 22, all with bath or shower, central heating, phone, hairdrier, TV, radio, balcony **Credit cards** AE, DC, MC, V **Closed** Mon **Languages** English, Frenchphone; some have TV **Credit cards** AE, DC, MC, V **Closed** Nov to mid-March **Languages** English

---

Converted castle, Jagsthausen

Burghotel Götzenburg

This friendly-looking moated castle, little changed over the centuries, loses its tranquil air most of the summer thanks to its theatre festival. Huge four-posters in the bedrooms and massive carved chests in the halls hardly fill the enormous spaces.

■ 74249 Jagsthausen **Tel** (07943) 2222 **Fax** (07943) 8200 **Meals** breakfast, lunch, dinner **Prices** rooms D-DDD with breakfast; meals DM15-40 **Rooms** 17, all with bath or shower, central heating, phone; some have TV **Credit cards** AE, DC, MC V **Closed** Nov to mid-March **Languages** English

---

Village inn, Lahr-Reichenbach

Adler

What was once a simple inn has been expensively transformed by Otto Fehrenbacher into a sophisticated restaurant. The interior , including the spacious bedrooms, is light and airy. Food can be a little pretentious, but simple snacks are available.

■ 77933 Lahr-Reichenbach, Reichenbacher Hauptstr 18 **Tel** (07821) 7035 **Fax** (07821) 7033 **Meals** breakfast, lunch, dinner, snacks **Prices** rooms D-DD with breakfast; meals DM25-88 **Rooms** 20, all with bath or shower, central heating, phone, hairdrier, TV, radio; some have minibar **Credit cards** MC, V **Closed** restaurant only, one week mid-Feb; Tue **Languages** English, French

---

Country hotel, Lahr-Sulz

Dammenmühle

Though pretty enough from the outside, this house is relatively ordinary within, with quite stylish modern furnishings. The setting, however, is rather special, with a big shady terrace beside the dam which powered the old oil mill (no longer here).

■ 77933 Lahr-Sulz **Tel** (07821) 93930 **Fax** (07821) 939393 **Meals** breakfast, lunch, dinner **Prices** D-DDD with breakfast; meals DM40 **Rooms** 17, all with bath or shower, central heating, phone, TV, hairdrier **Credit cards** MC, V **Closed** restaurant only, Mon, 3 weeks Jan/Feb; 2 weeks Sep/Oct **Languages** English, French

Baden-Württemberg

Converted castle, Leonberg-Höfingen

Schloß Höfingen

Far from being a typical gloomy castle, this one has been lovingly restored by Manuela Feckl, whose husband Franz is one of
Germany's rising culinary stars. Stylishly traditional dining-
rooms, rather plainer but spacious bedrooms.

■ 71229 Leonberg-Höfingen, Am Schloßberg 17 **Tel** (07152) 21049
Meals breakfast, lunch, dinner **Prices** rooms D-DD with breakfast;
meals DM70 **Rooms** 9, all with shower, central heating, phone, TV
Credit cards AE, DC, MC, V **Closed** 4 weeks Jul-Aug; Christmas;
national holidays; Sun & Mon **Languages** English

Town hotel, Lörrach

Villa Elben

An art nouveau villa in peaceful grounds, furnished with at least
some regard to its style. Club-like galleried sitting/reception
area, simpler breakfast room, well-proportioned bedrooms with
tasteful use of strong colours throughout.

■ 79539 Lörrach, Hünerbergweg 26 **Tel** (07621) 2066 **Fax** (07621)
43280 **Meals** breakfast **Prices** rooms DD **Rooms** 44, all with bath or
shower, central heating, phone, TV, radio, hairdrier **Credit cards** AE,
MC, V **Closed** never **Languages** English

Converted mill, Mahlstetten

Alte Lippachmühle

Delightfully unfussy inn for those who enjoy the simpler plea-
sures – walking, riding and scoffing hearty meals. Not for the
sybarite, but peace is guaranteed in idyllic setting by woods and
water, and the Eichels are warmly welcoming.

■ 78601 Mahlstetten **Tel** (07429) 2306 **Meals** breakfast, lunch, dinner
Prices rooms D **Rooms** 7, all with central heating **Credit cards** not
accepted **Closed** 2 weeks Jan; restaurant only, Tue **Languages** English,
French, Italian

Chalet hotel, Maierhöfen bei Isny

Gasthof zur Grenze

A long, low, chocolate-box chalet with all the trimmings – carved
balconies, flowers, murals. The jolly, bar-like dining-room has
benched seating and a *Kachelofen*. Most bedrooms have balconies overlooking the surrounding wooded hills.

■ 88167 Maierhöfen bei Isny, Schanz 103 **Tel** (07562) 3645 **Fax**
(07562) 55401 **Meals** breakfast, lunch, dinner **Prices** rooms D-DD with
breakfast; meals from DM28 **Rooms** 16, all with bath or shower, central
heating, phone, hairdrier, TV, radio **Credit cards** MC **Closed** 2 weeks
Mar/Apr, 3 weeks Nov/Dec; restaurant only, Mon,Tue
Languages English

Baden-Württemberg

Converted castle, Markdorf

Bischofschloß

The former summer residence of the Bishops of Constance, in the now-pedestrianized old town of Markdorf, has made a spacious, smart and elegant hotel – even if (to our eye) it does lack coherent style and warmth.

■ 88677 Markdorf, Schloßweg 2-8 **Tel** (07544) 8141 **Fax** (07544) 72313 **Meals** breakfast, lunch, dinner **Prices** rooms DD-DDD; meals from DM43 **Rooms** 43, all with bath, central heating, phone, TV, radio, minibar, hairdrier **Credit cards** AE, DC, MC **Closed** Christmas, New Year **Languages** English, French

---

Town inn, Meersburg

Weinstube Löwen

This jolly, wistaria-covered old tavern is on the marketplace, opposite the Zum Bären (full entry, page 000). The atmosphere in the simple, traditionally cosy dining-rooms is the highlight; plain but comfortable bedrooms.

■ 88709 Meersburg, Marktpl 2 **Tel** (07532) 43040 **Fax** (07541) 430410 **Meals** breakfast, lunch, dinner **Prices** rooms D-DD **Rooms** 21, all with bath or shower, central heating, phone, TV **Credit cards** AE, DC, MC, V **Closed** mid-Nov to mid-Dec **Languages** English

---

Riverside hotel, Neckargemünd

Hotel zum Ritter

This rambling old half-timbered inn enjoys a wonderful position on the banks of the River Neckar, with good river views from its popular restaurant. Noise from main road can be intrusive. Atmospheric cellar bar. Bedrooms quite stylish but rather stark.

■ 69151 Neckargemünd, Neckarstr 40 **Tel** (06223) 92350 **Fax** (06223) 73339 **Meals** breakfast, lunch, dinner **Prices** rooms D-DDD **Rooms** 38, all with bath or shower, central heating, phone **Credit cards** AE, MC, V **Closed** never **Languages** English, French, Italian

---

Converted castle, Neckarwestheim

Schloßhotel Liebenstein

An immaculate 1980s restoration of old buildings within the walls of a 16C hilltop castle, without an undulating 27-hole golf course. Atmospheric vaulted dining-room, tavern with terrace, spacious and tasteful bedrooms.

■ 74382 Neckarwestheim **Tel** (07133) 98990 **Fax** (07133) 6045 **Meals** breakfast, lunch, dinner, snacks **Prices** rooms DD-DDDD **Rooms** 24, all with bath or shower, central heating, phone, TV, radio, hairdrier **Credit cards** AE, DC, MC, V **Closed** Jan **Languages** German only

Baden-Württemberg

Converted castle, Neckarzimmern

Burg Hornberg

The ancient castle set high above the sweeping river Neckar, has comfortably modernized bedrooms, but the front ones can get too warm in summer. It is partly a museum so is very busy and near traffic.

■ 74865 Neckarzimmern **Tel** (06261) 92460 **Fax** (06261) 924644 **Meals** breakfast, lunch, dinner, snacks **Prices** rooms DD-DDD with breakfast **Rooms** 24, all with bath or shower, central heating, phone, TV, radio **Credit cards** MC, V **Closed** mid-Dec to Mar **Languages** English, French

---

Country inn, Oberkirch

Zur Oberen Linde

A complex of substantial timbered buildings, dating from the 17th century and extended more recently. Beside a busy road, but in a grassy garden. Traditional decoration, with tastefully furnished rooms.

■ 77704 Oberkirch, Haupstr 25 **Tel** (07802) 8020 **Fax** (07802) 3030 **Meals** breakfast, lunch, dinner, snacks **Prices** rooms DD-DDDD **Rooms** 40, all with bath, central heating, phone, TV, radio, minibar, hairdrier **Credit cards** AE, DC, MC, V **Closed** never **Languages** English, French

---

Chalet hotel, Oberwolfach

Hirschen

There is something for everyone at this pretty country hotel: traditional exterior and immaculate, tasteful interior, sauna, table-tennis, bowling alley, kids' toys, and good food – all backed up by a warm welcome from the three resident generations of the Junghanns family.

■ 77709 Oberwolfach, Schwarzwaldstr 2 **Tel** (07834) 366 **Fax** (07834) 6775 **Meals** breakfast, lunch, dinner, snacks **Prices** D-DD **Rooms** 42, all with central heating, phone **Credit cards** AE, DC, MC, V **Closed** 6th to 31st Oct **Languages** English

---

Town hotel, Offenburg

Hotel Sonne

A plain-looking hotel on the marketplace, with a 600-year history (Napoleon stayed here) but mainly modern and 19thC furnishings. Cosy panelled dining-room. Bedrooms vary in size as well as style – the best are very spacious.

■ 77652 Offenburg, Haupstr 94 **Tel** (0781) 71039 **Fax** (0781) 71033 **Meals** breakfast, lunch, dinner **Prices** rooms D-DD with breakfast **Rooms** 34, all with central heating **Credit cards** AE, MC, V **Closed** restaurant only, Jan & Feb **Languages** English, French

Baden-Württemberg

Country hotel, Pfalzgrafenweiler-Kälberbronn

Waldsägmühle

They don't come any more solid than this – wherever you look in Hans and Marta Ziegler's forest-girt hotel, you see massive beams (not necessarily very old ones). The best bedrooms, at the front of the house, have flower-decked balconies.

■ 72285 Pfalzgrafenweiler-Kälberbronn **Tel** (07445) 85150 **Fax** (07445) 6750 **Meals** breakfast, lunch, dinner **Prices** rooms D-DD with breakfast; meals about DM30 **Rooms** 37, all with bath or shower, central heating, phone, minibar, radio; most have TV **Credit cards** DC, V **Closed** 6th to 31st Jan; 4th to 21st Aug; restaurant only Sun afternoon, Mon **Languages** English

---

Country hotel, Rammingen

Landgasthaus Adler

Peacefully situated in a hamlet, this appealing creeper-clad hotel attracts visitors with its generous meals served in the beamed dining room, and comfortable bedrooms with painted furniture. The Apolloni family are friendly and welcoming hosts.

■ 89192 Rammingen, Riegestr 15 **Tel** (07345) 96410 **Fax** (07345) 964110 **Meals** breakfast, lunch, dinner **Prices** rooms D-DDD with breakfast; meals from DM25 **Rooms** 14, all with bath or shower, central heating, phone, hairdrier, minibar, radio **Credit cards** AE, DC, MC, V **Closed** Jan, Aug; restaurant only, Mon, Tue lunch **Languages** English, French, Italian

---

Hilltop hotel, Reutlingen

Achalm

An old estate converted to a rambling hotel, restaurant and conference complex sheltering under the ruins of the Achalm hillfort. The lofty beamed restaurant looks down towards Reutlingen, as do the modern bedrooms.

■ 72766 Reutlingen, Achalm **Tel** (07121) 4820 **Fax** (07121) 482100 **Meals** breakfast **Prices** rooms D-DDD with breakfast **Rooms** 46, all with bath or shower, central heating, phone, TV, minibar, radio **Credit cards** AE, DC, MC, V **Closed** never **Languages** English, French, Italian

---

Converted mill, Rielasingen

zur Alten Mühle

No half-measures here: the split-level bar/dining-room of this old mill surround you with beams, beams and more beams. The food is fairly ambitious, and successful. Bedrooms also are prettily furnished in rustic style.

■ 87239 Rielasingen, Singener Str 3 **Tel** (07731) 52055 **Fax** (07731) 52057 **Meals** breakfast, lunch, dinner **Prices** rooms D-DD with breakfast; **Meals** from DM25 **Rooms** 6, all with shower, central heating, phone, TV, minibar **Credit cards** MC, V **Closed** Mon **Languages** English, French, Italian

Baden-Württemberg

Country hotel, Rosenberg

Landgasthof Adler

The ancient exterior with green shutters beckons invitingly, and green with red is used in the informal breakfast room and *stüble*. But the bedrooms and dining-room serving haute cuisine are laboratory white – dogs certainly not allowed.

■ 73494 Rosenberg, Ellwanger Str 15 **Tel** (07967) 513 **Meals** breakfast, lunch, dinner , snacks **Prices** rooms D-DD breakfast DM12, meals DM20-45 **Rooms** 11, all with shower, central heating, phone, hairdrier **Credit cards** not accepted **Closed** 2 weeks Jan, 2 weeks Aug; restaurant only, Thu & Fri **Languages** English

---

Chalet hotel, Schopfheim-Schlechtbach

Gasthof Auerhahn

A picturesque, whitewashed, flower-decked chalet with views of the distant Alps. It is a simple place – compact bedrooms with flower-patterned furniture, and a modest, wood-panelled dining-room offering traditional fare. The prices are difficult to beat.

■ 79650 Schopfheim-Schlechtbach, Hauptstr 5 **Tel** (07620) 228 **Fax** (07620) 1559 **Meals** breakfast, lunch, dinner **Prices** rooms D with breakfast; meals DM16-50 **Rooms** 10, all with shower, central heating, **Credit cards** not acceepted **Closed** Wed dinner and Thu **Languages** English, French

---

Town hotel, Schwäbisch Hall

Der Adelshof

The marketplace is the focus of this pretty old town; the Goldener Adler has the slightly better position, but this suave hotel has the edge in comfort and style. Modern 'designer' bedrooms, handsome beamed dining-room.

■ 74523 Schwäbisch Hall, Am Markt 12-13 **Tel** (0791) 75890 **Fax** (0791) 6036 **Meals** breakfast, lunch, dinner **Prices** rooms DD with breakfast; meals from DM30 **Rooms** 47, all with bath or shower, central heating, phone, hairdrier, TV, minibar, radio **Credit cards** AE, DC, MC, V **Closed** restaurant only, Mon **Languages** English, French, Italian, Spanish

---

Coaching inn, Titisee-Neustadt

Adler Post

A comfortably solid hotel – in a health resort – with an old-fashioned atmosphere, run by the Ketterer family for 140 years. Massages and a daily clinic for *Kur*-seekers; traditional hospitality for the rest of us.

■ 79822 Titisee-Neustadt, Hauptstrasse 16, Ortsteil Neustadt **Tel** (07651) 5066 **Fax** (07651) 3729 **Meals** breakfast, lunch, dinner **Prices** D-DDD with breakfast **Rooms** 30, all with bath or shower, central heating, phone, TV, minibar **Credit cards** AE, DC, MC, V **Closed** 3 weeks before Easter **Languages** English, French, Italian

Baden-Württemberg

Country guest-house, Titisee-Neustadt

Traube

Herr Winterhalder happily welcomes families to his unpretentious solid chalet, quietly situated in the wooded hills north of the lake. Reliably rustic food, reliably rustic atmosphere, and comfortable to boot.

■ 79822 Titisee-Neustadt/Waldau, Sommerbergweg 1 **Tel** (07669) 755 **Fax** (07669) 1350 **Meals** breakfast, lunch, dinner **Prices** rooms D-DD with breakfast **Rooms** 30, all with bath or shower, central heating, phone, radio; some have minibar **Credit cards** not accepted **Closed** never **Languages** English, French

---

Country resort hotel, Triberg im Schwarzwald

Parkhotel Wehrle

A traditionally decorated hotel, family-run for centuries, with three further buildings tucked away in landscaped gardens with an outdoor heated pool, with another pool indoors. No pomposity here, despite the renowned food and luxurious fittings.

■ 78094 Triberg im Schwarzwald, Gartenstr 24 **Tel** (07722) 86020 **Fax** (07722) 860290 **Meals** breakfast, lunch, dinner **Prices** rooms D-DDD with breakfast; meals from DM40 **Rooms** 56, all with bath or shower, central heating, phone, hairdrier, TV, radio **Credit cards** AE, DC, MC, V **Closed** never **Languages** English, Italian, French

---

Lakeside hotel, Überlingen

Hotel Seegarten

There is an old-fashioned, home-like feel to this little hotel, behind the bland façade. Separated from Lake Constance only by a busy prom, guests can eat on the pretty terrace while watching the ferry plough to and fro.

■ 88644 Überlingen, Seepromenade 7 **Tel** (07551) 63498 **Fax** (07551) 3981 **Meals** breakfast, lunch, dinner, snacks **Prices** rooms D-DDD with breakfast; meals DM18.50-60 **Rooms** 21, all with bath or shower, central heating, phone, TV **Credit cards** MC **Closed** Dec to Feb **Languages** English, French

---

Lakeside hotel, Uhldingen-Mühlhofen

Hotel Fischerhaus

Booking is essential at this half-timbered hotel, and no wonder – with its private beach on Lake Constance, heated outdoor pool, tasteful bedrooms and dining-room (serving good food and fruit juices from the orchard - but for hotel guests only).

■ 88690 Uhldingen-Mühlhofen 1, Seefelden am Bodensee **Tel** (07556) 8563 **Fax** (07556) 6063 **Meals** breakfast, lunch, dinner **Prices** rooms DB&B DD-DDDD **Rooms** 27, all with bath or shower, central heating, phone, TV **Credit cards** not accepted **Closed** never **Languages** English, French

Baden-Württemberg

Town inn, Wangen im Allgäu

Hotel Alte Post

A well cared-for old inn with an excellent position in the traffic-free central area of Wangen. Elegantly furnished public areas and comfortably rustic bedrooms up in the roof space.

■ 88239 Wangen im Allgäu, Postpl 2 **Tel** (07522) 97560 **Fax** (07522) 22604 **Meals** breakfast, lunch, dinner **Prices** rooms D-DD **Rooms** 27, all with bath or shower, central heating, phone, TV, radio, minibar, hairdrier **Credit cards** AE, DC, MC, V **Closed** never **Languages** English, French

---

Bed-and-breakfast villa, Wangen im Allgäu

Hotel Postvilla

Elegant art nouveau villa in lush gardens, run by the same family as the Alte Post (above). Grand rooms with chandeliers and ornate furnishings create an air of formal luxury.

■ 88239 Wangen im Allgäu, Schönhalde 2 **Tel** (07522) 97460 **Fax** (07522) 29323 **Meals** breakfast **Prices** D-DDD with breakfast **Rooms** 17, all with central heating, phone, TV, radio, minibar, hairdrier **Credit cards** AE, DC, MC, V **Closed** 2 weeks Jan **Languages** German only

---

Town hotel, Weikersheim

Laurentius

The vaulted stone cellar accommodating a renowned restaurant is the only clue to the age of this functionally converted hotel, situated in an old square where Goethe once lived. The pretty courtyard terrace is pleasant for informal meals.

■ 97990 Weikersheim, Marktplatz 5 **Tel** (07934) 7007 **Fax** (07934) 7077 **Meals** breakfast, lunch, dinner **Prices** rooms D-DD with breakfast; meals from DM40 **Rooms** 14, all with bath or shower, central heating, phone; some rooms with phone, TV, radio **Credit cards** AE, DC, MC, V **Closed** Tue **Languages** English, French, Italian

---

Town hotel, Weikersheim

Gasthaus Zur Krone

Dating from 1572, the Hechler brothers' inn has no pretensions to being anything other than a good middle-class restaurant with simply furnished rooms. A riotously red dining room serves as an alternative to the other two rustic *Stuben*.

■ 79576 Weil, Hauptstr 58 **Tel** (07621) 71164 **Fax** (07621) 78963 **Meals** breakfast, lunch, dinner **Prices** rooms D-DD with breakfast; menus from DM52 **Rooms** 11, all with bath or shower, central heating, phone, TV, radio **Credit cards** AE, MC, V **Closed** restaurant only, Mon and Tue **Languages** English, French, Italian

Baden-Württemberg

Town hotel, Weikersheim

Gasthaus Zur Krone

Dating from 1572, the Hechler brothers' inn has no pretensions to being anything other than a good middle-class restaurant with simply furnished rooms. A riotously red dining room serves as an alternative to the other two rustic *Stuben*.

■ 79576 Weil, Hauptstr 58 **Tel** (07621) 71164 **Fax** (07621) 78963 **Meals** breakfast, lunch, dinner **Prices** rooms D-DD with breakfast; menus from DM52 **Rooms** 11, all with bath or shower, central heating, phone, TV, radio **Credit cards** AE, MC, V **Closed** restaurant only, Mon and Tue **Languages** English, French, Italian

---

Village inn, Weil-Haltingen

Zum Hirschen

This unassuming little inn, peacefully positioned away from the busy Rhine, has been in Angelika Ulfstedt's family for generations. The flower-filled garden is an appealing place in which to eat in the summer, and the modestly elegant rooms are value for money.

■ 79576 Weil-Haltingen, Grosse Gass 1 **Tel** (07621) 62344 **Meals** breakfast, lunch, dinner **Prices** rooms D-DD with breakfast; meals DM20-50 **Rooms** 9, all with bath or shower, central heating, phone **Credit cards** DC, MC, V **Closed** Mon **Languages** English, French, Finnish, Swedish

---

Restaurant with rooms, Weingarten

Walk'sches Haus

A delightfully rustic inn, both inside and out, yet far from simple. New owner, Dietmar Rübenbaker, also cooks. Carved and panelled dining-rooms are not quite matched in charm by the bedrooms, but comfort is not in doubt.

■ 76356 Weingarten, Marktplatz 7 **Tel** (07244) 2031 **Fax** (07244) 2034 **Meals** breakfast, lunch, dinner **Prices** rooms D-DD with breakfast; menus DM85-150 **Rooms** 14, all with bath or shower, central heating, air-conditioning, phone, hairdrier, TV, minibar, radio **Credit cards** AE **Closed** 1-10 Jan; Sun **Languages** English, French

---

Converted castle, Weitenburg

Schloß Weitenburg

A melting-pot of Renaissance, Baroque and Neo-Gothic styles in a historic castle high above the Neckar, with impressive views and some grandly elegant rooms. The indoor riding school, 18-hole golf course and indoor pool appeal to sports enthusiasts.

■ 72181 Weitenburg **Tel** (07457) 9330 **Fax** (07457) 933100 **Meals** breakfast, lunch, dinner, snacks **Prices** rooms DD-DDD with breakfast; meals DM40-90 **Rooms** 34, all with bath or shower, central heating, phone, TV, minibar, radio **Credit cards** AE, DC, MC, V **Closed** 24 & 25 Dec **Languages** English, French, Spanish

Northern Bayern

Hotels in Northern Bayern

The Danube flows in a great arc from west to east across Bayern (Bavaria), neatly dividing it into two; we have followed this division, putting cities on the Danube in our northern section. To the north of the river lies Franken, made up of the rolling plateaux of the Main basin and the great forested hills, including many National Parks, near the Czech border. The romantic heart of Germany, Franken was ruled by powerful prince bishops, who left the region a legacy of large fortified hilltop castles and laid the foundations of a rich cultural heritage.

The regional capital, Nürnberg, was one of Germany's most beautiful medieval cities until almost obliterated during World War II. We have one entry for the city, but its hotels are mostly new concrete blocks. The plush Atrium is one, but surrounded by parks, and centrally placed (Tel (0911) 47480, fax 4748420, 190 rooms). Within easy reach of the old town, there is the luxury-class Maritim (Tel 23630, fax 2363836, 307 rooms) or the comfortable, smaller bed-and-breakfast Am Jakobsmarkt, with 70 rooms (Tel 241440, fax 227634).

The historic towns of Bamberg and Bayreuth are well covered further on in the guide, but equally historic Coburg is ill served – try the newly renovated Coburger Tor, which has a talented chef, Ulrich Schaller (Tel (09561) 25074, fax 28874, 135 rooms), or the attractive Blankenburg (Tel 75005, fax 75674, 46 rooms) – with garden restaurant scented by herbs in the summer.

Aschaffenburg in the north-west is centre of a thriving textile industry, yet retains the atmosphere of a historic market town. Bon viveurs will want to stay at the Sonne, 8 km outside, for its excellent restaurant (Tel (06021) 470077, 10 rooms), while in the town itself, the Hofgut Fasanerie (Tel 91016, fax 98944, 6 rooms) offers simple rooms in a park-like setting.

In Würzburg, a busy city on the river Main, we have one entry. Alternatives include the Rebstock, a large, comfortable hotel with good restaurant (Tel (0931) 30930, fax 3093100, 79 rooms), but for superb views make your way up to the Schloß Steinburg, cluttered with castle kitsch (Tel (0931) 93061, fax 97121, 53 rooms). Or head south-east to Biebelried, where the Leicht (Tel (09302) 814, fax 3163, 66 rooms) has the rustic style befitting an ex-brewery, as well as home-made schnapps on offer.

Over on the eastern side of the region, industrial Marktredwitz has the thoroughly renovated turn-of-the-century Kaiserhof (Tel (09231) 1031, 16 rooms), while Weiden to the south is blessed with the 1970s Europa – much better from within than without, and with good food too (Tel (0961) 25051, fax 61562, 26 rooms).

This page acts as an introduction to the features and hotels of Northern Bayern, and gives brief recommendations of good hotels that for one reason or another have not made a full entry. The long entries for this 'Land' – covering the hotels we are most enthusiastic about – start on the next page. But do not neglect the shorter entries starting on page 184: these are all hotels that we would happily stay at. Southern Bayern starts on page 191.

Northern Bayern

Der Schafhof

The Benedictines certainly knew what they were doing when they set up here in the 15thC, and the Schafhof provides as much of a retreat from our world as it did from theirs. The 18thC red sandstone house that forms the hotel looks out across meadows to rolling, wooded hills, with scarcely another building in sight; the mellow stone outbuildings house sheep, hens and ducks for the table, the lake provides trout and carp. It is easy to get the feeling that life has hardly changed at the Schafhof in its 270 years. Everything from the bread, noodles, jams and confectionery to the apple juice is from the Schafhof's own kitchen (complete with smoke-house) or the local market.

The Winklers have kept the decoration simple, in harmony with the building's wooden beams, tiled floors and stonework. Fabrics are in soft pinks and creams, plastered walls are whitewashed. Bedrooms are cosy – simple pine beds nest beneath honey-coloured beams in those on the attic floor, others on the first floor accommodate grander antique furniture. There are plans for expansion – not, we hope, to an extent that will interfere with the present welcoming ambience.

Nearby baroque abbey church; bison reserve (10 km).

63916 Amorbach, Schafhof 1
Tel (09373) 97330
Fax (09373) 4120
Location in meadows, 3 km W of Amorbach; with ample car parking
Meals breakfast, lunch, dinner, snacks
Prices rooms DD-DDDD; lunch from DM49, dinner from DM98
Rooms 23 double, all with bath, (3 twins); all rooms have central heating, phone, TV, radio, hairdrier on request; some rooms have minibar **Facilities** dining-room, bar; terraces, courtyards, lake, tennis court, garden chess, bicycles, horse-drawn carriages **Credit cards** AE, DC, MC, V **Children** welcome **Disabled** access difficult **Pets** accepted in public rooms **Closed** never **Languages** English, French **Proprietor**s Lothar and Charlotte Winkler

Northern Bayern

Converted castle, Bad Neustadt

Kur- & Schloßhotel

This is the place to go for a pampering – 'a hotel with a special charme' as one German visitor has described it to us. Many people visit Bad Neustadt to take a *Kur*, and staying at the Schloßhotel, which is situated in the middle of the town, is a luxurious way of recharging the batteries in the name of healthy living. Even the food is geared towards being "anti-stress", or, intriguingly, "Lady-vital".

Michael Erichsen not only runs the kitchens, but also manages the hotel with his wife, Andrea; together they have recently restored this unassuming 18thC baroque castle with refreshing zest. Heavy silks and matching fabrics decorate the splendidly spacious bedrooms, handsome marble is used in the bathrooms, and the two rococo dining rooms are blessed with glorious, intricately moulded ceilings.

Yet for all this luxury, prices are surprisingly modest, especially given that Neustadt is in an area popular with tourists. This, however, will no doubt change as the Schloßhotel becomes better known, an inevitable consequence of being featured in a hotel guide.

Nearby Kurpark, old town; skiing, walking

97616 Bad Neustadt an der Saale, Kurhausstr 37
Tel (09771) 61610
Fax (09771) 2533
Location opposite Kurpark in middle of town; with car parking
Meals breakfast, lunch, dinner, snacks
Prices rooms D-DDD with breakfast; meals from DM30
Rooms 8 double, 6 suites; all rooms have central heating, phone, TV, minibar, radio
Facilities dining-rooms, bar, conference room; terrace
Credit cards AE, DC, MC, V
Children welcome
Disabled lift/elevator
Pets accepted
Closed never
Languages English
Proprietor Michael and Andrea Erichsen

Northern Bayern

Town hotel, Bad Neustadt

Schwan & Post

The popularity of Bad Neustadt's old town, with its inviting little shops set in narrow cobbled streets (many of which are for pedestrians only), makes parking difficult. All the more reason to head for the car park of the bustling little Schwan & Post, by the town's old entrance gate.

The hotel has a distinctive cream and grey façade, embellished by two splendid statues set in niches, and a tiny terrace. Inside, the decorative scheme is a restrained blend of old and new. A grand marble-painted staircase leads up from the large lobby to a traditional landing lined with modern oils and watercolours, and richly patterned rugs on the polished wooden floors. Wonderful antique doors lead into the pleasant, older bedrooms. The annexe contains soulless but comfortable modern rooms, simply fitted out in light ash, plus a sauna and whirlpool complex.

The attractively light dining-rooms are done in green, with menus written on a board and a long bar in one corner for pre-dinner drinks. The 'Postillion Stube' is less formal, with Provençal tiles on the floor and cartoons on the walls; the vaulted cellar bar has a charcoal grill and rustic feel.

Nearby Salzburg castle; skiing, walking.

97616 Bad Neustadt, Hohnstr 35
Tel (09771) 91070
Fax (09771) 910720
Location at entrance gate to old town; with car parking and some garages
Meals breakfast, lunch, dinner
Prices rooms D-DDD with breakfast; meals DM35-65
Rooms 15 twin, 15 single, all with bath; all rooms have central heating, phone, TV, minibar, radio
Facilities dining-room, bar, stube, whirlpool, solarium, fitness room
Credit cards AE, DC, MC, V
Children welcome
Disabled no special facilities
Pets accepted (DM15 per night) **Closed** never
Languages English
Proprietors Eva-Maria and Karlheinz Göb

Northern Bayern

Town wine-house, Bamberg

Weinhaus Messerschmitt

Set on a large island that splits the river Regnitz, the ancient core of the cathedral city of Bamberg is all cobbled streets, half-timbered and gabled houses and flower-filled courtyards. The 15thC Weinhaus Messerschmitt is very much a part of it in spirit, although physically it is set on a busy through-route.

The Weinhaus opened as a restaurant in 1832 and has remained in the Pschorn family since then; now Lydia Pschorn is in charge of the cooking and her husband Otto looks after the wine-cellars. The restaurant is well known for its regional specialities, including locally caught fish (or even eels, served in sage), and the Hubertusstube serves snacks and good wines throughout the day, while coffee and home-made cakes are available in the green oasis of the garden room.

The painted exterior of the hotel is immediately striking, and the inside does not disappoint – comfortingly traditional, with tiled floors, polished old wood and rustic decorations. The bedrooms are restfully decorated and comfortably furnished with good reproductions, and the tiled bathrooms decorated with antique fittings.

Nearby Gothic cathedral, episcopal and imperial palace.

96047 Bamberg,
Lange Str 41
Tel (0951) 27866
Fax (0951) 26141
Location in middle of Bamberg, near old part of town; with parking for 3 cars
Meals breakfast, lunch, dinner, snacks
Prices rooms D-DDD with breakfast; meals from DM24-70
Rooms 11 double with bath; 4 single, one with bath, 3 with shower; 2 suites; all rooms have central heating, phone, TV, minibar, radio
Facilities dining-room, drawing room, conference room; courtyard **Credit cards** AE, DC, MC, V **Children** accepted **Disabled** no special facilities **Pets** not accepted **Closed** never **Languages** English, French **Proprietor** Otto and Lydia Pschorn

Town hotel, Bamberg

Barock Hotel am Dom

Any irritation at the difficulty of finding this hotel (our inspector was reduced to kidnapping a local) is dispelled on arrival by the warmth of the welcome. Nothing is too much trouble for Frau Goller and her staff, from advising on where to eat, to rearranging cars for the convenience of the guests. Set in the middle of the old town, where car parking is a nightmare, this hotel scores heavily in having its own spaces just at the front.

Outside, the baroque building is splendidly ornate, despite its small scale. The interior has been renovated to create a comfortable hotel – but not one of great character or atmosphere. Only the breakfast room, with its rough-plastered, vaulted ceiling, reveals much of the building's antiquity. Although antiques line the hall and landings, the bedrooms are plainly furnished with modern fittings.

Frau Goller serves a hearty breakfast, with muesli, yogurts, meats and cheese, and constant smiles. The Barock Hotel am Dom is perfectly placed for exploring the old town of Bamberg, and there are many good *Stuben* in the area for lunch or dinner.
Nearby Old Town, Cathedral (Knight of Bamberg and Tomb of Heinrich II), Diocesan Museum.

96049 Bamberg, Vorderer Bach 4
Tel (0951) 54031
Fax (0951) 54021
Location in tiny street off pedestrian square near cathedral; with some car parking
Meals breakfast
Prices rooms D-DD with breakfast
Rooms 11 twin, 5 single, all with shower; one family room with bath; all rooms have central heating, phone, TV, minibar, radio
Facilities breakfast room
Credit cards AE, DC, MC, V
Children very welcome
Disabled access easy; lift/elevator
Pets accepted (DM5 per night)
Closed 6 Jan to 6 Feb
Languages English
Proprietor Inge Goller

Northern Bayern

Castle hotel, Bayreuth

Schloßhotel Thiergarten

This delightful late-baroque hunting lodge is set on a hill where the road from nearby Bayreuth winds up through farm and field. So it comes as a rather a shock to find that the *autobahn* the other side of the hill is visible and just audible. But the atmosphere of the little hotel itself is one of calm: most rooms and the terrace face east, where nothing interrupts the rural views and well-mannered service.

The downstairs rooms evoke another age, with well preserved stucco walls by Domencio Caddenazi, glorious chandeliers, candle-lit tables and large oil canvasses. You can eat in the elegant Wilhelmine Room, or the Venetian Room, named after its superb mirror and chandelier. There is also a pretty pink room with lovely fireplace for small parties, while larger receptions are held in the *Barocksaal*, a stunning domed rotunda with a glorious ceiling.

The bedrooms are all large and comfortable – some with green-stained furniture, others with varnished pine. Note, however, plans for massive development are afoot – enjoy the luxury of this hotel while it is still small.

Nearby Margrave Opera House, New Castle.

95448 Bayreuth, Oberthiergärtner Str 36
Tel (09209) 9840
Fax (09209) 98429
Location in countryside, 6 km SE of Bayreuth; with gardens, ample car parking and garages
Meals breakfast, lunch, dinner, snacks
Prices rooms DD-DDD with breakfast; meals DM20-75
Rooms 8 double, 6 with bath, 2 with shower; all rooms have central heating, phone, hairdrier, TV, minibar, radio
Facilities 2 dining-rooms, bar, conference room; sauna, terrace, outdoor pool
Credit cards AE, DC, MC, V
Children welcome
Disabled no special facilities
Pets accepted (DM10/night)
Closed never
Languages English
Proprietors Renate and Harald Kaiser

Northern Bayern

Hotel Eisenkrug

The pink-washed Eisenkrug may not have quite the sightseeing appeal of the nearby Deutsches Haus (page 181), but it shares the attraction of a central location in the the well preserved old town of Dinkelsbühl, overlooking the wine market, and in some respects is the more desirable place to stay.

Chief among these is the food – a blend of Franconian-Swabian specialities with more creative modern dishes – certainly the best in town, and good enough to earn a Michelin star. The main restaurant, Zum kleinen Obristen, is smart and pleasant, but with no particular character; its reproduction furniture is elegant. For more atmosphere you must descend to the Weinkeller, where, in the evenings, less ambitious food is served beneath low stone-vaulted ceilings. (Just hope that your visit does not coincide with that of a group enjoying a 'traditional Knight's banquet'.) For an afternoon coffee and cake, there is a little terrace in front of the building.

The bedrooms have been carefully furnished with a mixture of antiques and reproductions and the best are admirably spacious. A new guesthouse nearby has doubled the accommodation.

Nearby St George's church, Segringer Str, ramparts, Stadtmühle.

91550 Dinkelsbühl, Dr Martin-Luther-Str 1
Tel (09851) 6017
Fax (09851) 6020
Location in middle of old town, near wine market; public car parking nearby
Meals breakfast, lunch, dinner, snacks
Prices rooms D-DD, with breakfast; meals DM30-60
Rooms 18 double, one with bath, 17 with shower; 2 single with shower; one family room with bath; all rooms have central heating, phone, hairdrier, TV, minibar, safe
Facilities dining-room, bar, wine cellar, conference room; terrace
Credit cards AE, DC, MC, V
Children welcome
Disabled lift/elevator
Pets accepted (DM10 per night)
Closed never
Languages English, French
Proprietor Martin Scharff

Northern Bayern

Village inn, Erlangen-Frauenaurach

Schwarzer Adler

Tucked away from industrial Erlangen, in the outlying village of Frauenaurach, this delightful old *Weinstube* by the village church is a peaceful bolt-hole.

The rustic character of the timbered exterior means that the inside comes as no surprise to the visitor, other than in its extremely tasteful simplicity. A twisted oak stairway leads up to the two floors of bedrooms, passing an old rocking horse and grandfather clock on the landing. Bedrooms, each named after the birds hand-painted on its door, continue the good taste: 'Stork', for example, has an antique linenfold pine wardrobe and half-timbered and whitewashed walls. Despite the apparent simplicity of the bedrooms, all are fully equipped with modern conveniences.

Breakfast is accompanied (as the maid was pleased to point out to our inspector) by piped music. Although other main meals are not served at the Schwarzer Adler, snacks and drinks are available in the evenings, served either in the jolly *Weinstube* (wine-room) itself, with its decorative antlers and carved figures, or outside on the terrace.

Nearby Erlangen (5 km) – art gallery, castle garden.

91056 Erlangen-Frauenaurach, Herdegenpl 1
Tel (09131) 992051
Fax (09131) 993195
Location in small village square, 2 km from E45, SW of Erlangen; with ample public car parking
Meals breakfast, snacks
Prices rooms DD with breakfast
Rooms 9 twin, 5 single, one family room, all with shower; all rooms have central heating, phone, hairdrier, TV, minibar
Facilities *Stube*, terrace
Credit cards AE, DC, V
Children welcome
Disabled one ground-floor room **Pets** accepted
Closed mid-May to June, mid-Aug to Sep **Languages** English, some French
Proprietor Christiane Müller-Kinzel

Northern Bayern

Town inn, Feuchtwangen

Hotel Greifen-Post

This solid old hotel – plain and pink-washed without, but seductively warm and full of character within – has been in the business of refreshing the inner man since 1369. Recent updating has improved the facilities without spoiling the ambience. The dining-room has kept its coloured frescoes on the walls, but the kitchens use modern combinations, such as lamb with black olive sauce. More basic grills, cooked on an open wood fire, are available in the relaxed *Poststüble*, and there are another four quaint *Stuben*, each with its own flavour.

Bedrooms at the Greifen-Post have different styles, too, whether the ubiquitous Laura Ashley, the grander German Biedermeier (currently much beloved by British designers), or the rustic four-poster. Care and comfort are the unifying factors. The neighbouring building, the 16thC Neumeisterhaus, has been incorporated into the hotel, and this has given the Lorentzes another 2 apartments with separate sitting-rooms.

The swimming-pool, subject of much well-justified pride, is housed in what was, until the 1930s, an old stable block.

Nearby Roman cloisters, museum; Dinkelsbühl (10 km); Rothenburg ob der Tauber (25 km).

91555 Feuchtwangen, Marktplatz 8
Tel (09852) 6800 **Fax** 68068
Location in market square of old town 25 km SW of Ansbach; ample parking nearby
Meals breakfast, lunch, dinner
Prices rooms DD-DDD, with breakfast; 50% discount for children under 10; meals DM45-80
Rooms 32 double, 19 with bath, 13 with shower (4 twin); 6 single with shower; 3 family rooms with shower; all rooms have central heating, phone, hairdrier, TV, minibar, radio
Facilities 4 dining-rooms, library, 3 breakfast rooms, bar; bicycles **Credit cards** AE, DC, MC, V **Children** welcome
Disabled no special facilities
Pets accepted **Closed** never; restaurant only, Jan; Mon, Tue in winter **Languages** English, French, Italian
Proprietor Eduard Lorentz

Northern Bayern

Halbritter's Landgasthaus

The Halbritter money comes from the rag trade, we hear. Plenty of it must have been absorbed in the creation of this extraordinary country inn, newly built in traditional style, and designer-decorated and furnished with the kind of confident style that is rare enough in city-centre hotels – and virtually unknown in deepest Bavaria.

Wherever you go in this hotel, there is no getting away from the hand of the designer – the attention to detail is comprehensive, even oppressive. But, equally, there is no denying that the results are impressive. Traditional flourishes – swagged drapes above the windows in the public rooms, ornate wall-lights and door handles – go hand-in-hand with crisp contemporary wooden chairs. There is enough variety in the rich colour schemes to give each of the impressively comfortable bedrooms its own character.

The food in the main, coolly elegant dining-room is as fashionably modern as the bathrooms. In the simpler Grill-Stube you can have more robust country dishes, while surrounded by murals showing various indulgent scenes.

Nearby Saaleck Castle; Veitshocheim (40 km) – rococo gardens.

97797 Hammelburg, Hauptstr 4, Wartmannsroth
Tel (09737) 890
Fax (09737) 8940
Location in village 10 km NW of Hammelburg; with garden and ample car parking
Meals breakfast, lunch, dinner
Prices rooms DD-DDD with breakfast; meals from DM35
Rooms 11 double, all with bath; all rooms have central heating, phone, hairdrier, TV, minibar, radio
Facilities lobby, dining-room, piano bar, *Stube*, terrace, bicycles
Credit cards AE, MC, V
Children welcome **Disabled** no special facilities **Pets** not accepted **Closed** mid-Jan to mid-Feb, 2 wks Aug
Languages English
Proprietor Sepp Halbritter

Northern Bayern

Country hotel, Hohenau

Die Bierhütte

In the depths of the countryside near the Czechoslovakian border, the isolated position of this hotel does not seem to interfere with custom: on the occasion of our summer lunchtime visit the dining-rooms were busy serving anything from stuffed cabbage to marinated salmon. Puddings are particularly recommended, and the wine list is good and wide-ranging. But the Bierhütte's popularity has as much to do with the surroundings as the food. The outside terrace has large tables overlooking the hotel's pond, while inside the sophisticated *Wappen Stube* has a stunning painted ceiling and marble floor.

The bedrooms are housed in three different buildings: above the dining-rooms in the handsome, smartly renovated old brewery on which the hotel is based; in a chalet-style building where gingham and pine are much in evidence; or in the latest addition – another chalet, with modern leather armchairs and state-of-the-art lighting.

Ludwig Störzer runs an informal hotel very efficiently, and the staff are friendly. The hotel dominates the tiny village, its grounds encompassing neighbouring farm buildings.

Nearby winter sports, National Parkland woods.

94546 Hohenau, Bierhütte
10 **Tel** (08558) 96120
Fax (08558) 961270
Location in hamlet 4 km N of Freyung; with gardens and ample car parking
Meals breakfast, lunch, dinner, snacks
Prices rooms D-DDD with breakfast; meals DM35-75
Rooms 40 double, 16 with bath, 24 with shower; 3 single with shower; all rooms have central heating, phone, TV, minibar, radio; some rooms have hairdrier
Facilities 2 dining-rooms, breakfast room, *Stube*, terrace, playground
Credit cards AE, DC, MC, V
Children welcome **Disabled** no special facilities **Pets** welcome (DM10 per night)
Closed never **Languages** French, English, Italian
Proprietor Ludwig Störzer

Northern Bayern

Hotel zum Riesen

The 'oldest guest-house in Germany', the zum Riesen is in a prime position in the pedestrianized heart of pretty Miltenberg – and can be noisy as a result. Entrance is through a side door, as the main *Stube* downstairs is a separate business. Once in the lift to the hotel upstairs, however, you enter a different world.

Werner Jöst is justifiably proud of the luxurious atmosphere he has created in his hotel, where the rooms are named after past aristocratic guests. Trained as an architect, Herr Jöst has respected the age of the building. Some rooms are timbered and plastered, in others sandstone walls are left exposed, and each room has a different style – the Kaiser Friedrich has a beautifully painted yellow and white interior, with beams decorated in black and white; the Kaiserin Maria, with its own roof terrace, is very light and embellished with crystal ornaments. Some rooms have glorious antiques, some rustic or contemporary furniture.

Cilly Jöst's plentiful breakfasts are served in a rough-plastered room in the eaves, with pretty illustrations on the walls. For lunch or dinner, there is the downstairs *Stube* where Jürgen Lange cooks his patented 'no salt, pepper or paprika' meals.

Nearby Schnatterloch (Chattering Square), fountain.

63897 Miltenberg, Hauptstr 97
Tel (09371) 3644
Location half-way down main pedestrian street (with vehicular access for residents); with no private car parking
Meals breakfast only
Prices rooms D-DD with breakfast
Rooms 14 double, all with bath or shower; all rooms have central heating; most rooms have phone
Facilities breakfast room
Credit cards DC, MC
Children welcome
Disabled lift/elevator
Pets well behaved dogs only
Closed Dec to end Mar
Languages English and Italian
Proprietors Cilly and Werner Jöst

Northern Bayern

Restaurant with rooms, Muggendorf

Hotel Feiler

In a village tucked away up the green Wiesenttal, this half-timbered house has been in the hands of the Feiler family since 1890, and they have brought it to the height of rustic sophistication. It is a delight to sit on the glorious terrace, listening to the hotel's lovebirds singing below, and eating summer truffles collected and cooked by mushroom expert Horst Feiler. The menu is worth taking time over, and an appetiser is brought to the table while guests ponder over such specialities as fillets of sole with crayfish in a wood-mushroom sauce, and fillets of lamb in mustard sauce baked in a walnut pastry crust. The Feiler spaniels meander through diners' legs hunting for gourmet crumbs. It is that sort of hotel.

The 15 bedrooms strike the right note: spacious and prettily decorated in Laura Ashley prints, most looking out on to the flowery courtyard at the back. Attention to detail and flair are always in evidence – Dresden porcelain clocks and lovely lamps grace the dining-rooms, unusual art nouveau stained glass panels of the Four Seasons enliven the winter dining-room.

Nearby Ebermannstadt (5 km) – Gothic church, 17thC water wheel; Gößweinstein (10 km) – 11thC castle.

91346 Muggendorf, Oberer Markt 4
Tel (09196) 92450
Fax (09196) 362
Location in small village in Wiesental valley; with garden and ample car parking
Meals breakfast, lunch, dinner
Prices rooms DD-DDDD with breakfast; meals DM48-120
Rooms 9 double, 3 with bath; 5 with shower; one single with shower; 2 suites; 3 apartments with bath; all rooms have cen tral heating, phone, TV
Facilities dining-room; garden terrace
Credit cards AE, MC, V
Children welcome **Disabled** not suitable **Pets** accepted (DM10 per night) **Closed** Mon, between 15 Nov and 15 Mar **Languages** English
Proprietor Horst Feiler

Northern Bayern

Luxury inn, Pegnitz

Pflaums Posthotel

One of the most surprising and eccentric hotels in any of our guides, run by the Pflaums brothers. An old post house in Pegnitz, south of Bayreuth, the half-timbered exterior – dripping with trailing geraniums in summer – entirely belies what it contains. The proximity to Bayreuth gives the theme: Wagner. A screen in the lobby shows films of the composer's operas; rooms are named after Wagnerian characters and contain videos and CDs of his music. Some suites are ultra-modern interpretations of late-19thC Bayreuth stage designs. In one, you are cocooned between walls of buttoned red velvet; in another, a huge illustration of a church stage set acts as backdrop to the bed. In another, 'Parsifal', where Placido Domingo was the first guest, a thousand tiny stars pierce the dark at the flick of a switch. Some suites have gardens, and there is a special family suite, with play area for children. The futuristic treatment is carried through most of the hotel – there is also an Internet bar and a modern art gallery – although the *stübe* is in traditionally rustic style with cooking to match. The sophisticated restaurant acts as a palliative to all the stagey Design elsewhere. Great breakfasts, civilized service.
Nearby Bayreuth (19 km); Nürnberg (52 km).

91257 Pegnitz,
Nürnbergerstrasse 12-16
Tel (09241) 7250
Fax (09241) 80404
E-mail 100741.2016@compuserve.com
Location just outside Pegnitz, SW of town; ample parking
Meals breakfast, lunch, dinner
Prices rooms DDD-DDDD with breakfast; dinner DM60
Rooms 25 double, 25 suites all with bath; all rooms have central heating, TV, video, CD, radio, phone, hairdrier
Facilities dining-rooms, sitting-rooms, TV room, bar, meeting room, health club, indoor golf; terrace **Credit cards** AE, DC, MC, V
Children welcome **Disabled** 1 ground floor room; lift **Pets** by arrangement **Closed** never
Languages English, French
Proprietors Andreas and Hermann Pflaums

Northern Bayern

Converted castle, Riedenburg

Schloß Eggersberg

This solid 15thC castle was used by the von Bassus family as their hunting headquarters for over 250 years. The surrounding park still belongs to the Schloß, and while staying here you can play at being a country landowner – with nearby boating, fishing and 120 km of cycle-ways at your disposal. You can even stable horses here, and hack along the many bridle-ways. In winter, there are nursery slopes for the inexpert skier, with a drag-lift back to the house and marvellous trails for the *Langläufer.*

But you do not have to be athletic to appreciate Schloß Eggersberg; it is a warmly welcoming house, in a privileged country setting well off the beaten track, serving ambitious international food.

For the culturally inclined, there is a theatre in a converted granary. As for the bedrooms, they are, as you would hope, spacious and beautifully furnished; there are antiques of different periods, richly colourful Persian rugs on polished wooden floors, pictures against the whitewashed walls, and smart modern bathrooms.

Nearby Altmühl valley; Eichstätt (35 km) – 14thC cathedral, Residence Square (rococo palaces).

93339 Riedenburg
Tel (09442) 1498
Fax (09442) 2845
Location in rural park in Obereggersberg, 4 km W of Riedenburg; with ample car parking
Meals breakfast, lunch, dinner, snacks
Prices rooms D-DD with breakfast; children under 4 free; meals DM19-36
Rooms 10 double, 4 single, one family room, all with bath; all rooms have central heating, radio
Facilities dining-rooms, TV room; theatre; terrace, tennis, watersports, cycling, riding **Credit cards** AE, DC, MC, V **Children** very welcome **Disabled** access difficult **Pets** tolerated
Closed restaurant only, Mon
Languages English **Managers** Kirsten and Bernhard Leidl

Northern Bayern

Town hotel, Rothenburg ob der Tauber

Burg-Hotel

Gabriele Berger-Klatte appends her name to that of her elegant little hotel as a sort of subtitle, underlining her contribution to its character. The building, set in old monastery grounds on the edge of the historic town of Rothenburg, high above the Tauber valley, started life in the 12thC as a barn. The outside still has a monastic severity, but the interior is now notably feminine in its decoration and furnishings (and the place appears to be run entirely by women).

The views are magnificent, and best experienced when breakfasting on the terrace set into the medieval city walls; for dreary days, there is a pretty, soft pink breakfast room, with classically turned ash furniture, and a civilized little sitting-room. The bedrooms are equally elegant, decorated with peaceful, coordinating colours and fine furniture; some are notably spacious. It is worth asking for a room with a view of the Tauber, but the windows are scarcely panoramic.

If we were forced to choose, this would be our pick of the several hotels we list for Rothenburg.

Nearby Town Hall, the Plönlein, 14thC altarpiece in St-Jakob-Kirche, Herrngaße, Topplerschlösschen tower.

91541 Rothenburg ob der Tauber, Klostergasse 3
Tel (09861) 94890
Fax (09861) 948940
Location within old walls of medieval city, overlooking Tauber Valley; with cloister garden and car parking
Meals breakfast only
Prices rooms DD-DDDD with breakfast
Rooms 15 double, all with bath; all rooms have central heating, telephone, hairdrier, TV, minibar, radio; some rooms hav e safes
Facilities sitting-room, breakfast room; terrace
Credit cards AE, DC, MC, V
Children welcome
Disabled 2 ground-floor rooms **Pets** accepted
Closed never
Languages English, French
Proprietor Gabriele Berger-Klatte

Northern Bayern

Town hotel, Rothenburg ob der Tauber

Hotel Markusturm

Built as a customs house in 1264, the Markusturm fits snugly against the old tower (once part of the city ramparts) from which it takes its name, just on the edge of the traffic-free central area of romantic Rothenburg, near the market-place. The steeply pitched roof, yellow-washed exterior and powder blue shutters of the hotel are picturesque, and the traditional interior does not disappoint.

The place became an inn as long ago as 1488, but quite properly now prefers to be called a hotel. The bedrooms vary: many are furnished with comfortable antiques, and some have beamed ceilings, but others have a more modern look to them; all are decorated with taste and restraint, and the best are notably spacious. Downstairs, the decoration is rather more fussy – hanging planters, dried flower arrangements and ornamental *objets* abound.

The food is traditional, with seasonal game, fish from the hotel's own ponds, and good local dishes. From August until the end of October, the chef takes special delight in hunting for and serving up local mushrooms.

Nearby Town Hall, the Plönlein corner, the Burggarten.

91541 Rothenburg ob der Tauber, Rodergasse 1
Tel (09861) 2098
Fax (09861) 2692
Location in middle of town, next to Markusturm; with garages and car parking
Meals breakfast, lunch, dinner
Prices rooms DM140-300 with breakfast; meals DM20-45
Rooms 22 double, 13 with bath, 9 with shower (5 twin); 3 single, one with bath, 2 with shower; 3 family rooms with bath; all rooms have central heating, telephone, hairdrier, TV, radio
Facilities dining-rooms, sauna **Credit cards** DC, MC, V **Children** very welcome
Disabled no special facilities
Pets accepted **Closed** restaurant only, Jan
Languages English, French, Italian **Proprietor** Marianne and Stephan Berger

Northern Bayern

Town inn, Rothenburg ob der Tauber

Kloster-Stüble

Down a small side-street off the market-place, this little yellow-washed inn dating from 1540 offers something of an escape from the tourist traffic of Rothenburg. Step inside and you find a peaceful, dark hall with a painted mural and decorated chest.

The tranquillity extends to the bedrooms upstairs, which were renovated in 1987 and are prettily furnished with matching pine furniture, comfortable sofas and fresh lacy curtains. Space is at a premium in some of the rooms – but a four-poster has been squeezed into one bedroom and, with the pine-panelled walls, the overall effect is cosy rather than squashed. Bedrooms at the rear of the hotel have splendid views over the wooded Tauber valley as far as the distant Sauturm.

The *Stube* downstairs is simple, with dried flowers and rustic knick-knacks hanging from walls and ceiling, and a jovial mural depicting drinking and wenching; the dining-room beyond is pretty in pink, with fresh flowers on the tables and French windows on to the terraces at the side. Rudolf Hammel is both owner and cook, producing simple food that is refreshingly inexpensive.

Nearby old town, ramparts, town museum.

91541 Rothenburg ob der Tauber,
Heringsbronnengasse 5
Tel (09861) 6774
Fax (09861) 6474
Location in middle of town, near market-place; vehicle access restricted during day, public car parking nearby
Meals breakfast, lunch, dinner
Prices rooms D-DD with breakfast; meals DM25-50
Rooms 13 double with shower (2 twin); 2 single with shower; 5 family rooms, one with bath, 4 with shower; all rooms have central heating, TV; some rooms have minibar
Facilities dining-room, *Stube;* terraces **Credit cards** V
Children welcome
Disabled not suitable
Pets accepted **Closed** restaurant only, Jan and Feb
Languages English
Proprietor Rudolf Hammel

Northern Bayern

Town inn, Volkach

Zur Schwane

On the banks of the mighty river Main, Volkach is a little town surrounded by rolling vine-covered hills. Housed in one of the prettiest buildings in the town, the zur Schwane has been serving customers since 1404, and is one of the area's oldest inns. To enter, you pass through an old archway into the cobbled courtyard. In summer, this is a charming spot for lunch, especially when the sun filters through the soft vines trailing overhead – and vines are very important to the Pfaff family, who have their own vineyards and sell their award-winning wines at the hotel.

The kitchens are more than a match for the hotel's cellars, providing good wholesome food with a regional slant. For informal meals, the ancient *Stüberl* has wood-panelled walls and a stunning painted wood ceiling; there is also a more formal dining-room – light and pretty, with white plaster pillars, old oil portraits of local worthies, and elegant silver candlesticks.

Bedrooms vary in style, the older being plain but perfectly comfortable, and the newer rooms more refined, with pretty striped wallpaper, delicate lighting and swish bathrooms.
Nearby walks, river trips, wine-tasting.

97332 Volkach,
Haupstrasse 12
Tel (09381) 80660
Fax (09381) 806666
Location on main street of small town, 25 km E of Würzburg; private car parking
Meals breakfast, lunch, dinner
Prices rooms D-DDDD with breakfast; meals DM39-110
Rooms 16 double, 11 single, all with shower; 2 apartments with bath; all rooms have central heating, phone, TV; most rooms have radio; some rooms have hairdrier, minibar **Facilities** 2 dining-rooms, *stube*, conference room **Credit cards** AE, DC, MC, V **Children** welcome
Disabled no special facilities
Pets small dogs only accepted
Closed restaurant only , 20 Dec to 20 Jan **Languages** English **Proprietor**s Petra and Michael Pfaff

Northern Bayern

Posthotel

Once upon a time there was a famous Knight of Wirsberg, who ruled his poor subjects from a castle on the hill above the village. The castle has fallen; only the gardens remain for the use of guests of this former coaching inn; and the forest-girt village of Wirsberg is now a popular health resort.

The Posthotel occupies a central position overlooking the market square. There is no traffic noise, but loud taped music assaults you in the lobby. That apart, this is an exceedingly elegant and comfortable place to stay – bedrooms are of a high standard, with fabrics and papers in Laura Ashley style and high-quality reproduction furniture. Some of the back bedroom windows open out to the sound of the nearby river.

The main dining-room is large, with white-washed walls offsetting its lack of windows, and barley twist pillars giving diners something to look at if the uneven service is having an off-day. Breakfast is served in a pretty, light room with lovely Indian rugs.

One of the hotel's main attractions is its superb indoor pool, looking like a Roman bath.

Nearby medieval market place, steam engine museum; Kulmbach (10 km) – beer, Plassenburg castle.

95339 Wirsberg, Marktplatz 11
Tel (09227) 2080
Fax (09227) 5860
Location in market square of village, 21 km N of Bayreuth; with ample public parking
Meals breakfast, lunch, dinner, snacks
Prices rooms DD-DDD with breakfast; meals DM18-98
Rooms 24 double, 7 single, 5 apartments, 10 suites, all with bath; all rooms have central heating, phone, hairdrier, TV, minibar, radio; most rooms have air-conditioning
Facilities sitting-room, breakfast room, dining-room, bar, conference room, indoor swimming-pool, sauna
Credit cards AE, DC, MC, V
Children welcome **Disabled** no special facilities **Pets** accepted **Closed** never
Languages English, French, Italian
Proprietor Herta Herrmann

Village inn, Altenkunstadt

Hotel Gondel

Behind the neat, traditional, white-and-timber façade is a warm interior of carved doors and beams, with rough-cast walls painted white, and unassuming bedrooms above. It has been owned by the jovial Herr Jahn's family since 1900.

■ 96264 Altenkunstadt, Marktplatz 7 **Tel** (09572) 3661 **Fax** (09572) 4596 **Meals** breakfast, lunch, dinner **Prices** rooms D-DD with breakfast; meals DM18-40 **Rooms** 38, all with bath or shower, central heating, phone, TV **Credit cards** not accepted **Closed** one week early Jan, one week Aug; restaurant only, Fri **Languages** English, Italian

City hotel, Ansbach

Hotel Bürger-Palais

A grand town house, expensively renovated in keeping with the beautiful baroque exterior. A profusion of Bavarian crystal chandeliers and silk damask in the bedrooms, marble in the bathrooms, rough wooden walls in the *Stüble*. Pretty garden and terrace .

■ 91522 Ansbach, Neustadt 48 **Tel** (0981) 95131 **Fax** (0981) 95600 **Meals** breakfast, lunch, dinner **Prices** rooms DD-DDD with breakfast; meals from DM26 **Rooms** 12, all with bath, central heating, phone, TV **Credit cards** AE, DC, MC, V **Closed** never **Languages** English, French

Town hotel, Bad Kissingen

Laudensacks Parkhotel

This turn-of-the-century house set in large gardens has been gutted by Hermann and Susanne Laudensack to make a gracious *Kurhotel*. Food is suberb, they are charming hosts, furnishings are of the contemporary sophisticated sort – this is a winner.

■ 97688 Bad Kissingen, Kurhausstr 28 **Tel** (0971) 72240 **Fax** (0971) 722444 **Meals** breakfast, lunch, dinner, snacks **Prices** rooms DD-DDD with breakfast; meals from DM68 **Rooms** 19, all with bath, central heating, phone, hairdrier, TV, minibar, radio **Credit cards** AE, DC, MC, V **Closed** mid-Dec to end Jan; restaurant only, Thu **Languages** English

Town hotel, Bayreuth

Hotel Königshof

The utilitarian exterior hides a graciously furnished hotel, well positioned close to the Festival Theatre, and opposite the station. Bedrooms come in all shapes and sizes, priced accordingly, and Uwe Werner has decorated them with style.

■ 95444 Bayreuth, Bahnhofstr 23 **Tel** (0921) 24094 **Fax** (0921) 12264 **Meals** breakfast, lunch, dinner **Prices** rooms DD-DDDD with breakfast; meals DM27-130 **Rooms** 35, all with bath or shower, central heating, phone, TV, minibar **Credit cards** AE, DC, MC, V **Closed** never **Languages** English, French

Northern Bayern

Country guest-house, Bayreuth

Gastätte im Park der Eremitage

Elegant, slightly austere rooms in the romantic formal gardens of Princess Wilhelmina's Schloß – some in a converted coach - house, some in the water-tower that feeds the fountains. Wonderfully peaceful. Sadly, neither food nor service would win awards.

■ 95448 Bayreuth, Schlossallee **Tel** (0921) 99287 **Meals** breakfast, lunch, dinner **Prices** rooms D-DD with breakfast; meals from DM15 **Rooms** 10, all with bath or shower, central heating; some have telephone, TV **Credit cards** not accepted **Closed** 15 Sep to 1 Mar; Tue in low season **Languages** English

---

Converted castle, Colmberg

Burg Colmberg

A mighty Bavarian edifice that whisks guests back 1000 years, while still offering modern creature comforts. Some glorious bed rooms. With a golf course, children's playground and animal park, no lack of activities.

■ 91598 Colmberg, An der Burgenstr **Tel** (09803) 615 **Fax** (09803) 262 **Meals** breakfast, lunch, dinner **Prices** rooms D-DDD **Rooms** 27, all with bath or shower, central heating, phone; some have hairdrier **Credit cards** MC **Closed** Jan; Tue **Languages** English

---

Town inn, Dinkelsbühl

Gasthof zum Goldenen Anker

Away from the crowded main streets, this pretty, family-run inn offers traditional-style panelled rooms downstairs and spacious, but slightly anonymous, modern bedrooms upstairs.

■ 91550 Dinkelsbühl, Untere Schmiedsgasse 22 **Tel** (09851) 57800 **Fax** (09851) 578080 **Meals** breakfast, lunch, dinner, snacks **Prices** D-DD with breakfast **Rooms** 16, all with bath or shower, central heating, phone, TV, radio, minibar **Credit cards** AE, DC, MC, V **Closed** 3 weeks Jan **Languages** German only

---

Town inn, Dinkelsbühl

Deutsches Haus

History oozes from every nook of this ancient inn, filled with wall paintings, painted ceilings and doors, antique furniture – a housekeeper's nightmare. Recent updating has breathed life into once worn bedrooms. Frau Kellerbauer is unfailingly charming.

■ 91550 Dinkelsbühl, Weinmarkt 3 **Tel** (09851) 6058 **Fax** (09851) 7911 **Meals** breakfast, lunch, dinner, snacks **Prices** D-DDD **Rooms** 8, all with bath or shower, central heating, phone, TV, minibar, radio **Credit cards** AE, DC, MC, V **Closed** 24 Dec to 10 Jan **Languages** English

Northern Bayern

Country inn, Eschau-Hobbach

Gasthof Engel

Even here, in a 200-year-old inn hidden in the quiet Elsavatal on the edge of the Spessart nature reserve, there are seminar rooms. But don't be put off: the beamed *Stuben* are welcoming, and the new bedroom extension is comfortable.

■ 63863 Eschau-Hobbach, Bayernstrasse 47 **Tel** (09374) 388 **Fax** (09374) 7831 **Meals** breakfast, lunch, dinner **Prices** rooms D-DD with breakfast; meals from DM22 **Rooms** 24, all with bath or shower, central heating, phone, balcony **Credit cards** not accepted **Closed** Fri **Languages** some English

---

Converted winery, Frickenhausen

Hotel Meintzinger

More an expansion of a winery than a conversion, since the long-established Meintzinger wine business continues to prosper alongside this newer venture. Bedrooms are spacious if not particulary stylish, the breakfast room light and cheerful.

■ 8701 Frickenhausen **Tel** (09331) 3077 **Fax** (09331) 7578 **Meals** breakfast, snacks **Prices** rooms D-DDD **Rooms** 21, all with bath or shower, central heating, phone, TV, radio **Credit cards** AE, MC, V **Closed** never **Languages** English

---

Converted castle, Fürsteneck

Schloß Fürsteneck

Unpretentious pension housed in 12thC castle dominating a tiny Bavarian village. Bedrooms are simply furnished in country style, dining-rooms are rustic, the food equally so. A good, simple base from which to tour the pretty area.

■ 94142 Fürsteneck, Schloßweg 5 **Tel** (08505) 1473 **Meals** breakfast, lunch, dinner **Prices** rooms D-DDDD with breakfast; meals D **Rooms** 10, all with central heating **Credit cards** AE, MC **Closed** Jan; restaurant only, Wed **Languages** English

---

Chalet hotel, Grafenau

Säumerhof

Overlook the unprepossessing exterior: a friendly welcome awaits you in this modern chalet, along with stylish comfort in both the bedrooms and the dining-room. And Gebhard Endl's equally modern cooking earns high praise.

■ 94481 Grafenau, Steinberg 32 **Tel** (08552) 2401 **Fax** (08552) 5343 **Meals** breakfast, lunch, dinner **Prices** rooms D-DD with breakfast; meals DM50-120 **Rooms** 11, all with shower, central heating, phone, hairdrier, TV, radio **Credit cards** AE **Closed** restaurant only, Mon to Thu lunch **Languages** English

Northern Bayern

Town hotel, Gunzenhausen

Hotel zur Post

No expense has been spared in the renovation of this fine old post-house into a comfortable modern hotel – the panelled public rooms being particularly successful. The cuisine too is rich, and beautifully presented, if over-ambitious at times.

■ 91710 Gunzenhausen, Bahnhofstr 7 **Tel** (09831) 7061 **Fax** (09831) 9285 **Meals** breakfast, dinner, snacks **Prices** rooms D-DDD with breakfast; dinner from DM14 **Rooms** 26, all with shower, central heating, phone, hairdrier, TV, minibar **Credit cards** AE, DC, MC, V **Closed** 23 Dec to 6 Jan; restaurant only Sun & Mon **Languages** English

Village hotel, Kainsbach bei Hersbruck

Kainsbacher Mühle

The mill wheel (or a replica) still turns, but there is little else antique about this modern hotel, richly ornamented in the best Bavarian neo-rustic style, at least in the public areas – bedrooms are relatively bland. Pleasant garden, indoor pool.

■ 91230 Kainsbach bei Hersbruck **Tel** (09151) 7280 **Fax** (09151) 728162 **Meals** breakfast, lunch, dinner, snacks **Prices** rooms DD-DDD with breakfast; meals DM29-50 **Rooms** 34, all with bath or shower, central heating, phone, TV, minibar, radio **Credit cards** DC, MC, V **Closed** never **Languages** English

Farmhouse hotel, Kötzting

Landsitz Gut Ulmenhof

Unfussy farmhouse accommodation for all the family. No refinements to worry anxious parents, who can let the kids enjoy the surrounding parkland. Donkeys and ponies to ride, fishing, mini-golf and indoor pool also on offer.

■ 93444 Kotzting, Bonried 31 **Tel** (09945) 632 **Meals** breakfast, dinner **Prices** rooms D-DD with breakfast; dinner from DM23 **Rooms** 18, all with bath or shower, central heating, radio **Credit cards** not accepted **Closed** never **Languages** German only

Country hotel, Lohr am Main-Land

Buchenmühle

A handsome, mellow stone house in a peaceful woodland setting, with a large sunny terrace. Inside, welcoming rustic dining-rooms, decorated with more enthusiasm than taste, and bedrooms that may lack character but not comfort.

■ 97816 Lohr am Main, Buchentalstr 23 **Tel** (09352) 3424 **Fax** 6824 **Meals** breakfast, lunch, dinner **Prices** rooms D-DD with breakfast; meals from DM35 **Rooms** 15, all with bath or shower, central heating, phone, TV **Credit cards** MC **Closed** Feb; Mon **Languages** English, French

Northern Bayern

Town hotel, Marktbreit

Hotel Löwen

The welcome here may be cool but the building is splendid: a 15thC half-timbered affair. Inside there are cool medieval hallways, dark-panelled *Stuben* and an extraordinary high-ceilinged rustic dining-room. Some impressive bedrooms, too.

■ 97340 Marktbreit, Marktstr 8 **Tel** (09332) 3085 **Fax** (09332) 9438 **Meals** breakfast, lunch, dinner **Prices** rooms D-DD with breakfast; meals from DM20 **Rooms** 25, all with shower, central heating, phone; some have TV **Credit cards** AE, DC, MC, V **Closed** never **Languages** English

---

Town hotel, Marktheidenfeld

Anker

A prosperous modern hotel, stronger on comfort and housekeeping than style – enthusiastically run by the 12th generation of the Deppisch family, who look on it as a calling, not a job. Breakfast can be taken as easily at midday as at 7am. Michelin starred restaurant, as well as wine cellar for lighter means.

■ 97828 Marktheidenfeld, Obertorstr 6-8 **Tel** (09391) 60040 **Fax** (09391) 600477 **Meals** breakfast, lunch, dinner **Prices** DD-DDD with breakfast **Rooms** 39, all with bath, central heating, phone, TV, radio, minibar, hairdrier **Credit cards** AE, MC, V **Closed** never **Languages** English, French, Italian

---

Town inn, Miltenberg

Jagd Hotel Rose

An inviting wisteria-hung exterior, with red and white striped shutters, and a charming interior – airy, light dining-rooms, with terracotta floors and natural woods, all as neat as Frau Schneider's sparkling little bedrooms.

■ 63897 Miltenberg, Hauptstr 280 **Tel** (09371) 40060 **Fax** (09371) 400617 **Meals** breakfast, lunch, dinner **Prices** rooms DD breakfast DM15; meals DM40-79 **Rooms** 23, all with shower, central heating, phone, hairdrier, TV, minibar, radio **Credit cards** AE, DC, MC, V **Closed** Sun dinner **Languages** English, French, Swedish

---

Country hotel, Nürnberg

Hotel Zirbelstube

'Small and charming' is the motto of this modest canalside hotel, and it lives up to it. Other plus points: an idyllic situation on the Ludwig canal, a richly panelled dining-room, pretty little bedrooms with rich fabrics, and a sunny terrace.

■ 90455 Nürnberg-Worzeldorf 60, Friedrich-Overbeck-Str 1 **Tel** (0911) 998820 **Meals** breakfast, dinner **Prices** rooms DD with breakfast; meals DM120 **Rooms** 8, all with shower, central heating, phone, TV, minibar, radio **Credit cards** AE, MC **Closed** 2 weeks Jan/Feb, 3 weeks Jul/Aug; Mon **Languages** English, French

Northern Bayern

Country hotel, Ochsenfurt

Polisina

'Wald- und Sporthotel' runs the subtitle, accurately conveying
the charm of the setting and extent of facilities (4 tennis courts,
splendid indoor pool with adjacent spectators' sitting-room).
The warm ambience of the stone-and-wood house is a bonus.

■ 97199 Ochsenfurt, Marktbreiter Str 265 **Tel** (09331) 3081
Fax (09331) 8440 meals breakfast, lunch, dinner **Prices** rooms DD-
DDDD with breakfast; **Meals** from DM34 **Rooms** 93, all with bath or
shower, central heating, phone, TV, minibar, radio **Credit cards** AE, DC,
MC, V **Closed** never **Languages** English, French

Town hotel, Passau

Hotel Wilder Mann

Aristocracy have used this rococo-style hotel in droves over the
past 150 years. The bedrooms still retain a regal air, and those
overlooking the garden are protected from street noise.
Gourmet restaurant – Michelin star.

■ 94032 Passau, Am Rathausplatz **Tel** (0851) 35071 **Fax** (0851)
31712 **Meals** breakfast, lunch, dinner **Prices** rooms D; breakfast
DM17; meals from DM39 **Rooms** 49, all with bath or shower, central
heating, phone, TV, radio; some have minibar **Credit cards** AE, DC,
MC, V **Closed** never **Languages** English

Chalet guest-house, Regen

Burggasthof Weißenstein

Peacefully positioned under the ruins of an old castle, this unso-
phisticated little chalet has a wide terrace looking over wooded
Bavarian hills. Inside, dining-rooms are colourful, often further
enlivened by live music; bedrooms are pristine but modest.

■ 94209 Regen, Weißenstein 32 **Tel** (09921) 2259 **Meals** breakfast,
lunch, dinner **Prices** rooms D with breakfast; meals DM12-25
Rooms 15, all with bath or shower, central heating **Credit cards** not
accepted **Closed** Tue; Nov to mid-Dec **Languages** some English

Town hotel, Rothenburg ob der Tauber

Hotel Meistertrunk

A new hotel in an historic building, the Meistertrunk is distinguished by spacious, elegantly furnished bedrooms and a warmly traditional, panelled breakfast room.

■ 91541 Rothenburg ob der Tauber, Herrngasse 26 **Tel** (09861) 6077
Fax (09861) 86871 **Meals** breakfast, lunch, dinner **Prices** D-DDD with
breakfast **Rooms** 15, all with bath or shower, central heating, phone,
radio **Credit cards** AE, MC, V **Closed** Jan & Feb **Languages** English
Credit cards AE, DC, MC, V **Closed** 23-25 Dec **Languages** German
only

Northern Bayern

Town inn, Rothenburg ob der Tauber

Hotel Reichs-Küchenmeister

Largely rebuilt since World War II, this central little inn remains faithful to its 14thC origins, although it now overlaps in to building oppposite. The rustic decorations are not excessive and there are some delightful bedrooms

■ 91541 Rothenburg ob der Tauber, Kirchpl 8-10 **Tel** (09861) 2046 **Fax** (09861) 86965 **Meals** breakfast, dinner, snacks **Prices** DD with breakfast **Rooms** 50, all with central heating, phone, TV, radio **Credit cards** AE, DC, MC, V **Closed** never **Languages** English

Town hotel, Rothenburg ob der Tauber

Hotel Bären

In a tourist town bursting with hotels, the Müllers have invested heavily to outshine the opposition: the result is tastefully opulent. Extra plus-points are Fritz Müller's modern cooking and the peaceful position.

■ 91541 Rothenburg ob der Tauber, Hofbronnengasse 9 **Tel** (09861) 6033 **Fax** (09861) 4 875 **Meals** breakfast, dinner (lunch Fri-Sun and public holidays) **Prices** rooms DD-DDDD with breakfast; meals DM35-135 **Rooms** 35, all with bath, central heating, phone, TV **Credit cards** MC, V **Closed** Jan to Mar **Languages** English

Modern country hotel, Wirsberg

Reiterhof

A lovingly created luxury hotel in a peaceful setting much favoured by skiers, riders and tennis players. Artifice is rife: palm trees by the pool, carved panelling and gilt chandeliers in the public rooms. The food is as rich as the guests.

■ 95339 Wirsberg, Sessenreuther Str 50 **Tel** (09227) 2040 **Fax** (09227) 7058 **Meals** breakfast, lunch, dinner **Prices** rooms DD-DDD with breakfast; meals *à la carte* from DM40 **Rooms** 51, all with bath or shower, central heating, phone, hairdrier, TV, minibar, radio **Credit cards** AE, DC, MC, V **Closed** never **Languages** English

City inn, Würzburg

Zur Stadt Mainz

This inn's dark dining-room, with rustic artefacts hanging from the walls and an extensive traditional menu (written in 5 languages and Braille), befits a history going back to 1430. Bedrooms are pretty and floral, but can be affected by street noise.

■ 97070 Würzburg, Semmelstr 39 **Tel** (0931) 53155 **Fax** (0931) 58510 **Meals** breakfast, lunch, dinner **Prices** DD with breakfast **Rooms** 15, all with shower, central heating, phone, TV, radio **Credit cards** AE, MC, V **Closed** 20 Dec to 20 Jan; restaurant only, Sun din, Mon **Languages** English, French

Southern Bayern

Hotels in Southern Bayern

Lederhosen, dirndl skirts and overflowing *steins* of beer are the foreigner's standard image of Bavarians, and it's all true; however, the region is one of outstanding beauty: steep mountains plunge to meet large, clear lakes, fairy-tale castles perch on top of snow-capped hills, flowers tumble from the wooden balconies of Alpine chalets, and onion-domed spires top the churches. It is also a sportsman's dream, with hiking, climbing, and sailing in the summer; skiing and skating in the winter.

The northern plains and gentle hills of the region are criss-crossed by rivers – perfect wine-growing country. Augsburg, birth-place of Bertholt Brecht, is situated on the 'Romantic Road', and has the Hotel Gregor and its Cheval Blanc restaurant (Tel (0821) 80050, fax 800569, 40 rooms) – the best of a mediocre bunch, although the Fischertor is quiet and comfortable enough, if gloomy-looking from the outside (Tel (0821) 156051, fax 30702, 21 rooms).

Munich bursts with life and sophistication, good shops and more than its fair share of excellent hotels, but there is a dearth of worthwhile accommodation on its northern side. However, to the south and east, the choices are wide; worthwhile additions to our full entries include the 16-bed Terrassenhotel Kolbergarten (Tel (08041) 9067, fax 9069) in the delightful spa town of Bad Tölz, and the big but well-manicured 89-bed Gut Ising at Chieming, a riding and sports hotel (Tel (08667) 790) by the Chiemsee. With the Alps as background, the Chiemsee has powerful attractions, not least the tragic King Ludwig II's Schloß Herrenchiemsee. An alternative to our full entries is the picturesque Yachthotel at Prien (Tel (08051) 6960, fax 5171).

Füssen on the Forggensee is another popular tourist destination, not only for the lake, but also for its proximity to more of Ludwig II's castles – the fantastic Neuschwanstein and his family home, Hohenschwangau. Both the Alpen-Schlößle (Tel (08362) 39847, 10 rooms) and the Hirsch (Tel 5080, fax 508113, 46 rooms) are family-run chalets, the former with excellent food.

Right on the Austrian border, Mittenwald is a jewel of an Alpine resort and sadly suffers from over-popularity as a result. However, the breakfast-only Gästehaus Franziska is peaceful, despite its central location, and well furnished (Tel (08823) 5051, fax 3893, 20 rooms). Also small, the high-altitude Latscheneck offers good regional cooking to overnight guests only (Tel 1419, fax 1058, 13 rooms), and the Wipfelder (Tel 1057, fax 4077, 15 rooms) is another favourite; although rooms could be deemed somewhat spartan, breakfasts are anything but.

This page acts as an introduction to the features and hotels of Southern Bayern, and gives brief recommendations of good hotels that for one reason or another have not made a full entry. The long entries for this 'Land' – covering the hotels we are most enthusiastic about – start on the next page. But do not neglect the shorter entries starting on page 206: these are all hotels that we would happily stay at. Northern Bayern starts on page 163.

Southern Bayern

Landhotel Schloßwirtschaft

Real excellence in a genuinely small and personal hotel is a rarity in Germany, and in our terms the Schloßwirtschaft is something of a gem. With less than a dozen rooms it is one of the smaller establishments in this guide (only about 40 are smaller), and it is one of the few that creates an entirely successful ambience, free of pretentious elegance on the one hand and rustic clutter on the other. It is reasonably priced, too.

Or at least the rooms are reasonably priced. In some eyes, Eberhard Aspacher is one of Germany's top chef's (though Michelin awards only a single star), and his dishes are priced accordingly; if you dine here you are likely to multiply your overnight bill by three or four. For many travellers, the style of the food may be as off-putting as the prices: intricately modern in conception, artistic in presentation.

The house, overseen by Eberhard's jolly young wife Renate, is mellow, tasteful and relaxing. There is pine panelling and a *Kachelofen* in the beamed dining-room, plain walls and prettily painted furniture in the bedrooms. Only the lobby/bar area strikes a wrong note, with its rather dreary armchairs.

Nearby Memmingen (20 km) – House of Seven Roofs.

89281 Illereichen, Kirchpl 2
Tel (08337) 8045
Fax (08337) 460
Location in village 20 km N of Memmingen, down no-through-road next to church; with garden, garages and ample car parking
Meals breakfast, lunch, dinner
Prices rooms DD-DDD with breakfast; meals DM132-150; children's menu
Rooms 11 double, all with bath; all rooms have central heating, phone, TV, minibar
Facilities breakfast-room, dining-room, bar; terrace, children's playground
Credit cards AE, DC, MC, V
Children very welcome
Disabled ground-floor room
Pets accepted (DM15 per night) **Closed** Sun evening, Mon **Languages** English, French, Italian
Proprietor Eberhard Aspacher

Southern Bayern

Residenz Heinz Winkler

'Restaurant-with-rooms' might be the best description of this imposing temple of gastronomy. In the picture-perfect village of Aschau, opposite the church with its distinctive onion domes, a striking red-and-white shuttered 17thC coaching inn has become the luxurious domain of award-winning chef Heinz Winkler, who wins two Michelin stars for his inventive and expensive creations.

In the time available to you between the smoothly served dinner (which attracts non-residents from miles around) and the coious breakfast next morning, you can retire to bedrooms which are spacious and elegant, mixing pretty fabrics, warm lighting and antique and modern furniture. Though solidly Bavarian in the main, the old inn has various architectural touches which recall Italy and the Renaissance, such as the hexagonal oriol windows at each corner, and the pyramid roof with its geometric decoration on the underside. This gave the theme for the flights of fancy – walls decorated with painted flowers and *trompe l'oeil* murals – which proliferate in the large lobby and dining-rooms. There is an Estee Lauder beauty centre, but no sitting-room. The Winklers are caring and assiduous hosts.

Nearby Schloss Hohenaschau; Salzburg (80 km).

3229 Aschau-im-Chiemgau, Kirchplatz 1
Tel (08052) 17990
Fax (08052) 179966
E-mail 106536.3667@compuserve.com
Location in village centre, 82 km SE of Munich; garage and car park
Meals breakfast, lunch, dinner
Prices rooms DDD-DDDD breakfast DM30; dinner from DM178
Rooms 13 double, 6 deluxe double, 13 suites, all with bath; all rooms have central heating, phone, TV, radio, hairdrier
Facilities restaurants, bar, TV room, meeting room; terrace; sauna
Credit cards AE, DC, MC, V
Children accepted
Disabled some rooms on ground floor **Pets** by arrangement **Closed** never
Languages English, French
Proprietor Heinz Winkler

Southern Bayern

Brauereigasthof Hotel Aying

This inn takes its name from the village in which it is set – a village with over 500 years' tradition of brewing a famous Bavarian beer. The modern Aying brewery and the inn are next door to one another, and you are very much here for the beer (the beer list is longer than some hotels' wine lists, with seasonal special brews prominent).

Rampant vines almost obscure the inn's doorway and windows. Within, banquets for up to 200 are served beneath a splendid painted ceiling, but there is also an intimate *à la carte* dining-room. The cooking is robust, weighted heavily towards pork; beer is, of course, on tap, but there is also a fair selection of wines. Outside, naturally, is a beer garden – very inviting on a summer's day, with red-checked table-cloths and green slatted chairs emphasizing the rural atmosphere.

An inn of this sort can get by with modest bedrooms, but here they are spacious, decorated with restraint and furnished with style – some with gloriously colourful painted furniture and canopied beds. Bathrooms are large and immaculately clean,
Nearby beer-tasting; skiing in Bavarian Alps; Munich (30 km); Rosenheim (30 km).

85653 Aying, Zornedinger Str 2
Tel (08095) 705
Fax (08095) 2053
Location in village, 26 km SE of Munich; take Hofolding exit from E45; with ample car parking
Meals breakfast, lunch, dinner, snacks
Prices rooms DD-DDD with breakfast; meals DM30-80
Rooms 18 double, 7 with bath, 9 with shower; 3 single with shower; 7 family rooms with bath; all rooms have central heating, telephone, TV, radio
Facilities dining-room, banquet room; beer garden
Credit cards AE, DC, MC, V
Children very welcome
Disabled not suitable
Pets accepted
Closed mid to end Jan
Languages English, some Italian **Proprietor** Franz Inselkammer

Southern Bayern

Town hotel, Bad Aibling

Hotel Lindner

With its yellow-washed front and jazzy, green-and-white striped shutters, the Lindner's aristocratic exterior reflects its castle origins over 1000 years ago. The interior effortlessly retains its historical atmosphere, too. The public rooms are spanned by vaulted ceilings, the landing is decorated with antique tables and old family portraits in oils, and pretty Renaissance-style curtains hang at the windows. Bavarian crystal chandeliers add to the charm, although the wood-panelling in the dining-room and breakfast room gleams under modern spotlights and state-of-the-art lighting.

The bedrooms are pleasant and spacious, happily recently updated. Most are furnished with a mix of antiques, with Impressionist reproductions on the walls. Some bedrooms are housed in a new building at the back, separated by a courtyard, and overlooking the hotel's informal, grassy garden. The annexe also has a small bar-cum-library, and drinks can be served in the garden. Erna Lindner's elegant daughter, Gabi, is a charming and efficient hostess, happy to carry on the family's 150-year ownership of the hotel.

Nearby Miesbach (10 km) – waterlily gardens; Salzburg; Munich.

83043 Bad Aibling, Marienplatz 5
Tel (08061) 90630
Fax (08061) 30535
Location in middle of town by marketplace; with garden, and ample car parking and garages
Meals breakfast, lunch, dinner
Prices rooms D-DDD with breakfast; meals DM19-70
Rooms 16 double, with bath; 16 single, 11 with bath; all rooms have central heating; most have phone, hairdrier, TV **Facilities** dining-room, breakfast room, conference room; garden, terrace; bicycles, golf **Credit cards** AE, DC, MC, V **Children** very welcome **Disabled** some ground-floor rooms **Pets** welcome (DM7 per night) **Closed** never **Languages** English and French **Proprietors** Erna Lindner and Gabi Jung

Southern Bayern

Restaurant with rooms, Bad Tölz

Altes Fährhaus

Altes Fährhaus means 'old ferry house'. The mighty Isar, rich in iodine, winds through Bad Tölz: on one side of the river is the old town, where the Fährhaus is situated; on the other is the spa town. Hence the need for a ferry. The ferry boathouse (actually situated below the old town) has been converted into this smart restaurant with rooms, and, although difficult to find, its secluded location by the river is obviously a tremendous draw.

The building, set into a dark rocky hillside, is unimpressive, apart from its lovely tree-shaded terrace directly over the water. Inside, the two dining-rooms are light and airy, one decorated with art deco lamps and fruitwoods, the other with ribbons and pink butterflies. The bedrooms all have riverside balconies and are comfortably furnished in contemporary style.

Elly Reißer is not only owner of the Fährhaus, she is also head chef in a renowned kitchen. Her cooking is classically based, with a bias towards fish dishes such as perch in filo pastry and turbot in *beurre blanc*. Game is well represented too.

It is worth staying the night for the breakfasts alone –parma ham and marinated salmon, as well as home-baked breads.
Nearby Old town (Marktstraße, Maria Himmelfahrt Church).

83646 Bad Tölz, An der Isarlust 1
Tel (08041) 6030
Location on bank of Isar river, on NE edge of town; with small garden and limited car parking
Meals breakfast, lunch, dinner
Prices rooms DD with breakfast; menus DM85-130
Rooms 5 twin, all with bath; all rooms have central heating, phone, TV, minibar, radio
Facilities 2 dining-rooms; terrace
Credit cards not accepted
Children welcome
Disabled not suitable
Pets accepted in public rooms only
Closed for holidays as needed; restaurant, Mon, Tue lunch **Languages** English
Proprietor Elly Reißer

Southern Bayern

Village inn, Bayrischzell

Postgasthof Rote Wand

Situated in a valley surrounded by Alps, this is very much a no-frills hiker's and skier's hotel. The furnishings are plain at best. But the bedrooms are comfortable and the bathrooms large, with ample hot water for aching limbs. The real attraction (apart from the setting) is the warmth of the Gaukler-Pellkofer family's welcome. Nothing is too much trouble for them, and children and dogs are made much of.

The dining-rooms, one of which is non-smoking, are plainly furnished and dotted with rustic ornaments, family shooting trophies, and photos of Herr Gaukler-Pellkofer skiing in the 1936 Winter Olympics. There is a lovely outside terrace, part of which is covered to give shade, where hot walkers can come in off the mountains for a cool beer. There is a large *Kachelofen* to dry out against in winter, and ample helpings of sustaining food (the smell of which can waft around the hotel) cooked by Michael Gaukler, the son of the house. Note, however, that early hours are kept here and the kitchens are supposed to cease serving at 8.00pm, although this did not seem to be adhered to on the busy Saturday summer's evening that our inspector visited.

Nearby Rotwand mountain (1885 m); Wendelstein cable-car.

83735 Bayrischzell, Geitau 15
Tel (08023) 661
Fax (08023) 656
Location in hamlet, 5 km NE of Bayrischzell; with gardens and ample car parking
Meals breakfast, lunch, dinner, snacks
Prices rooms D-DD with breakfast (50% reduction for children); meals DM25-60
Rooms 20 double, 4 with bath, 16 with shower; 10 single with shower; one family room with shower; all rooms have central heating, phone **Facilities** 2 dining-rooms, TV room, *Stube*, terrace **Credit cards** AE, MC, V **Children** very welcome **Disabled** no special facilities **Pets** welcome **Closed** restaurant only, Tue, Wed lunch **Languages** English **Proprietor**s Gaukler-Pellkofer family

Southern Bayern

Country guest-house, Eisenberg

Magnushof

At the foot of the Alps, close to beautiful lakes and surrounded by field and wood, the position alone would make this an appealing place to stay; combined with a stunning interior and a relaxed and welcoming air, the Magnushof is exceptional.

Its personality has been stamped on it by previous owners so there is now an eclectic mix of furniture, ranging from traditionally painted and canopied beds to modern pink leather armchairs. The effect may sound wild, but it has been all put together with taste – and not only works, but works superbly well. The large bedrooms, named after wild ducks, have a feeling of home, being well supplied with books, pictures and games. The smart pool and fitness rooms beguile even the idle to leave the cosy confines of the sitting-room – a lovely room, with a large open fireplace, a wonderful red-and-blue stained glass wall and a marble bust looking on from a niche.

The Deuschles, who have recently taken over, are now offering a range of regional dishes in the new restaurant, accompanied by a choice of wines from the excellent cellar. Breakfasts are generous. Reports on the changes would be welcome.

Nearby Neuschwanstein & Hohenschwangau (5 km) – castles.

87637 Eisenberg,
Unterreuten 51
Tel (08363) 91120
Fax (08363) 911250
Location in hamlet, up signposted lane between Eisen-berg and Hopferau, 10 km NW of Füssen; car parking
Meals breakfast, lunch, dinner
Prices rooms D-DD with breakfast **Rooms** 9 twin, 1 with bath, 8 with shower; one single with shower; all rooms have central heating, phone, TV, radio **Facilities** dining-room, sitting-room; indoor swimming-pool, sauna, solarium, fitness room **Credit cards** MC, V **Children** welcome **Disabled** not suitable **Pets** by arrangement **Closed** never **Languages** some English **Proprietors** Deuschle family

Southern Bayern

Country hotel, Frasdorf

Landgasthof Karner

Only a stone's throw from the motorway to Austria conveniently situated equidistant between Munich and Salzburg, this is a popular weekend retreat for high-powered city types, the women bejewelled and the men smooth, who want to get away from it all – but not too far away.

The Karner is not your run of the mill Alpine chalet – that much is obvious from the outside, with its pristine, powder-blue shutters, immaculate whitewash and stunning carved doors. Inside, it is equally impressive. The dining-room is stylish, with polished wood floors, old panelling and simple, beautifully made curtains. Bedrooms are furnished with rustic furniture and a scattering of good quality rugs.

Although awarded a Michelin star, the food at the Karner has been criticized for attempting bizarre combinations of ingredients, but it certainly draws the crowds – especially on a sunny afternoon in high season, when the lovely garden terrace can be filled to bursting. It would make a pleasant base for walkers who enjoy creature comforts along with their exercise.

Nearby skiing, hang-gliding; Wildenwart (5 km) – castle; Chiemsee (15 km).

83112 Frasdorf, Nußbaumstr 6
Tel (08052) 4071
Fax (08052) 4711
Location in side-street of village, 78 km SE of Munich; with garden and ample car parking
Meals breakfast, lunch, dinner
Prices rooms D-DD with breakfast and dinner
Rooms 18 double, 9 with bath, 9 with shower (one twin); 2 single with shower; 3 apartments with bath; all rooms have cen tral heating, phone, TV, radio
Facilities dining-room, *stube*, indoor swimming-pool; garden terrace, sauna
Credit cards AE, EC, MC, V
Children accepted
Disabled no special facilities
Pets accepted **Closed** never
Languages English
Proprietors Christel and Günter Karner

Southern Bayern

Alpenhof

Grainau is almost a rustic suburb of Garmisch-Partenkirchen, and shares the major resort's majestic Alpine outlook; the mountain railway up the Zugspitze (Germany's highest peak, on the border with Austria) passes through the village.

In an area where modern, flower-decked chalet hotels are two-a-penny, the Alpenhof – undistinguished from the outside – stands out for its restrained use of traditional styles within; the wood panelling in the main dining-rooms is not over-heavy, and the gilt light fittings that bring out its warmth are not over-ornate. Another high-ceilinged room has an amusing *trompe l'oeuil* mural, depicting the outside of an imaginary building. The admirably spacious bedrooms are plainer in style, but not disappointingly so (as in so many rival chalets); the antique furnishings and muted modern fabrics are just sufficient to relieve the plain white walls.

The attention to detail extends to the indoor pool, which is unusually stylish and looks out on to the lush garden – where there is a brightly furnished terrace in summer. Special 'theme evenings' enliven the hotel's summer social calendar.

Nearby skiing, hiking, Alpine gardens, Zugspitze.

82491 Grainau, Alpspitzstr 34
Tel (08821) 9870
Fax (08821) 98777
Location in middle of village 6 km SW of Garmisch-Partenkirchen; in grounds with ample car parking
Meals breakfast, lunch, dinner, snacks
Prices rooms D-DDDD with breakfast; children under 4 free; meals from DM20
Rooms 29 double, 12 with bath, 17 with shower; 7 single with shower; all rooms have central heating, phone, hairdrier, T V, minibar
Facilities dining-rooms, *Stuberl*, sitting-room; terrace, sauna, indoor pool, bicycles
Credit cards DC, MC, V
Children welcome
Disabled no special facilities
Pets not accepted
Closed mid-Nov to mid-Dec
Languages English
Proprietors Albert and Margaret Falkenstein

Southern Bayern

Town hotel, Landshut

Hotel Fürstenhof

Although this little hotel's position on the outskirts of this lovely town is uninteresting, the interior of the Fürstenhof is anything but. Hertha Sellmair has true flair and the public areas of her tall, ornately gabled house – from the welcoming reception to the dining-rooms – are enchanting. Flowers, both fresh and dried, fill the corners, the lighting is delicate, the colours soft blues and pinks, betraying the feminine influence behind the scenes.

Frau Selmair's flair is also obvious in the decoration of the bedrooms – pink-washed walls are teamed with powder-blue carpets. There is a non-smoking floor of three suites, and this, too, sparkles with taste. Designer curtains enhance elegant furniture, and fittings are chosen with care.

There are three dining-rooms: the *Herzogstüberl*, wood panelled and rustic; the *Fürstenzimmer*, beribboned and sophisticated; and the light, pretty Pavilion, looking out to the garden beyond. Food is 'modern German', and creative with its flavours and sauces, producing such delights as perch served on a bed of vegetables with sesame.

Nearby St Martin's cathedral, Trausnitz castle.

84034 Landshut, Stethaimer Str 3
Tel (0871) 92550
Fax (0871) 925544
Location on main road in suburb N of old town; with garden and ample car parking
Meals breakfast, lunch, dinner
Prices rooms DD-DDD with breakfast; meals DM 34-42
Rooms 11 double, 2 with bath, 9 with shower; 10 single with shower; 3 suites with bath; all rooms have central heating, phone, hairdrier, TV, minibar, radio
Facilities sitting-room, 2 dining-rooms, bistro in conservatory, sauna, solarium; garden terrace
Credit cards AE, DC, MC, V
Children accepted **Disabled** not suitable **Pets** accepted (DM10 per night)
Closed restaurant only, Sun
Languages English, French
Proprietor Hertha Sellmair

Southern Bayern

Town chalet, München

Schrenkhof

From the outside, the Schrenkhof looks like a run-of-the-mill modern Alpine chalet, but the interior of this delightful hotel (on the southern outskirts of Munich) is stunningly different from the norm. Although the house was built as recently as 1988, old materials and styles have been lavishly used to create an atmosphere of antiquity, and no expense has been spared in the detailed marquetry and paintwork which decorate both the public rooms and the bedrooms.

The hotel is certainly Alpine in style, but there is nothing rustic about the bedrooms. Although the same beautiful fabric and boldly striped carpet are used, each room is individually decorated in a particular historical style – some are painted in tiny detail, some are carved – giving each room its own appeal. Even the lighting is discreet, mixing antique with the best of modern as appropriate.

The breakfast room is a match for the bedrooms, with a Renaissance tiled stove as its centrepiece. By comparison, the restaurant of the same name next door seems ordinary, but by everyday standards it too is stylish and welcoming.

Nearby Sights of Munich; Bavarian Alps within driving distance.

82008 München,
Leonhardsweg 6,
Unterhaching
Tel (089) 610 0910
Fax (089) 6100 9150
Location in residential area,
10 km S of city along
Tegernseer Landstr and B13;
with 4 underground garages
and ample car parking
Meals breakfast only;
restaurant next door under
same ownership
Prices rooms DD-DDD with
breakfast
Rooms 20 double, 5 single,
all with bath; all rooms have
central heating, telephone,
hairdrier, TV, minibar, radio
Facilities breakfast room,
sauna, solarium
Credit cards AE, DC, MC, V
Children accepted
Disabled suitable
Pets accepted
Closed 20 Dec to 8 Jan
Languages English, French
Proprietor Petra Durach

Southern Bayern

City hotel, München

Hotel Rafael

One of the international Relais & Châteaux chain, the Rafael is at the top end of our size and price range; the furniture is purpose-made and the decoration is relatively uniform. But the hotel makes an impression – particularly on the local business community – by virtue of its suave combination of discreet luxury, stylish elegance and attentive service. If this is the sort of thing you like, you'll like it very much.

An enormous amount of care as well as money has gone into the conversion of the 20thC Renaissance-style building to a hotel. The public areas combine modern and traditional elements (downlighters, glass tables, antique prints, curvaceous chairs) in a carefully controlled fashion, with warm-toned wood in the furniture and occasional wall panel contributing to the warm, harmonious atmosphere. There are comfortable places for a rendezvous in the lobby bar (where snacks are served) and the smooth piano bar next door to the restaurant.

The bedrooms and suites are deeply comfortable, impressively spacious and extremely well equipped. Bathrooms are a highlight, with extravagant baths and bold use of marble.

Nearby English Garden, Nymphenburg Palace, Alte Pinakothek.

80331 München,
Neuturmstr 1
Tel (089) 290980
Fax (089) 222539
Location in middle of city behind Hofbräuhaus; with private parking for 40 cars
Meals breakfast, lunch, dinner, snacks
Prices rooms DDDD with breakfast; meals from DM52
Rooms 56 double (5 twin), 18 suites, all with bath; all rooms have central heating,
air- conditioning, phone, hairdrier, TV, minibar, radio
Facilities lobby, dining-room, bar; roof terrace (with pool)
Credit cards AE, DC, MC, V
Children very welcome
Disabled lift/elevator; wheelchair available
Pets accepted in bedrooms only
Closed never
Languages English, French, Italian, Spanish
Manager Hartmut E. Zunk

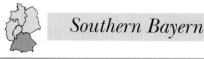

Southern Bayern

Kur hotel, Oberstaufen

Hotel zum Löwen

Housed in one of the most beautiful buildings in a fashionable spa town – an elaborately decorated chalet – the zum Löwen is a *Kur* hotel which is not taken over completely by physical activities and treatments. Yes, the blue and green indoor pool is stunning, the fitness rooms are spacious and well equipped, and the diet sheets as punishing as anywhere. But the ordinary holiday-maker is immediately captivated by the hotel's stylish aura, starting with the façade's floral frescoes and window boxes, and the light, welcoming lobby.

The three dining-rooms are in different styles: one modern in bright green; one panelled and rustic; the third intimate and pretty. All serve ambitious food that earns high praise from Michelin and Gault-Millau: roulade of salmon and perch, truffle-stuffed pigeon breasts, for example. For those following a *Kur*, superior lettuce leaves are available, but there is a wide-ranging wine list to alleviate the pain.

Bedrooms are spacious, with high quality built-in beds, modern furniture, jazzy modern art prints, and ritzy bathrooms. All have balconies, with views over the surrounding hills.

Nearby museum, theatre, skiing.

LOW003 87534 Oberstaufen, Kirchplatz 8
Tel (08386) 4940 **Fax** 494222
Location in pedestrian square in middle of town; garden, garages, and ample parking
Meals breakfast, lunch, dinner, snacks
Prices rooms DD-DDDD with breakfast; meals DM20-38
Rooms 20 twin with shower; 10 single with shower; one apartment with bath; all have central heating, phone, radio, hairdrier, cable TV, minibar
Facilities sitting-room, café, 3 dining-rooms, sauna, indoor swimming-pool, fitness room
Credit cards AE, DC, V
Children welcome **Disabled** access easy; lift/elevator **Pets** by arrangement **Closed** mid-Nov to mid-Dec; restaurant only, Wed **Languages** English, French, Italian, Spanish
Proprietors Emerich family

Southern Bayern

Lakeside hotel, Seebruck

Malerwinkel

The 'painter's nook' is well-named – its position overlooking the Chiemsee is magical and the hotel makes the most of it. Large French windows open from the dining-room on to the terrace, where the view to the lake and Alps beyond would keep a painter busy for days.

The dining-room is split in two by a partition: on one side is the winter dining-room, warmed by a large green *Kachelofen*, on the other a summer pavilion with a natural wood support at its centre echoing the spars of the sailing boats moored on the hotel's jetty. The kitchens are very much part of the dining area and some noise does intrude, but the food is so richly satisfying, and the welcome so friendly, that this hardly matters. Taking their cue from the aimiable Anni Loh, staff are unruffled by late arrivals and will cheerfully provide a superb meal after the appointed hour for the kitchens to close.

Bedrooms are tastefully decorated, with a mixture of antique and carefully chosen modern furniture. Rooms at the back can suffer from road noise and there is a premium to pay for those with a view of the lake.

Nearby sailing; Herrninsel, Fraueninsel (islands).

83358 Seebruck, Lambach 23
Tel (08667) 488
Fax (08667) 1408
Location on NW shore of Chiemsee, 3 km SW of Seebruck; with garden and ample car parking
Meals breakfast, lunch, dinner, snacks
Prices rooms D-DDD with breakfast; meals DM40-75
Rooms 13 double, one single, 6 family rooms, all with shower; all rooms have central heating, phone, TV, radio
Facilities dining-room, conference room, sauna; lakeside terrace, jetty
Credit cards MC
Children very welcome
Disabled not suitable **Pets** accepted (DM5 per night)
Closed never
Languages English, French
Proprietor Anni Loh

Southern Bayern

Chalet hotel, Bayrischzell

Die Meindelei

A colourful, family-run pension with extra accommodation in chalet bungalows dotted around the peaceful garden. The Schwerdtfegers are amiable hosts, and take great pride in their comfortable, if cluttered, hotel.

■ 83735 Bayrischzell, Michael-Meindl Str 13 **Tel** (08023) 318 **Fax** 1480 **Meals** breakfast, dinner **Prices** rooms D-DD with breakfast; meals DM28-42 **Rooms** 12, all with bath or shower, central heating, phone, TV; some rooms have hairdrier **Credit cards** AE, DC, MC **Closed** mid-Nov to mid-Dec; Tue **Languages** English, French

---

Country hotel, Berchtesgaden-Stanggaß

Hotel Geiger

A converted Bavarian farmhouse, greatly extended and refurbished, and a long-standing Berchtesgaden favourite. Sitting- and dining-rooms are cosy and rustic; bedrooms are furnished more simply, and in a modern style.

■ 83471 Berchtesgaden, Berchtesgadener Str 103-115 **Tel** (08652) 9653 **Fax** (08652) 965400 **Meals** breakfast, dinner **Prices** rooms DD-DDDD with breakfast; meals from DM30 **Rooms** 51, all with central heating, phone; most have minibar; some have hairdrier, TV **Credit cards** V **Closed** 1Nov to 18 Dec **Languages** English, French, Spanish

---

Converted monastery, Burghausen

Klostergasthof Raitenhaslach

Definitely secular these days, this large wing of an old monastery attracts coachloads of beer drinkers by day and jolly diners by night. Vaulted dining-rooms are huge and welcoming, bedrooms comfortable. Some lovely antiques and pictures.

■ 84489 Burghausen, Raitenhaslach 9 **Tel** (08677) 7062 **Fax** (08677) 66111 **Meals** breakfast, lunch, dinner, snacks **Prices** D-DD with breakfast **Rooms** 14, all with shower, central heating, phone, TV, radio **Credit cards** AE, MC,V **Closed** 1-9 Nov **Languages** English, French

---

Country restaurant with rooms, Dietmannsried/Probstried

Landhaus Haase

Wilfried Haase runs his chalet hotel and restaurant with brio. The two tasteful dining-rooms (one luxurious, the other countrified) are popular with locals – booking is advised; spacious bedrooms are well-designed and comfortable.

■ 87463 Dietmannsried/Probstried, Wohlmutser Weg 2 **Tel** (08374) 8010 **Fax** (08374) 6655 **Meals** breakfast, lunch, dinner **Prices** rooms D-DD with breakfast; meals from DM40 **Rooms** 8, all with bath or shower, central heating, phone, TV, radio **Credit cards** AE, DC, MC, V **Closed** restaurant only, Sat lunch **Languages** English, French

Southern Bayern

Town hotel, Eichstätt

Hotel Adler

The lovely old baroque exterior disguises an expensively done interior – essentially modern and plain, but with traditional embellishments such as chandeliers. Formula furnishings but impressive amounts of space in the bedrooms.

■ 85072 Eichstätt, Marktpl 22 **Tel** (08421) 6767 **Fax** (08421) 8283 **Meals** breakfast only **Prices** rooms DD with breakfast **Rooms** 38, all with bath, central heating, phone, minibar, TV, radio **Credit cards** AE, DC, MC, V **Closed** 15 Dec to 15 Jan **Languages** English, French

---

Village inn, Ettal

Zur Post

A pleasant chalet in a village on the main road to Oberammergau. Pretty panelled dining-rooms (with piped music); bedrooms are mixed – some furnished with good reproductions, some ordinarily modern.

■ 82488 Ettal, Kaiser Ludwig Pl 18 **Tel** (08822) 3596 **Fax** (08822) 6971 **Meals** breakfast, lunch, dinner, snacks **Prices** D-DD with breakfast **Rooms** 22, all with bath or shower, central heating, TV, radio **Credit cards** AE, DC, MC, V **Closed** Nov to mid-Dec **Languages** English, Italian

---

Country inn, Freilassing

Gasthof Moosleitner

On the old trade route between Salzburg and Munich, this delighful old inn is run by the personable Traudl and Hans Niederbuchner. They have furnished it with great taste, while preserving the flavour of 700 years' history.

■ 883395 Freilassing, Wasserburger Str 52 **Tel** (08654) 2081 **Fax** (08654) 62010 **Meals** breakfast, lunch, dinner **Prices** rooms D-DD with breakfast; meals from DM18 **Rooms** 50, all with bath or shower, central heating, phone, hairdrier, TV, minibar, radio **Credit cards** AE, DC, MC, V **Closed** 2-6 Jan **Languages** English, French

---

Chalet hotel, Garmisch-Partenkirchen

Gasthof Fraundorfer

A hostelry with festive murals on the exterior and an equally cheerful interior. An evening's entertainment may include yodelling. Beds are idiosyncratic, some carved to look like cars.

■ 82467 Garmisch-Partenkirchen, Ludwigstr 24 **Tel** (08821) 71071 **Fax** (08821) 70173 **Meals** breakfast, lunch, dinner, snacks **Prices** D-DD with breakfast **Rooms** 33, all with central heating, phone, TV **Credit cards** AE, MC, V **Closed** restaurant only, Nov **Languages** English, French, Spanish

Southern Bayern

Chalet hotel, Garmisch-Partenkirchen

Hotel Garmischer Hof

A delightful find in the middle of Garmisch – a chalet furnished with unusual taste and style. The lush garden (where simple lunches are served) gives glorious views of the Alps.

■ 82467 Garmisch-Partenkirchen, Chamonixstr 10 **Tel** (08821) 9110 **Fax** (08821) 51440 **Meals** breakfast, lunch, snacks **Prices** D-DDD with buffet breakfast **Rooms** 43, all with bath or shower, central heating, phone, TV, minibar **Credit cards** AE, DC, MC, V **Closed** never **Languages** English

---

Chalet hotel, Garmisch-Partenkirchen

Hotel Staudacherhof

The onion-domed tower disguises a large modern chalet, its interior a mix of Spanish arches and Bavarian hearts and flowers. Spectacular mountain views from the recently renovated bedrooms. Indoor and outdoor pools for all weathers.

■ 82467 Garmisch-Partenkirchen, Höllentalstr 48 **Tel** (08821) 9290 **Fax** (08821) 929333 **Meals** breakfast, snacks **Prices** D-DDDD with breakfast; meals DM18 **Rooms** 37, all with bath or shower, central heating, phone, TV, minibar, radio, hairdrier **Credit cards** MC, V **Closed** mid-Nov to mid-Dec **Languages** English, French, Swedish, Italian

---

Lakeside hotel, Garmisch-Partenkirchen

Rießersee

The low modern chalet-style building is pleasant enough inside and out, though some of the furniture is rather routine. But what a position: from the sunny terrace you look across a small lake to a view of the Zugspitze that Hollywood would not have dared to invent.

■ 82467 Garmisch-Partenkirchen, Riess 6 **Tel** (08821) 50181 **Meals** breakfast, lunch, dinner **Prices** rooms DD with breakfast; meals from DM15 **Rooms** 5, all with bath or shower, central heating, phone, TV, minibar, radio **Credit cards** AE, DC, MC, V **Closed** Mon; Nov to 20 Dec **Languages** English

---

Town hotel, Garmisch-Partenkirchen

Posthotel Partenkirchen

The genuine article: a Bavarian coaching inn with its heritage carefully preserved behind the painted façade. Ceilings are beamed, vaulted or coffered, walls moulded or panelled. For once, there are some bedrooms in the same style.

■ 82467 Garmisch-Partenkirchen, Ludwigstr 49 **Tel** (08821) 51067 **Fax** (08821) 78568 **Meals** breakfast, lunch, dinner, snacks **Prices** rooms DD-DDDD with breakfast; meals from DM35 **Rooms** 59, all with bath, central heating, phone, TV, radio, minibar **Credit cards** AE, DC, MC, V **Closed** never **Languages** English, French

Southern Bayern

Alter Wirt

Conveniently situated just off the road into Munich, and with more appeal than that might suggest. Light and airy bedrooms contrast with the more sombre, wood-beamed public rooms. Leafy terrace on which to enjoy a mid-morning snack.

■ 82039 Grünwald, Marktpl 1 **Tel** (089) 6417855 **Fax** (089) 6414266 **Meals** breakfast, lunch, dinner **Prices** rooms DD with breakfast; meals DM53 **Rooms** 49, all with bath or shower, central heating, phone, TV, radio **Credit cards** AE, MC, V **Closed** 24 Dec **Languages** English, French, Spanish, Italian

---

Chalet hotel, Herrsching am Ammersee

Piushof

A member of the Silencehotel chain, Hans Moser's colourful chalet is not typical of the genre, being smaller and more tasteful than most – although every available surface has been painted in Bavarian style.

■ 82211 Herrsching am Ammersee, Schönbichlstr 18 **Tel** (08152) 1007 **Fax** (08152) 8328 **Meals** breakfast, lunch, dinner **Prices** rooms DD with breakfast; meals DM20-95 **Rooms** 21, all with central heating, phone, TV, minibar, radio **Credit cards** AE, DC, MC, V **Closed** restaurant only, Sun dinner and Mon lunch **Languages** English

---

Country hotel, Hirschegg-Kleinwalsertal

Walserhof

A modern chalet with respectable sports facilities, built down the hillside beside the road, with views across the beautiful Kleinwalsertal. Warmly rustic rooms inside, particularly the rough-timbered, low-ceilinged bar, and imaginative pool room.

■ 87568 Hirschegg, Walserstr 11 **Tel** (08329) 5684 **Fax** (08329) 5938 **Meals** breakfast, lunch, dinner, snacks **Prices** rooms D-DD with breakfast; meals DM13.50-36 **Rooms** 35, all with bath or shower, central heating, phone, TV, radio **Credit cards** MC **Closed** Nov to mid-Dec **Languages** English, French

---

Chalet hotel, Iffeldorf

Landgasthof Osterseen

Large terraces overlooking a peaceful lake attract diners to this busy chalet, equipped inside with the usual over-abundance of moulded pine. The Link family run the hotel with much charm and it is spotlessly clean.

■ 82393 Iffeldorf, Hofmark 9 **Tel** (08856) 1011 **Fax** (08856) 9606 **Meals** breakfast, lunch, dinner, snacks **Prices** rooms DD-DDD with breakfast; meals DM25-80 **Rooms** 24, all with bath, central heating, phone, TV, radio **Credit cards** AE, DC, MC, V **Closed** 7th to 24th Jan; restaurant only, Tue **Languages** English

Southern Bayern

Village hotel, Inzell

Zur Post

At first sight, the archetypal Bavarian post-hotel: a solid old building, painted and balconied, next to the church in a village ringed by mountains. But inside, beyond the vaulted hallways, more elegance than rustic charm, and very popular it is too.

■ 83334 Inzell, Reichenhaller Str 2 **Tel** (08665) 9850 **Fax** (08665) 985100 **Meals** breakfast, lunch, dinner **Prices** rooms D-DD with breakfast; meals from DM10 **Rooms** 45, all with bath or shower, central heating, phone, TV, radio **Credit cards** DC, MC, V **Closed** mid-Nov to mid-Dec **Languages** English, Italian

---

Town hotel, Kaufbeuren

Goldener Hirsch

The dominant hotel of Kaufbeuren, but none the worse for that – a plain but handsome house, dating from the 17th century, sensitively and tastefully modernized with some old features retained. Designer-decorated bedrooms.

■ 87600 Kaufbeuren, Kasier-Max Str 39 **Tel** (08341)43030 **Fax** (08341) 430369 **Meals** breakfast, lunch, dinner **Prices** rooms D-DDD; meals from DM40 **Rooms** 42, all with bath or shower, central heating, phone, TV, minibar, radio **Credit cards** AE, DC, MC, V **Closed** never **Languages** English, French

---

Lakeside hotel, Lindau Island

Lindauer Hof

Its wonderful position overlooking the harbour on the island of Lindau, with Lake Constance beyond, is the chief attraction of this pleasant hotel. A recent face-lift has given the old building an elegantly contemporary feel.

■ 88105 Lindau/Insel, An der Seepromenade **Tel** (08382) 4064 **Fax** (08382) 24203 **Meals** breakfast, lunch, dinner, snacks **Prices** D-DDDD with breakfast **Rooms** 25, all with bath, central heating, phone, TV, radio, minibar, safe **Credit cards** AE, MC, V **Closed** never **Languages** English, French

---

City hotel, München

Hotel Splendid

A central hotel with a private-house atmosphere. Elegant antiques emphatically traditional decoration and spacious bedrooms. No restaurant but a terrace for drinks and snacks.

■ 80538 München 22, Maximilianstr 54 **Tel** (089) 296606 **Fax** (089) 291 3176 **Meals** breakfast, snacks **Prices** DD-DDDD with breakfast **Rooms** 40, all with central heating, phone, TV, radio **Credit cards** AE, DC, MC, V **Closed** never **Languages** German only

Southern Bayern

Converted water-mill, München

Insel-Mühle

Like other industrial buildings, old water-mills can be dark inside, and this one is no exception. But it has been converted with taste, in rustic style: rooms in the eaves are especially attractive, and the situation by the river is idyllic.

■ 80999 München, Von-Kahr-Str 87 **Tel** (089) 81010 **Fax** (089) 812 0571 **Meals** breakfast, lunch, dinner **Prices** rooms DD-DDDD with breakfast; meals from DM30 **Rooms** 37, all with shower, central heating, phone, TV, radio **Credit cards** DC, MC, V **Closed** restaurant only, Sun **Languages** English, French

---

City hotel, München

Hotel Prinzregent

Undistinguished to look at, this hotel just the wrong side of the river Isar has surprises in store: beams, panelling and baroque ornaments to rival Bavaria's best. Bedrooms, too, are furnished with character. Breakfast in swish new conservatory.

■ 81675 München, Ismaninger Str. 42-44 **Tel** (089) 416050 **Fax** (089) 41605466 **Meals** breakfast, snacks **Prices** rooms DD-DDDD with breakfast; children free in parents' room **Rooms** 66, all with bath or shower, central heating, phone, hairdrier, TV **Credit cards** AE, DC, MC, V **Closed** Christmas **Languages** English, French, Italian, Spanish

---

Chalet hotel, Murnau am Staffelsee

Alpenhof Murnau

The view across lawns and fields to the Alps is one of the key attractions of this glossy Relais & Château hotel – together with ambitious modern cooking (very un-Bavarian) and restrained traditional decor.

■ 82418 Murnau am Staffelsee, Ramsachstr 8 **Tel** (08841) 4910 **Fax** (08841) 5438 **Meals** breakfast, lunch, dinner **Prices** DD-DDDD with breakfast **Rooms** 44, all with bath, central heating, phone, radio **Credit cards** AE, MC, V **Closed** Jan **Languages** German only

---

Chalet hotel, Oberammergau

Gasthof zur Rose

Herr and Frau Stückl have retired, and it is now their daughter Renate who runs this jolly little inn with her husband, Ludwig. Antiques, colourful paintings, flowers and pretty fabrics create a warm, cared-for atmosphere. Bedrooms are simple, food is ample, if somewhat erratically served in a bright dining-room. Hard place to find, an American visitor reports .

■ 82487 Oberammergau, Dedlerstr 9 **Tel** (08822) 4706 **Fax** (08822) 6753 **Meals** breakfast, lunch, dinner **Prices** rooms D-DD with breakfast; meals from DM10 **Rooms** 24, all with bath or shower, central heating; some rooms have TV **Credit cards** AE, DC, MC, V **Closed** Nov **Languages** English

Southern Bayern

Bed and breakfast guest-house, Oberstdorf

Haus Wiese

Otto Wiese is a retired ship's cook from Hamburg, who has immortalised his love of the city in a mural of Deichstrasse beside the pool. Hand-carved furniture and panelling are also a source of pride in this pristine family home.

■ 87561 Oberstdorf, Stillachstr 4a **Tel** (08322) 3030 **Meals** breakfast **Prices** D-DDD with breakfast **Rooms** 13, all with bath or shower, central heating, phone, TV **Credit cards** not accepted **Closed** never **Languages** German only

---

Chalet hotel, Pfronten

Hotel Bavaria

A large but friendly hotel with modern façade and luxurious, traditional interior, in glorious setting at head of peaceful valley. Large open fires in winter – necessary for those using the oudoor pool heated to 30°C. Indoor pool, suana and solarium too.

■ 87459 Pfronten-Dorf, Kienbergstr 62 **Tel** (08363) 9020 **Fax** (08363) 6815 **Meals** breakfast, lunch, dinner, snacks **Prices** DD-DDD with breakfast **Rooms** 48, all with bath or shower, central heating, phone, TV radio **Credit cards** AE, MC **Closed** restaurant only, Nov **Languages** English, French, Italian

---

Chalet guest-house, Seeg

Pension Heim

Mountains to the south, rolling hills to the north: peace and glorious scenery surround this little chalet. Although a bit ordinary in terms of decoration and furnishings, it is neat, clean and run in friendly fashion by the welcoming Heim family.

■ **Meals** breakfast **Prices** D-DD with breakfast **Rooms** 16, all with bath or shower, central heating, phone, TV **Credit cards** not accepted **Closed** 1 Nov to 25 Dec **Languages** English

---

Country hotel, Wallgau

Parkhotel Wallgau

With magnificent mountains as a backdrop, everything about this sumptuous, chalet-style hotel is rustically ornate. Detailed wood-carvings abound, from the panelling in the bar to the chairs in the galleried dining-room.

■ 82499 Wallgau, Barmseestr 1 **Tel** (08825) 290 **Fax** (08825) 366 **Meals** breakfast, dinner, snacks **Prices** DB&B DD-DDD **Rooms** 52, all with bath or shower, central heating, phone, hairdrier, TV, minibar, radio; some have air-conditioning **Credit cards** not accepted **Closed** 7 weeks Nov to Dec **Languages** English, French, Italian

Index of hotel names

In this index, hotels are arranged in order of the most distinctive part of their name; in many cases, other parts of the name are also given after the main part, but very common prefixes such as 'Hotel', 'Gasthof' and 'Das' are omitted. Where a hotel's name begins with Schloß or Schloßhotel, it will normally be indexed under the word that follows. Hotels covered in the several Area introductions are not indexed.

Index of hotel names

Index of hotel names

Index of hotel names

Index of hotel names

Index of hotel locations

In this index, hotels are arranged by the name of the city, town or village they are in or near. Where a hotel is located in a very small place, it may be indexed under a nearby place which is more easily found on maps.

Index of hotel locations

Index of hotel locations

Index of hotel locations

Index of hotel locations

Special Offer

Buy your *Charming Small Hotel Guide* by post directly from the publisher and you'll get a worthwhile discount. *

Titles available:	Retail price	Discount price
Austria	£9.99	**£8.50**
Britain & Ireland	£9.99	**£8.50**
Britain's Most Distinctive Bed & Breakfasts	£9.99	**£8.50**
USA: Florida	£9.99	**£8.50**
France	£9.99	**£8.50**
France: *Bed & Breakfast*	£8.99	**£7.50**
Germany	£9.99	**£8.50**
Italy	£9.99	**£8.50**
USA: New England	£8.99	**£7.50**
Paris	£9.99	**£8.50**
Southern France	£9.99	**£8.50**
Spain	£9.99	**£8.50**
Switzerland	£9.99	**£8.50**
Tuscany & Umbria	£9.99	**£8.50**
Venice	£9.99	**£8.50**

Also available: *Independent Traveller's Guides/Versatile/ Travel Planner & Guides*: all-purpose travel guides.

Titles available:	Retail price	Discount price
Australia	£12.99	**£10.50**
California	£12.99	**£10.50**
Central Italy	£12.99	**£10.50**
Florida	£12.99	**£10.50**
France	£12.99	**£10.50**
Greece	£12.99	**£10.50**
Italy	£12.99	**£10.50**
Spain	£12.99	**£10.50**
Thailand	£12.99	**£10.50**
Turkey	£12.99	**£10.50**
England & Wales *Walks Planner &Guide*	£12.99	**£10.50**

Please send your order to:

Book Sales, Duncan Petersen Publishing Ltd, **31 Ceylon Road, London W14 OPY**

enclosing: 1) the title you require and number of copies 2) your name and address 3) your cheque made out to: **Duncan Petersen Publishing Ltd**

Offer applies to UK only.

**CHARMING
SMALL HOTEL
GUIDES**

Would you like to receive
information about special
discounts at hotels in the
***Charming Small
Hotel Guide***
series?

☆

Many of our hotels are
offering big savings on
standard room rates if you
book at certain times of
the year.

☆

If so, send your name and
address to:

***Reader Information
Charming Small
Hotel Guides***
Duncan Petersen Publishing
31 Ceylon Road
London W14 OPY

☆